新丝路“中文 + 职业技能”系列教材编写委员会
（中文 + 计算机网络技术）

新丝路“中文+职业技能”系列教材
New Silk Road "Chinese + Vocational Skills" Series

中文+计算机网络技术
Chinese + Computer Networking Technology

高级 Advanced

新丝路“中文+职业技能”系列教材编写委员会　编

北京语言大学出版社
BEIJING LANGUAGE AND CULTURE UNIVERSITY PRESS

图书在版编目（CIP）数据

中文＋计算机网络技术．高级 ／ 新丝路“中文＋职业技能”系列教材编写委员会编．-- 北京 ：北京语言大学出版社，2024．12．--（新丝路“中文＋职业技能”系列教材）．-- ISBN 978-7-5619-6655-6

Ⅰ．H195.4；TP393.08

中国国家版本馆 CIP 数据核字第 2024Z0N106 号

中文 + 计算机网络技术（高级）

ZHONGWEN + JISUANJI WANGLUO JISHU (GAOJI)

排版制作：北京创艺涵文化发展有限公司
责任印制：周　燚

出版发行：北京语言大学出版社
社　　址：北京市海淀区学院路 15 号，100083
网　　址：www.blcup.com
电子信箱：service@blcup.com
电　　话：编 辑 部　8610-82303647/3592/3395
　　　　　国内发行　8610-82303650/3591/3648
　　　　　海外发行　8610-82303365/3080/3668
　　　　　北语书店　8610-82303653
　　　　　网购咨询　8610-82303908
印　　刷：北京富资园科技发展有限公司

版　　次：2024 年 12 月第 1 版　　印　　次：2024 年 12 月第 1 次印刷
开　　本：889 毫米 × 1194 毫米　1/16　　印　　张：12.75
字　　数：233 千字
定　　价：118.00 元

PRINTED IN CHINA
凡有印装质量问题，本社负责调换。售后 QQ 号 1367565611，电话 010-82303590

编写说明

新丝路“中文＋职业技能”系列教材是把中文作为第二语言，结合专业和职业的专门用途、职业用途的中文教材，不是专业理论教材，不是一般意义的通用综合中文教材。本系列教材定位为职场生存中文教材、立体式技能型语言教材。教材研发的目标是既要满足学习者一般中文环境下的基本交际需求，又要满足学习者职业学习需求和职场工作需求。它和普通的国际中文教材的区别不在语法，而在词汇的专门化程度，在中文的用途、使用场合、应用范围。目前，专门用途、职业用途的中文教材在语言分类和研究成果上几近空白，本系列教材的成功研发开创了中文学习的新视野、新领域、新方向，将“中文＋职业技能＋X等级证书”真正融合，使学习者在学习中文的同时，也可通过实践掌握职业技能，从而获得X等级证书。

适用对象

本系列教材将适用对象定位为双零基础（零语言基础、零技能基础）的来华学习中文和先进技能的长期或者短期进修生，可满足初、中、高各层次专业课程的教学需要。教材亦可供海内外相关的培训课程及“走出去”的中资企业培训本土化员工使用。

结构规模

本系列教材采取专项语言技能与职业技能训练相结合的中文教学及教材编写模式。教材选择当前热门的物流管理、汽车服务工程技术、电子商务、机电一体化、计算机网络技术、酒店管理等六个专业，培养各专业急需急用的技术岗位人才。每个专业教材均包括初、中、高级三册。每一册都配有专业视频教学资源，还附有“视频脚本”“参考答案”等配套资源。

编写理念

本系列教材将词语进行分类，区分普通词语和专业词语，以通用语料为基础，以概念性、行为性词语为主，不脱离职场情境讨论分级，做到控制词汇量，控制工作场景，控制交流内容与方式，构建语义框架。将语言的分级和专业的分级科学地融合，是实现本系列教材成功编写的关键。

教材目标

语言技能目标：

初级阶段，能熟练掌握基础通用词语和职场的常用专业词语，能使用简短句子进行简单的生活及工作交流。中级阶段，能听懂工作场合简单的交谈与发言，明白大意，把握基本情况，能就工作中重要的话题用简单的话与人沟通。高级阶段，能听懂工作场合一般的交谈与发言，抓住主要内容和关键信息，使用基本交际策略与人交流、开展工作，能初步了解与交际活动相关的文化因素，掌握与交际有关的一般文化背景知识，能排除交际时遇到的文化障碍。交际能力层次的递进实现从初级的常规礼节、基本生活及工作的交流能力，到中级的简单的服务流程信息交流能力，最后达到高级的复杂信息的交流和特情处理的能力。

职业技能目标：

以满足岗位需求为目标，将遴选出的当前热门的专业工作岗位分为初、中、高三级。物流管理专业初、中、高级对应的岗位分别是物流员、物流经理、物流总监；汽车服务工程技术专业初、中、高级对应的岗位分别是汽车机电维修工、汽车服务顾问、技术总监；电子商务专业初、中、高级对应的岗位分别是电子商务运营助理、电子商务运营员、电子商务客服；机电一体化专业初、中、高级对应的岗位分别是机电操作工、机电调整工、机电维修工；计算机网络技术专业初、中、高级对应的岗位分别是宽带运维工程师、网络运维专员、网络管理员；酒店管理专业初、中、高级对应的岗位分别是前厅基层接待员、前厅主管、前厅经理。每个专业分解出三十个工作场景 / 任务，学习者在学习后能够全面掌握此岗位的概况及基本程序，实现语言学习和专业操作的双重目标。

编写原则

1. 语言知识技能与专业知识技能并进，满足当前热门的、急需急用的岗位需求。

2. 渐进分化，综合贯通，拆解难点，分而治之。

3. 语言知识与专业知识科学、高效复现，语言技能与专业技能螺旋式上升，职场情境、语义框架、本体输入方式相互配合。

4. 使用大量的图片和视频，实现专业知识和技能呈现形式可视化。

5. 强化专业岗位实操性技能。本系列教材配有专业技术教学的视频，突出展示专业岗位的实操性技能，语言学习难度与技能掌握难度的不匹配可通过实操性强的视频和实训环节来补充。

特色追求

本系列教材从初级最基础的语音知识学习和岗位认知开始，将“中文 + 职业技能”融入在工作场景对话中，把工作分解成一个个任务，用图片认知的方式解决专业词语的认知问题，用视频展示的方法解决学习者掌握中文词语与专业技能的不匹配问题，注重技能的实操性，注重“在做中学”。每一单元都设置了“学以致用”板块，目的不仅仅是解决本单元任务的词语认知问题，更是将学习的目标放在“能听”“能用”“能模仿说出”上。我们力争通过大量图片的使用和配套视频的展示，将教材打造成立体式、技能型语言教材，方便学习者能够更好地自主学习。

使用建议

1. 本系列教材每个专业分为初、中、高级三册，每册10单元，初级每单元建议8～10课时完成，中级 10 ～ 12 课时完成，高级 12 ～ 14 课时完成。

2. 教材注释和说明着力于简明扼要，注重实操性，注重听说技能培养，对于教材涉及的语法知识，教师可视情况予以细化和补充。

3. “单元实训”板块可以在课文和语言点学完之后作为课堂练习使用，建议 2 课时完成。教师要带着学习者按照实训步骤一步步完成，实训步骤不要求学习者能够看懂，读懂，重要的是教师要引领操作，实现学习者掌握专业技能的目标。

4. “单元小结”板块是对整个单元关键词语和核心内容的总结，对于这部分内容，教师要进行听说练习，以便更好地帮助学习者了解本单元的核心工作任务。

5. 教师上课时要充分利用教材设计的练习，引导学习者多听多练，听说结合，学做合一。

6. 教师要带着学习者熟练诵读课文，要求学习者把每课的关键词语和句子、课堂用语背诵下来。

特别感谢

感谢教育部中外语言交流合作中心将新丝路“中文＋职业技能”系列教材列为重点研发项目，为我们教材编写增添了动力和责任感。教材编写委员会负责整套教材的规划、设计与编写协调，并先后召开上百次讨论会，对每册教材的课文编写、体例安排、注释说明、练习设计、图片选择、视频制作等进行全方位的评估、讨论和审定。感谢编写委员会成员和所有编者高度的敬业精神、精益求精的编写态度，以及所投入的热情和精力、付出的心血与智慧。感谢关注本系列教材并贡献宝贵意见的国际中文教育教学界专家和全国各地的同人。

新丝路“中文＋职业技能”系列教材编写委员会

2023 年 4 月

Compilation Instructions

The New Silk Road "Chinese + Vocational Skills" is a series of Chinese textbooks for specialized and vocational purposes that combine professional and vocational technologies with Chinese as a second language. Instead of being specialized theoretical textbooks, or comprehensive or universal Chinese textbooks in a general sense, this series is intended to be Chinese textbooks for career survival, and three-dimensional skills-based language textbooks. The textbooks are developed with a view to meeting students' basic communication needs in general Chinese environment, and their professional learning needs and workplace demands as well. They are different from ordinary Chinese textbooks for foreigners in the degree of specialization of vocabulary, in the purpose, usage occasion, and application scope of Chinese (not in grammar). At present, Chinese textbooks for specialized and vocational purposes are virtually non-existent in terms of language classification and research results, so the successful development of this series has opened up new horizons, new fields and new directions for Chinese learning, and virtually integrated "Chinese + Vocational Skills + X-Level Certificates", which enables students to practically master vocational skills and obtain X-level certificates while learning Chinese.

Applicable Targets

This series is targeted at long-term or short-term students who come to China to learn Chinese and advanced skills with zero language basis and zero skill basis, which can meet the teaching needs of the elementary, intermediate and advanced specialized courses. This series can also be used for relevant training courses at home and abroad and for Chinese-funded enterprises that "go global" to train local employees.

Structure and Scale

This series adopts a Chinese teaching and textbook compilation model combining special language skills and vocational skills training. The series includes the textbooks for six popular majors such as logistics management, automotive service engineering technology, e-commerce, mechatronics, computer networking technology, and hotel management to cultivate technical talents in urgent need. The textbooks for each major consist of the textbooks at the elementary, intermediate and advanced levels. Each textbook is equipped with professional video teaching resources, and "video scripts", "reference answers" and other supporting resources as well.

Compilation Concept

This series classifies the vocabulary into general vocabulary and specialized vocabulary. Based on the general vocabulary, it focuses on conceptual and behavioral words, not deviating from workplace situations, so as to control the vocabulary, work scenarios and content and means of communication, and build the semantic framework. The scientific integration of language classification and specialty classification is the key to the successful compilation of textbooks.

Textbook Objectives

Language Skill Objectives

For students at the elementary level, they are trained to be familiar with basic general vocabulary and common specialized vocabulary in the workplace, and be able to use short sentences for simple communication in life and at work. For those at the intermediate level, they are trained to understand simple conversations and speeches in the workplace, comprehend the main ideas, grasp the basic situations, and communicate with others in simple words on important topics at work. For those at the advanced level, they are trained to be able to understand general conversations and speeches in the workplace, grasp the main content and key information, use basic communication strategies to communicate with others and carry out the work, have a preliminary understanding of cultural factors related to communication activities, master the general communication-related cultural background knowledge, and overcome cultural barriers encountered during communication. The progression in level of communicative competence helps them to leap forward from routine etiquette, basic communication in life and at work at the elementary level, to simple information exchange of service processes at the intermediate level, and finally to complex information exchange and handling of special circumstances at the advanced level.

Vocational Skill Objectives

To meet job requirements at the elementary, intermediate and advanced levels, the professional positions that are most urgently needed overseas are selected. The positions corresponding to logistics management at the elementary, intermediate and advanced levels are logistics staff, logistics managers and logistics directors; the positions corresponding to automotive service engineering technology at the elementary, intermediate and advanced levels are automotive electromechanical maintenance staff, automotive service consultants and technical directors; the positions corresponding to e-commerce at the elementary, intermediate and advanced levels are electronic operation assistants, e-commerce operators and e-commerce customer service staff; the positions corresponding to mechatronics at the elementary, intermediate and advanced levels are mechanical and electrical operators, mechanical and electrical adjusters, and mechanical and electrical maintenance staff; the positions corresponding to computer networking technology at the elementary, intermediate and advanced levels are broadband operation and maintenance engineers, network operation and maintenance specialists, and network administrators; the positions corresponding to hotel management at the elementary, intermediate and advanced levels are lobby receptionists, lobby supervisors and lobby managers. Through 30 work scenarios/tasks set for each major, learners can fully grasp the general situations and basic procedures of the position after learning, and achieve the dual goals of language learning and professional operation.

Principles of Compilation

1. Language knowledge skills and professional knowledge skills go hand in hand to meet the demands of current popular and urgently needed job positions;

2. It makes progressive differentiation and comprehensive integration, breaking down, dividing and conquering difficult points;

3. Language knowledge and professional knowledge recur scientifically and efficiently, language skills and professional skills spiral upward, and the situational stage, semantic framework, and ontology input methods cooperate with each other;

4. Professional knowledge and skills are visualized, using a lot of pictures and videos;

5. It strengthens the practical skills in professional positions. This series of textbooks is equipped with videos of professional technical training, highlighting the practical skills for professional positions. It addresses the mismatch between the difficulty of language learning and that of mastering skills by supplementing with practical videos and practical training.

Characteristic Pursuit

Starting from the basic phonetic knowledge learning and job cognition at the elementary level, this series integrates “Chinese + Vocational Skills” into the working scene dialogues, breaking down the job into various tasks, solving lexical problems by means of picture cognition, solving the problem of the mismatch between students' mastery of Chinese vocabulary and professional skills by means of displaying videos, stressing the practicality of skills, and focusing on "learning by doing". Each unit has a "Practicing What You Have Learnt" module, which not only solves the problem of lexical cognition of this unit, but also takes "being able to comprehend", "being able to use" and "being able to imitate" as the learning objectives. We strive to use a large number of pictures and display supporting videos to build the textbooks into three-dimensional skills-based language teaching materials, so that learners can learn more independently.

Recommendations for Use

1. Each major of this series consists of three volumes at the elementary, intermediate, and advanced levels, with 10 units in each volume. For each unit, it is recommended to be completed in 8-10 class hours at the elementary level, 10-12 class hours at the intermediate level, and 12-14 class hours at the advanced level.

2. The notes and explanations in the textbooks focus on conciseness, practicality, and the training of listening and speaking skills. The grammar knowledge in the textbooks can be detailed and supplemented by teachers as the case may be.

3. "Unit Practical Training" module can be used as a classroom exercise after the texts and language points, preferably to be completed in two class hours. Teachers should guide students to complete the training tasks step by step. Students are not required to read and understand the training steps. It is important that teachers guide students to achieve the goal of mastering professional skills.

4. "Unit Summary" module summarizes the keywords and core content of the entire unit. Through listening and speaking exercises, this part can better help learners understand the core tasks of this unit.

5. Teachers should make full use of the exercises designed in the textbooks during class, and guide students to listen more and practice more, combine listening and speaking, and integrate learning with practice.

6. Teachers should guide students to proficiently read the texts aloud, asking them to recite the keywords, sentences and classroom expressions in each unit.

Acknowledgements

We are grateful to the Center for Language Education and Cooperation of the Ministry of Education for listing the New Silk Road "Chinese + Vocational Skills" series as a key research and development project, which adds motivation and a sense of responsibility to our textbook compilation. The Textbook Compilation Committee is responsible for the planning, design, compilation and coordination of the entire set of textbooks, and has held hundreds of seminars to conduct a comprehensive evaluation, discussion, examination and approval of text compilation, style arrangement, notes and explanations, exercise design, picture selection, and video production of each textbook. We are indebted to the members of the Compilation Committee and all compilers for their professional dedication, unwavering pursuit of perfection in the compilation, as well as their enthusiasm, hard work and wisdom. We are thankful to the experts in international Chinese language education and colleagues from all over the country who have kept a close eye on this series and contributed their valuable opinions.

Compilation Committee of New Silk Road "Chinese + Vocational Skills" Series

April 2023

gǎngwèi jièshào

岗位介绍

Introduction to Posts

wǎngluò gōngchéngshī

网络 工程师

Network Engineer

wǎngyè shèjìshī

网页设计师

Web Designer

wǎngzhàn wéihùyuán

网站 维护员

Website Maintainer

jìsuànjī xìtǒng wéihùyuán

计算机系统维护员

Computer System Maintainer

shùjùkù guǎnlǐ yǔ wéihù gōngchéngshī

数据库管理与维护 工程师

Database Management and Maintenance Engineer

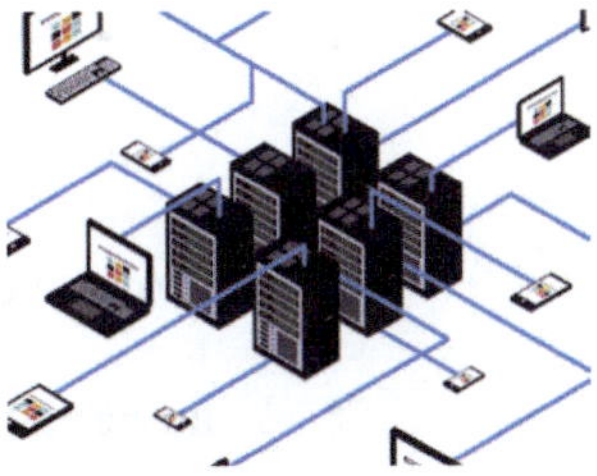

语法术语及缩略形式参照表
Abbreviations of Grammar Terms

Grammar Terms in Chinese	Grammar Terms in Pinyin	Grammar Terms in English	Abbreviations
名词	míngcí	noun	n.
专有名词	zhuānyǒu míngcí	proper noun	pn.
代词	dàicí	pronoun	pron.
数词	shùcí	numeral	num.
量词	liàngcí	measure word	m.
数量词	shùliàngcí	quantifier	q.
动词	dòngcí	verb	v.
助动词	zhùdòngcí	auxiliary	aux.
形容词	xíngróngcí	adjective	adj.
副词	fùcí	adverb	adv.
介词	jiècí	preposition	prep.
连词	liáncí	conjunction	conj.
助词	zhùcí	particle	part.
拟声词	nǐshēngcí	onomatopoeia	onom.
叹词	tàncí	interjection	int.
前缀	qiánzhuì	prefix	pref.
后缀	hòuzhuì	suffix	suf.
成语	chéngyǔ	idiom	idm.
短语	duǎnyǔ	phrase	phr.
主语	zhǔyǔ	subject	S
谓语	wèiyǔ	predicate	P
宾语	bīnyǔ	object	O
定语	dìngyǔ	attributive	Attrib
状语	zhuàngyǔ	adverbial	Adverb
补语	bǔyǔ	complement	C

CONTENTS

目录

第一单元 RIP 组建网络 Unit 1 RIP Networking 1

第一部分 课文 Texts 2

一、热身 Warm-up 2

二、课文 Texts 5

三、视听说 Viewing, Listening, and Speaking 9

四、学以致用 Practicing What You Have Learnt 10

五、小知识 Tips 10

第二部分 汉字 Chinese Characters 11

一、汉字知识 Knowledge about Chinese Characters 11

汉字的偏旁（1） Radicals of Chinese characters (1)

口 囗 女 亻 日

二、汉字认读与书写 The Recognition and Writing of Chinese Characters 12

第三部分 日常用语 Daily Expressions 13

第四部分 单元实训 Unit Practical Training 13

RIP 路由的配置 RIP Routing Configuration 13

第五部分 单元小结 Unit Summary 14

第二单元 OSPF 组建网络 Unit 2 OSPF Networking 17

第一部分 课文 Texts 18

一、热身 Warm-up 18

二、课文 Texts 20

三、视听说 Viewing, Listening, and Speaking 25

四、学以致用 Practicing What You Have Learnt 26

五、小知识 Tips 27

第二部分 汉字 Chinese Characters 28

一、汉字知识 Knowledge about Chinese Characters 28

汉字的偏旁（2） Radicals of Chinese characters (2)

氵 讠 艹 辶

二、汉字认读与书写 The Recognition and Writing of Chinese Characters 29

第三部分 日常用语 Daily Expressions 30

第四部分 单元实训 Unit Practical Training 30
OSPF 路由的配置 OSPF Routing Configuration 30
第五部分 单元小结 Unit Summary 31

第三单元 动态虚拟局域网 Unit 3 Dynamic VLAN 33

第一部分 课文 Texts 34
一、热身 Warm-up 34
二、课文 Texts 36
三、视听说 Viewing, Listening, and Speaking 40
四、学以致用 Practicing What You Have Learnt 41
五、小知识 Tips 44
第二部分 汉字 Chinese Characters 44
一、汉字知识 Knowledge about Chinese Characters 44
汉字的偏旁（3） Radicals of Chinese characters (3)
扌 木 纟 心 𧾷
二、汉字认读与书写 The Recognition and Writing of Chinese Characters 45
第三部分 日常用语 Daily Expressions 46
第四部分 单元实训 Unit Practical Training 46
动态 VLAN 的设置 Dynamic VLAN Settings 46
第五部分 单元小结 Unit Summary 48

第四单元 VLAN 间路由 Unit 4 Inter-VLAN Routing 51

第一部分 课文 Texts 52
一、热身 Warm-up 52
二、课文 Texts 54
三、视听说 Viewing, Listening, and Speaking 58
四、学以致用 Practicing What You Have Learnt 59
五、小知识 Tips 60
第二部分 汉字 Chinese Characters 61
一、汉字知识 Knowledge about Chinese Characters 61
汉字的偏旁（4） Radicals of Chinese characters (4)
阝(左) 宀 又 月 钅 王
二、汉字认读与书写 The Recognition and Writing of Chinese Characters 62
第三部分 日常用语 Daily Expressions 62

第四部分 单元实训 Unit Practical Training 62
配置 VLAN 间路由 Configuring Inter-VLAN Routing 63
第五部分 单元小结 Unit Summary 63

第五单元 DHCP 中继代理配置 Unit 5 DHCP Relay Agent Configuration 65

第一部分 课文 Texts 66
一、热身 Warm-up 66
二、课文 Texts 68
三、视听说 Viewing, Listening, and Speaking 72
四、学以致用 Practicing What You Have Learnt 73
五、小知识 Tips 74
第二部分 汉字 Chinese Characters 75
一、汉字知识 Knowledge about Chinese Characters 75
汉字的偏旁（5） Radicals of Chinese characters (5)
巾 广 小 ⺌ 八 刂
二、汉字认读与书写 The Recognition and Writing of Chinese Characters 76
第三部分 日常用语 Daily Expressions 76
第四部分 单元实训 Unit Practical Training 77
DHCP 中继代理配置 DHCP Relay Agent Configuration 77
第五部分 单元小结 Unit Summary 78

第六单元 链路聚合 Unit 6 Link Aggregation 81

第一部分 课文 Texts 82
一、热身 Warm-up 82
二、课文 Texts 85
三、视听说 Viewing, Listening, and Speaking 90
四、学以致用 Practicing What You Have Learnt 93
五、小知识 Tips 95
第二部分 汉字 Chinese Characters 96
一、汉字知识 Knowledge about Chinese Characters 96
汉字的偏旁（6） Radicals of Chinese characters (6)
⺮ 灬 衤 ⻗ 土
二、汉字认读与书写 The Recognition and Writing of Chinese Characters 97
第三部分 日常用语 Daily Expressions 98

第四部分 单元实训 Unit Practical Training 98
链路聚合配置 Link Aggregation Configuration 98
第五部分 单元小结 Unit Summary 99

第七单元 网络安全 Unit 7 Network Security 101

第一部分 课文 Texts 102
一、热身 Warm-up 102
二、课文 Texts 105
三、视听说 Viewing, Listening, and Speaking 109
四、学以致用 Practicing What You Have Learnt 110
五、小知识 Tips 113
第二部分 汉字 Chinese Characters 114
一、汉字知识 Knowledge about Chinese Characters 114
汉字的偏旁（7） Radicals of Chinese characters (7)
走 忄 攵 饣 禾
二、汉字认读与书写 The Recognition and Writing of Chinese Characters 115
第三部分 日常用语 Daily Expressions 115
第四部分 单元实训 Unit Practical Training 115
ACL 配置及应用 ACL Configuration and Application 115
第五部分 单元小结 Unit Summary 116

第八单元 网络地址转换 Unit 8 Network Address Translation 119

第一部分 课文 Texts 120
一、热身 Warm-up 120
二、课文 Texts 122
三、视听说 Viewing, Listening, and Speaking 126
四、学以致用 Practicing What You Have Learnt 127
五、小知识 Tips 128
第二部分 汉字 Chinese Characters 129
一、汉字知识 Knowledge about Chinese Characters 129
汉字的偏旁（8） Radicals of Chinese characters (8)
门 疒 冂 车 贝
二、汉字认读与书写 The Recognition and Writing of Chinese Characters 129
第三部分 日常用语 Daily Expressions 130

第四部分 单元实训 Unit Practical Training 130
配置静态网络地址转换 Configuring Static NAT 130
第五部分 单元小结 Unit Summary 131

第九单元 点到点协议 PPP Unit 9 Point-to-Point Protocol PPP 133

第一部分 课文 Texts 134
一、热身 Warm-up 134
二、课文 Texts 137
三、视听说 Viewing, Listening, and Speaking 141
四、学以致用 Practicing What You Have Learnt 143
五、小知识 Tips 145
第二部分 汉字 Chinese Characters 146
一、汉字知识 Knowledge about Chinese Characters 146
汉字的偏旁（9） Radicals of Chinese characters (9)
耳 攵 冫 彳
二、汉字认读与书写 The Recognition and Writing of Chinese Characters 147
第三部分 日常用语 Daily Expressions 147
第四部分 单元实训 Unit Practical Training 147
配置 PPP Configuring PPP 148
第五部分 单元小结 Unit Summary 149

第十单元 网络管理 Unit 10 Network Management 151

第一部分 课文 Texts 152
一、热身 Warm-up 152
二、课文 Texts 155
三、视听说 Viewing, Listening, and Speaking 159
四、学以致用 Practicing What You Have Learnt 161
五、小知识 Tips 162
第二部分 汉字 Chinese Characters 163
一、汉字知识 Knowledge about Chinese Characters 163
汉字的偏旁（10） Radicals of Chinese characters (10)
穴 田 力 牛
二、汉字认读与书写 The Recognition and Writing of Chinese Characters 163
第三部分 日常用语 Daily Expressions 164

第四部分 单元实训 Unit Practical Training 164
应用网络管理系统 Application of Network Management System 164
第五部分 单元小结 Unit Summary 165

附录 Appendixes 167

词语总表 Vocabulary 167
视频脚本 Video Scripts 176
参考答案 Reference Answers 182

1

RIP zǔjiàn wǎngluò

RIP 组建网络

RIP Networking

RIP lùyóu pèizhì de cāozuò bùzhòu

RIP 路由配置的操作步骤

Operation Steps of RIP Routing Configuration

xiàzài bìng ānzhuāng eNSP ruǎnjiàn

下载并安装 eNSP 软件

Download and Install the eNSP Software

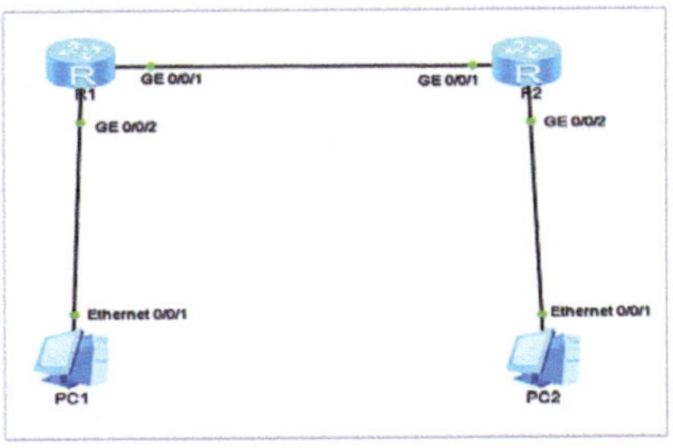

dǎkāi eNSP ruǎnjiàn, huìzhì wǎngluò tuòpūtú

打开 eNSP 软件，绘制网络拓扑图

Open the eNSP Software and Draw the Network Topology Diagram

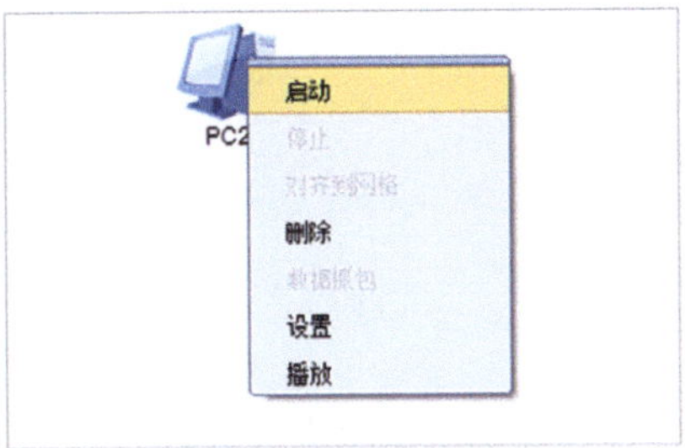

qǐdòng suǒ xū shèbèi

启动所需设备

Start the Required Equipment

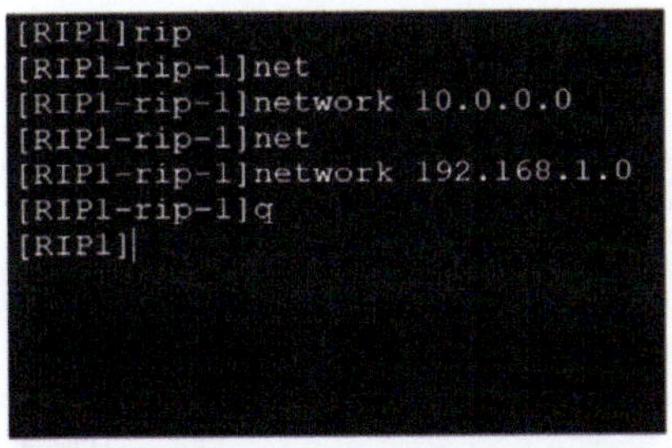

dǎkāi lùyóuqì, jìnxíng RIP lùyóu pèizhì

打开路由器，进行 RIP 路由配置

Turn on the Router and Perform RIP Routing Configuration

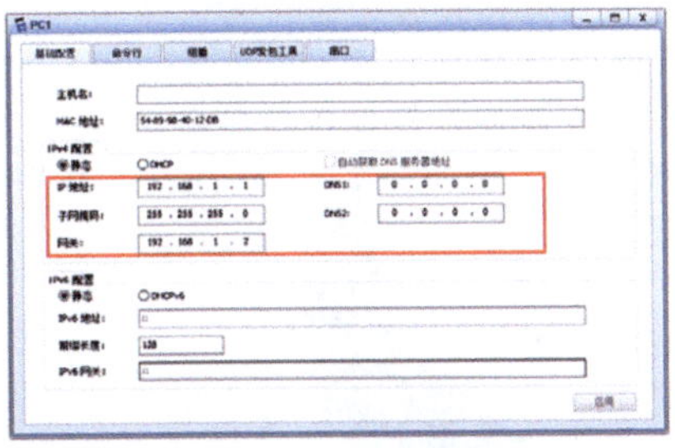

dǎkāi jìsuànjī, pèizhì IP dìzhǐ、zǐwǎng yǎnmǎ hé wǎngguān

打开计算机，配置 IP 地址、子网掩码和网关

Turn on the Computer, and Configure the IP Address, Subnet Mask and Gateway

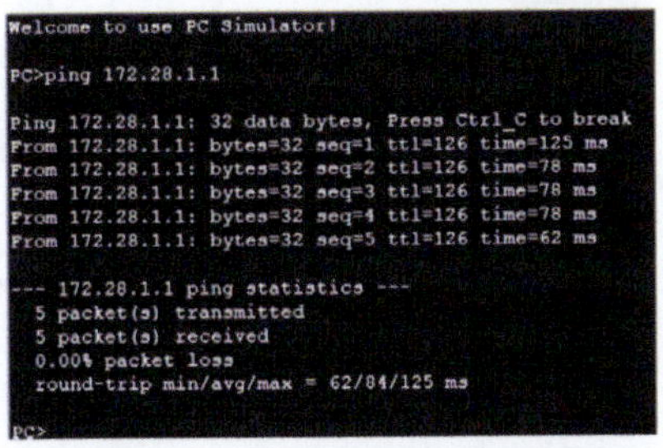

bǎocún pèizhì, bìng cèshì jìsuànjī liántōngxìng

保存配置，并测试计算机连通性

Save the Configuration and Test the Computer Connectivity

题解 Introduction

1. 学习内容：RIP 组建网络的安装流程、RIP 路由配置的基本步骤和作业要求。

   Learning content: The installation process of RIP networking, basic steps and working requirements of RIP routing configuration

2. 知识目标：掌握 RIP 组建网络的关键词语，了解汉字的偏旁“口”“囗”“女”“亻”“日”，学写相关汉字。

   Knowledge objectives: To master the keywords for RIP networking, understand the Chinese radicals “口”, “囗”, “女”, “亻”, “日”, and learn to write the related Chinese characters

3. 技能目标：学会配置 RIP 路由，让计算机之间可以互通。

   Skill objective: To master RIP routing configuration and enable computers to communicate with each other

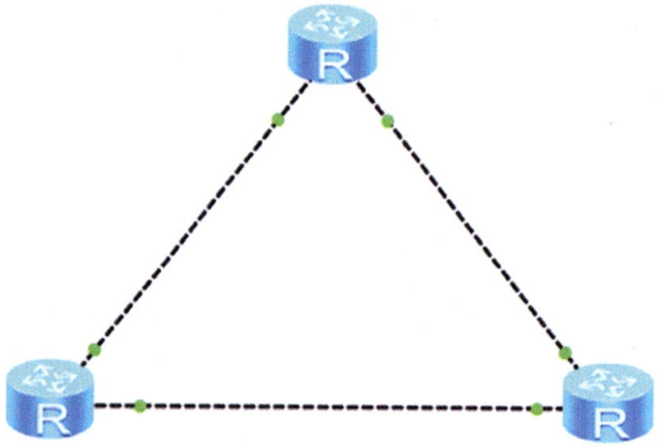

第一部分 Part 1

课文 Texts

一、热身 rèshēn Warm-up

1. 给词语选择对应的图片。Choose the corresponding pictures for the words.

A.

B.

C.

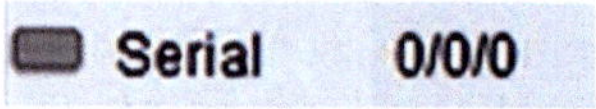

D.

E.

F.

E kǒu
① E 口________________
E port

jìsuànjī
② 计算机________________
computer

lùyóuqì
③ 路由器________________
router

④ eNSP________________

G kǒu
⑤ G 口________________
G port

S kǒu
⑥ S 口________________
S port

2. 观看介绍在 eNSP 中绘制网络拓扑图的流程的视频，将流程中的步骤和相应的图片连线。

Watch the video introducing the process of drawing network topology diagram in eNSP, and match the steps in the process with the corresponding pictures.

Qǐdòng eNSP ruǎnjiàn.
① 启动 eNSP 软件。
Start the eNSP software.

Xuǎnzhòng zuǒbian de "lùyóuqì" shèbèi jí xínghào, tuōdòng lùyóuqì dào gōngzuòqū, chóngfù cǐ bùzhòu, zài tuōdòng lìng yì tái lùyóuqì dào gōngzuòqū.
② 选中左边的"路由器"设备及型号，拖动路由器到工作区，重复此步骤，再拖动另一台路由器到工作区。
Select the "router" device and model on the left, drag the router to the work area, and repeat this step to drag another router to the work area.

Xuǎnzé zuǒshàngjiǎo de "zhōngduān shèbèi", xuǎnzhòng zuǒ cè de PC tuō dào gōngzuòqū, chóngfù cǐ bùzhòu, zài tuōdòng lìng yì tái PC dào gōngzuòqū.
③ 选择左上角的"终端设备"，选中左侧的PC拖到工作区，重复此步骤，再拖动另一台PC到工作区。
Select the "terminal device" in the upper left corner, drag the selected PC on the left to the work area, and repeat this step to drag another PC to the work area.

Xuǎnzhòng suǒyǒu shèbèi, àn qǐdòngjiàn qǐdòng shèbèi.
④ 选中所有设备，按启动键启动设备。
Select all the devices and press the start button to start the devices.

Xuǎnzé zuǒshàngjiǎo de "shèbèi liánxiàn", xuǎnzhòng copper xiàn.
⑤ 选择左上角的"设备连线"，选中 copper 线。
Select the "equipment connection" in the upper left corner and select the copper line.

Zài lùyóuqì shang yòu jī shǔbiāo, xuǎnzhòng G kǒu, tuōdòng xiànlǎn dào lìng yì tái lùyóuqì, yòu jī shǔbiāo, xuǎnzé G kǒu jìnxíng shèbèi liánxiàn, chóngfù cǐ bùzhòu, wánchéng lùyóuqì yǔ PC jī zhījiān de liánxiàn.
⑥ 在路由器上右击鼠标，选中G口，拖动线缆到另一台路由器，右击鼠标，选择G口进行设备连线，重复此步骤，完成路由器与PC机之间的连线。
Right-click the mouse on the router to select G port, drag the cable to another router, right-click the mouse to select G port for equipment connection, and repeat this step to complete the connection between the routers and the PC.

A.
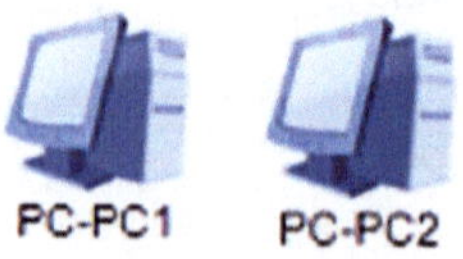

B.
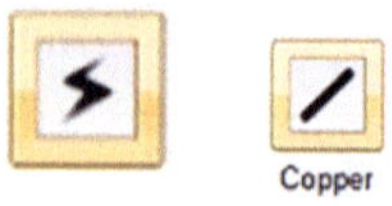

C.
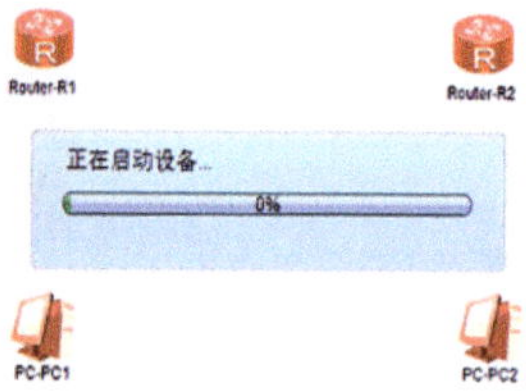

D.

E.
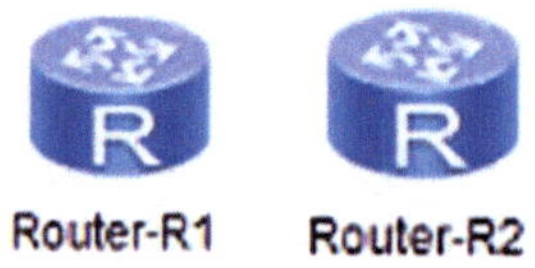

F.
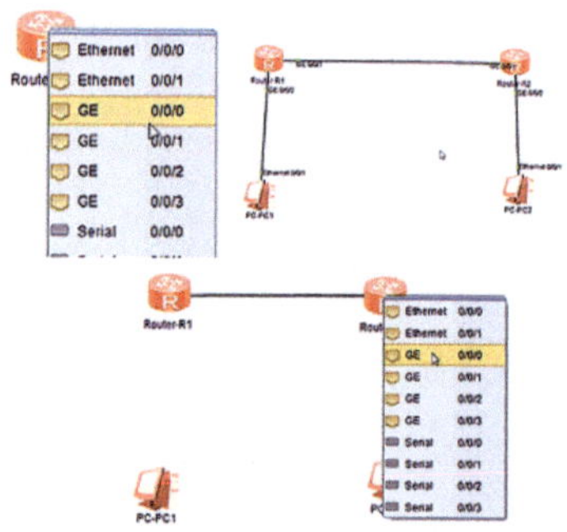

二、课文 kèwén Texts

A 01-01

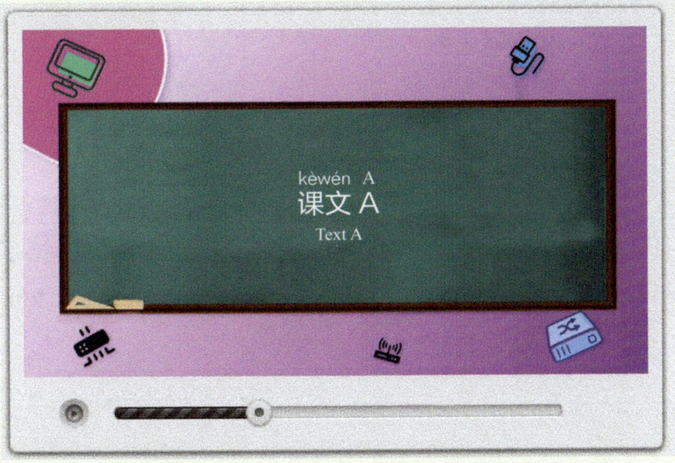

túdì: Shīfu, dòngtài lùyóu zěnme pèizhì?
徒弟：师傅，动态路由怎么配置？

shīfu: Pèizhì dòngtài lùyóu shǒuxiān xūyào xiàzài bìng ānzhuāng eNSP ruǎnjiàn; ránhòu zài eNSP jièmiàn zhōng huìzhì wǎngluò tuòpūtú; jiēzhē qǐdòng suǒyǒu shèbèi, dǎkāi eNSP zhōng de lùyóuqì, jìnxíng RIP dòngtài lùyóu de pèizhì.
师傅：配置动态路由首先需要下载并安装 eNSP 软件；然后在 eNSP 界面中绘制网络拓扑图；接着启动所有设备，打开 eNSP 中的路由器，进行 RIP 动态路由的配置。

túdì: Pèizhì wán RIP dòngtài lùyóu yǐhòu, zài zuò shénme?
徒弟：配置完 RIP 动态路由以后，再做什么？

shīfu: Pèizhì wán RIP dòngtài lùyóu yǐhòu, zài dǎkāi eNSP zhōng de jìsuànjī, pèizhì IP dìzhǐ、zǐwǎng yǎnmǎ hé wǎngguān. Zuìhòu bǎocún pèizhì, bìng cèshì jìsuànjī liántōngxìng.
师傅：配置完 RIP 动态路由以后，再打开 eNSP 中的计算机，配置 IP 地址、子网掩码和网关。最后保存配置，并测试计算机连通性。

túdì: Nà RIP xiéyì rúhé gēngxīn lùyóubiǎo ne?
徒弟：那 RIP 协议如何更新路由表呢？

shīfu: RIP huì zhōuqīxìng guǎngbō zhěnggè lùyóubiǎo, jíshǐ wǎngluò tuòpū méiyǒu fāshēng rènhé biànhuà, RIP yě huì měi gé 30 miǎo zhōuqīxìng de fāsòng zhěnggè lùyóubiǎo gěi xiānglín de lùyóuqì.
师傅：RIP 会周期性广播整个路由表，即使网络拓扑没有发生任何变化，RIP 也会每隔 30 秒周期性地发送整个路由表给相邻的路由器。

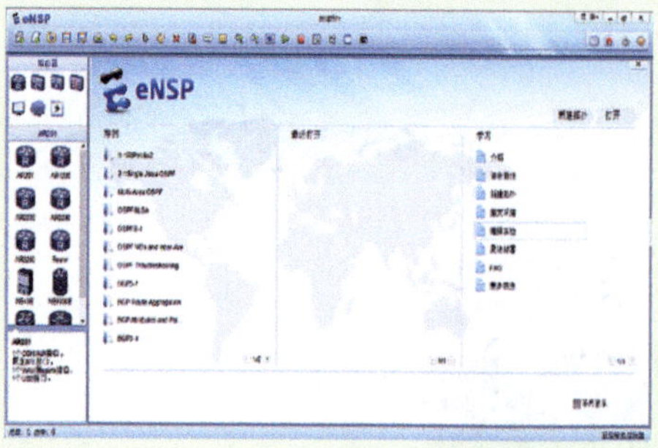

eNSP jièmiàn
eNSP 界面
eNSP interface

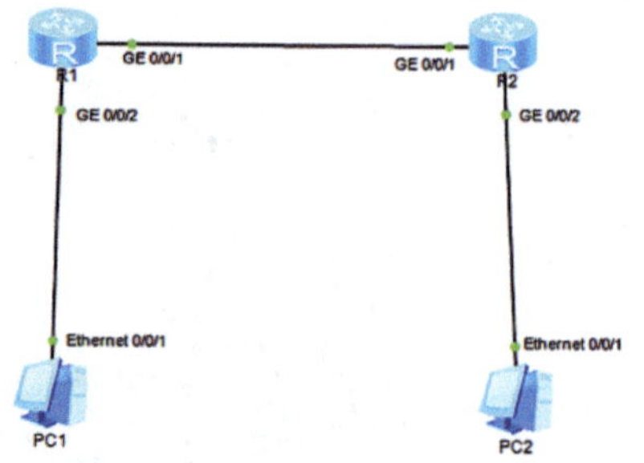

wǎngluò tuòpūtú
网络拓扑图
Network topology

译文 yìwén Text in English

Apprentice: Master, how can I configure dynamic routing?

Master: To configure dynamic routing, first download and install the eNSP software; draw the network topology diagram in the eNSP interface; start all the devices, turn on the router in eNSP, and configure RIP dynamic routing.

Apprentice: What shall I do after configuring RIP dynamic routing?

Master: After configuring RIP dynamic routing, switch on the computer in eNSP and configure the IP address, subnet mask and gateway. Finally, save the configuration and test the computer connectivity.

Apprentice: How does the RIP protocol update the routing table?

Master: RIP broadcasts the entire routing table periodically. Even if the network topology has not changed, RIP will periodically send the entire routing table to adjacent routers every 30 seconds.

普通词语 pǔtōng cíyǔ General Vocabulary

01-02

1.	打开	dǎ//kāi	v.	turn on, switch on
2.	完	wán	v.	finish
3.	更新	gēngxīn	v.	update
4.	广播	guǎngbō	v.	broadcast
5.	整个	zhěnggè	adj.	whole
6.	即使	jíshǐ	conj.	even if
7.	发生	fāshēng	v.	happen
8.	任何	rènhé	pron.	any
9.	变化	biànhuà	n.	change
10.	隔	gé	v.	(be) after/at an interval
11.	秒	miǎo	m.	second
12.	发送	fāsòng	v.	send
13.	相邻	xiānglín	adj.	adjacent

专业词语 zhuānyè cíyǔ Specialized Vocabulary

01-03

1.	动态路由	dòngtài lùyóu	phr.	dynamic routing
2.	eNSP 软件	eNSP ruǎnjiàn	phr.	eNSP software
3.	RIP 动态路由	RIP dòngtài lùyóu	phr.	RIP dynamic routing
4.	路由表	lùyóubiǎo	n.	routing table
5.	周期性	zhōuqīxìng	n.	periodicity

B 01-04

túdì: Shénme shì RIP lùyóu?
徒弟：什么是 RIP 路由？

shīfu: RIP shì yì zhǒng jīyú jùlí shǐliàng de lùyóu xiéyì, yǐ lùyóu tiàoshù zuòwéi jìshù dānwèi, shìhé yòngyú xiǎoxíng de wǎngluò huánjìng.
师傅：RIP 是一种基于距离矢量的路由协议，以路由跳数作为计数单位，适合用于小型的网络环境。

túdì: Shīfu, zài pèizhì RIP lùyóu qián xūyào zuò shénme ne?
徒弟：师傅，在配置 RIP 路由前需要做什么呢？

shīfu: Wǒmen xūyào ānzhuāng eNSP, huìzhì wǎngluò tuòpūtú.
师傅：我们需要安装 eNSP，绘制网络拓扑图。

túdì: RIP lùyóu zěnme pèizhì ne?
徒弟：RIP 路由怎么配置呢？

shīfu: Xiān zài lùyóuqì de liǎng gè duānkǒu pèizhì IP dìzhǐ, ránhòu jìnxíng RIP lùyóu de pèizhì. Zài jìsuànjī shang, wǒmen xūyào pèizhì hǎo IP dìzhǐ、zǐwǎng yǎnmǎ hé wǎngguān.
师傅：先在路由器的两个端口配置 IP 地址，然后进行 RIP 路由的配置。在计算机上，我们需要配置好 IP 地址、子网掩码和网关。

túdì: Nà wǒmen zěnme cái néng zhīdào pèizhì hǎo le ne?
徒弟：那我们怎么才能知道配置好了呢？

shīfu: Wǒmen kěyǐ yòng display ip routing-table chákàn lùyóu de pèizhì xìnxī, ránhòu cèshì jìsuànjī zhījiān de liántōngxìng.
师傅：我们可以用 display ip routing-table 查看路由的配置信息，然后测试计算机之间的连通性。

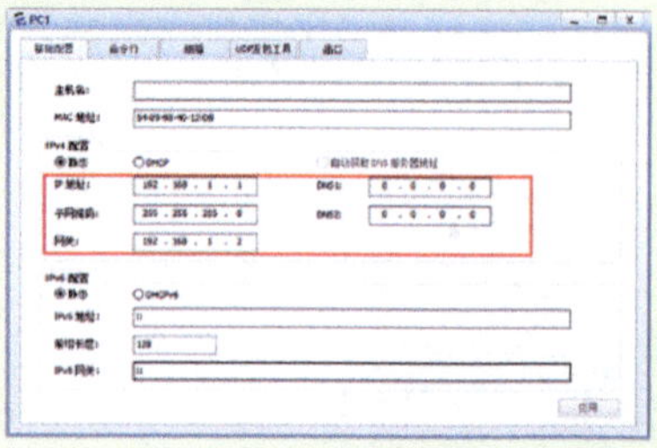

IP dìzhǐ
IP 地址
IP address

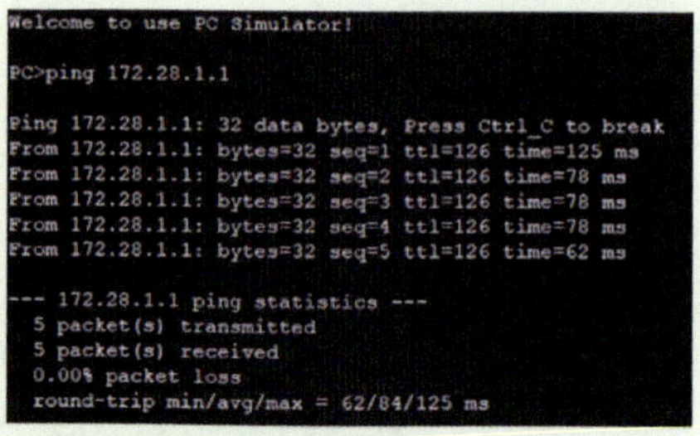

cèshì liántōngxìng
测试连通性
Test the connectivity

译文 yìwén Text in English

Apprentice: What is RIP routing?

Master: RIP is a routing protocol based on distance vector, which takes routing hop counts as the counting unit. It is suitable for small network environment.

Apprentice: Master, what shall I do before configuring RIP routing?

Master: We need to install eNSP and draw the network topology diagram.

Apprentice: How can I configure RIP routing?

Master: First, configure IP addresses on the two ports of the routers, and then configure RIP routing. On the computer, we need to configure the IP address, subnet mask and gateway.

Apprentice: How can we know that the configuration is ready?

Master: We can use *display ip routing-table* to view the routing configuration information, and then test the connectivity between computers.

普通词语 pǔtōng cíyǔ General Vocabulary

01-05

1.	适合	shìhé	v.	be suitable for
2.	作为	zuòwéi	v.	regard as
3.	小型	xiǎoxíng	adj.	small, small-scale

专业词语 zhuānyè cíyǔ Specialized Vocabulary

01-06

1.	距离矢量	jùlí shǐliàng	phr.	distance vector

2.	路由跳数	lùyóu tiàoshù	phr.	routing hop count
3.	计数单位	jìshù dānwèi	phr.	counting unit

三、视听说 shì-tīng-shuō Viewing, Listening, and Speaking

1. 看视频，掌握 RIP 路由配置的基本内容和要求，将相关内容进行连线。

Watch the video to master the basic contents and requirements for RIP routing configuration, and match the related content.

qiánqī zhǔnbèi
① 前期准备
early-stage preparations

jīběn pèizhì
② 基本配置
basic configuration

cèshì yǔ bǎocún
③ 测试与保存
testing and saving

pèizhì jìsuànjī de IP dìzhǐ
A. 配置计算机的 IP 地址
configuring the computer's IP address

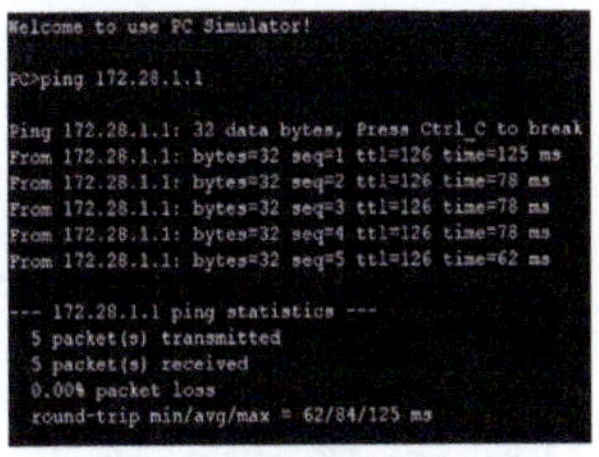

cèshì jìsuànjī liántōngxìng
B. 测试计算机 连通性
testing the connectivity between computers

xiàzài bìng ānzhuāng eNSP ruǎnjiàn
C. 下载并 安装 eNSP 软件
downloading and installing the eNSP software

bǎocún pèizhì
D. 保存配置
saving the configuration

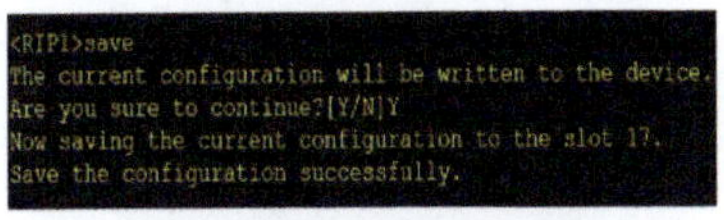

pèizhì RIP lùyóu
E. 配置 RIP 路由
configuring RIP routing

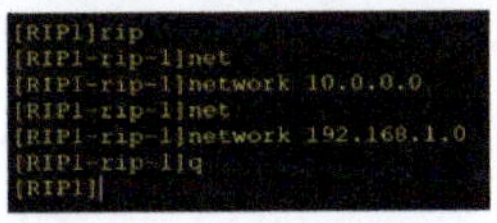

huìzhì wǎngluò tuòpūtú
F. 绘制 网 络 拓扑图
drawing the network topology diagram

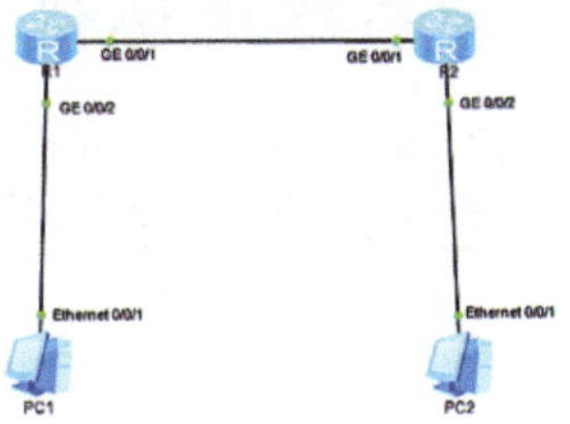

2. 说一说　Let's talk

说一说 RIP 路由配置的基本内容和要求。

Talk about the basic contents and requirements for RIP routing configuration.

四、学以致用　xuéyǐzhìyòng　Practicing What You Have Learnt

观看实际操作中 RIP 路由配置的视频，给安装步骤排序。

Watch the video on RIP routing configuration in actual operation, and arrange the installation steps in order.

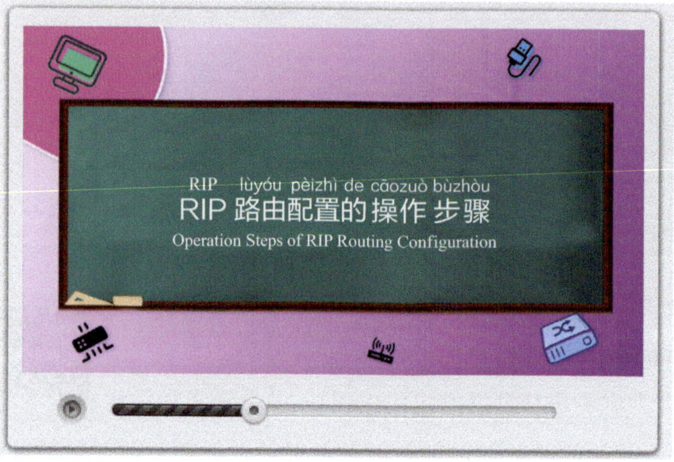

ānzhuāng ruǎnjiàn
A. 安装 软件
Install the software

cèshì liántōngxìng
B. 测试连通性
Test the connectivity

qǐdòng shèbèi
C. 启动 设备
Start the equipment

pèizhì RIP lùyóu
D. 配置 RIP 路由
Configure the RIP routing

huìzhì tuòpūtú
E. 绘制拓扑图
Draw the topology diagram

pèizhì jìsuànjī IP
F. 配置计算机 IP
Configure the computer IP

① ________ ② ________ ③ ________ ④ ________ ⑤ ________ ⑥ ________

五、小知识　xiǎo zhīshi　Tips

RIP dòngtài lùyóu xiéyì
RIP 动态 路由 协议

RIP (Routing Information Protocol, lùyóu xìnxī xiéyì) shì shǐyòng zuì jiǔ de dòngtài lùyóu xiéyì zhīyī. Tā shì yì zhǒng jīyú jùlí xiàngliàng de lùyóu xuǎnzé xiéyì, zhǔyào shìyòng yú xiǎo guīmó de wǎngluò huánjìng. RIP xiéyì zhǔyào yòngyú yí gè AS (Autonomous

RIP（Routing Information Protocol，路由信息协议）是使用最久的动态路由协议之一。它是一种基于距离向量的路由选择协议，主要适用于小规模的网络环境。RIP 协议主要用于一个 AS（Autonomous

System, zìzhì xìtǒng) nèi lùyóu xìnxī de chuándì, měi 30 miǎo fāsòng yí cì lùyóu xìnxī
System，自治系统）内路由信息的传递，每 30 秒发送一次路由信息

gēngxīn. RIP yìngyòng yú OSI wǎngluò qī céng móxíng de yìngyòngcéng. Gè chǎngjiā dìngyì de
更新。RIP 应用于 OSI 网络七层模型的应用层。各厂家定义的

guǎnlǐ jùlí (AD, jí yōuxiān jí) rúxià: Huáwéi dìngyì de yōuxiānjí shì 100, Sīkē
管理距离（AD，即优先级）如下：华为定义的优先级是 100，思科

dìngyì de yōuxiānjí shì 120.
定义的优先级是 120。

RIP Dynamic Routing Protocol

RIP (Routing Information Protocol) is one of the longest-lived dynamic routing protocols. It is a routing protocol based on distance vector, which is mainly suitable for small-scale network environment. The RIP protocol is mainly used for the transmission of routing information in an AS (Autonomous System), and it sends the routing information update every 30 seconds. RIP is applied to the application layer of the OSI (Open System Interconnection) network 7-layer model. The Administrative Distance (AD, i.e. priority) defined by various manufacturers are as follows: the priority defined by Huawei is 100 and that defined by Cisco is 120.

补充专业词语 bǔchōng zhuānyè cíyǔ Supplementary Specialized Vocabulary

01-07

1.	ping 通	ping tōng	phr.	ping each other
2.	作业要求	zuòyè yāoqiú	phr.	operation requirement
3.	距离向量	jùlí xiàngliàng	phr.	distance vector
4.	自治系统	zìzhì xìtǒng	phr.	As (Autonomous System)
5.	应用层	yìngyòngcéng	n.	application layer
6.	管理距离	guǎnlǐ jùlí	phr.	administrative distance

第二部分 Part 2

汉字 Chinese Characters

一、汉字知识 Hànzì zhīshi Knowledge about Chinese Characters

汉字的偏旁（1） **Radicals of Chinese characters (1)**

偏旁 Radicals	例字 Examples	部件组合 Combinations	结构图示 Illustrations
口	吗	口＋马	⿰
	呢	口＋尼	⿰
	哪	口＋那	⿰

（续表）

偏旁 Radicals	例字 Examples	部件组合 Combinations	结构图示 Illustrations
口	吃	口＋乞	
	啊	口＋阿	
	叫	口＋丩	
囗	国	囗＋玉	
	图	囗＋冬	
女	妈	女＋马	
	她	女＋也	
	姓	女＋生	
	娜	女＋那	
亻	你	亻＋尔	
	他	亻＋也	
	们	亻＋门	
	作	亻＋乍	
	什	亻＋十	
	做	亻＋故	
日	时	日＋寸	
	晚	日＋免	
	明	日＋月	
	早	日＋十	
	星	日＋生	

二、汉字认读与书写 Hànzì rèndú yǔ shūxiě The Recognition and Writing of Chinese Characters

认读下列词语，并试着读写构成词语的汉字。

Recognize the following words, and try to read and write the Chinese characters forming these words.

括号　　视图　　比如　　信件　　临时

括	号	视	图
比	如	信	件
临	时		

第三部分 Part 3

日常用语 *Daily Expressions*

① 我还要再确认吗？ Wǒ hái yào zài quèrèn ma? Do I have to make a reconfirmation?
② 我要等多久呢？ Wǒ yào děng duōjiǔ ne? How long do I have to wait?
③ 有其他的航班吗？ Yǒu qítā de hángbān ma? Do you have any other flights?

第四部分 Part 4

单元实训 *Unit Practical Training*

RIP 路由的配置 RIP lùyóu de pèizhì RIP Routing Configuration

实训目的 Training purpose

掌握 RIP 路由配置的步骤，并能独立完成配置，让计算机之间可以互通。

To master the steps of RIP routing configuration, and be able to complete the configuration independently to enable the computers to communicate with each other.

实训组织 Training organization

每组 4 人，选出一个组长。

Each group consists of four people, and a group leader is selected.

实训内容 Training content

RIP 路由的配置。

Configuration of RIP routing.

实训步骤 Training steps

① 将参加人员分成若干小组，每组 4 人。

Divide the trainees into groups of 4.

② 第一个人安装 eNSP APP。

The first person installs the eNSP App.

③ 第二个人绘制拓扑图，准备配置 RIP 路由。

The second person draws the topology diagram and prepares to configure RIP routing.

④ 第三个人启动设备，配置 RIP 路由和 PC 机地址。

The third person starts the device and configures RIP routing and PC address.

⑤ 第四个人测试计算机连通性。

The fourth person tests the connectivity between computers.

⑥ 实训结束，教师总结评价。

The training ends. The teacher makes a summary and an evaluation.

第五部分 Part 5

单元小结 Unit Summary

cíyǔ
词语
Vocabulary

普通词语 General Vocabulary

1.	打开	dǎ//kāi	v.	turn on, switch on
2.	完	wán	v.	finish
3.	更新	gēngxīn	v.	update
4.	广播	guǎngbō	v.	broadcast
5.	整个	zhěnggè	adj.	whole
6.	即使	jíshǐ	conj.	even if
7.	发生	fāshēng	v.	happen
8.	任何	rènhé	pron.	any
9.	变化	biànhuà	n.	change
10.	隔	gé	v.	(be) after/at an interval
11.	秒	miǎo	m.	second
12.	发送	fāsòng	v.	send
13.	相邻	xiānglín	adj.	adjacent
14.	适合	shìhé	v.	be suitable for
15.	作为	zuòwéi	v.	regard as
16.	小型	xiǎoxíng	adj.	small, small-scale

专业词语 Specialized Vocabulary

1.	动态路由	dòngtài lùyóu	phr.	dynamic routing
2.	eNSP 软件	eNSP ruǎnjiàn	phr.	eNSP software
3.	RIP 动态路由	RIP dòngtài lùyóu	phr.	RIP dynamic routing
4.	路由表	lùyóubiǎo	n.	routing table

cíyǔ
词语
Vocabulary

5.	周期性	zhōuqīxìng	n.	periodicity
6.	距离矢量	jùlí shǐliàng	phr.	distance vector
7.	路由跳数	lùyóu tiàoshù	phr.	routing hop count
8.	计数单位	jìshù dānwèi	phr.	counting unit

补充专业词语 Supplementary Specialized Vocabulary

1.	ping 通	ping tōng	phr.	ping each other
2.	作业要求	zuòyè yāoqiú	phr.	operation requirement
3.	距离向量	jùlí xiàngliàng	phr.	distance vector
4.	自治系统	zìzhì xìtǒng	phr.	AS (Autonomous System)
5.	应用层	yìngyòngcéng	n.	application layer
6.	管理距离	guǎnlǐ jùlí	phr.	administrative distance

jùzi
句子
Sentences

1. 配置动态路由首先需要下载并安装 eNSP 软件；然后在 eNSP 界面中绘制网络拓扑图；接着启动所有设备，打开 eNSP 中的路由器，进行 RIP 动态路由的配置；再打开 eNSP 中的计算机，配置 IP 地址、子网掩码和网关；最后保存配置，并测试计算机连通性。
2. RIP 是一种基于距离矢量的路由协议，以路由跳数作为计数单位，适合用于小型的网络环境。
3. 我们可以用 display ip routing-table 查看路由的配置信息，然后测试计算机之间的连通性。

2

OSPF　　zǔjiàn　wǎngluò

OSPF 组建网络

OSPF Networking

OSPF　lùyóu pèizhì de bùzhòu

OSPF 路由配置的步骤

Steps of OSPF Routing Configuration

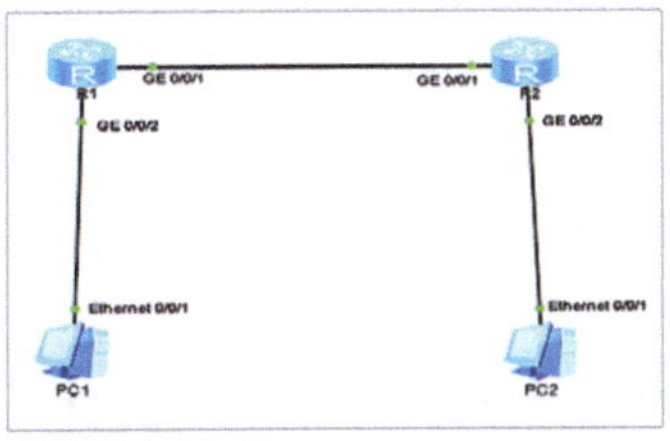

xiàzài bìng ānzhuāng eNSP ruǎnjiàn,　dǎkāi

下载并　安装 eNSP 软件，打开

eNSP ruǎnjiàn, huìzhì wǎngluò　tuòpūtú

eNSP 软件，绘制　网络　拓扑图

Download and Install the eNSP Software, Open the eNSP Software and Draw the Network Topology Diagram

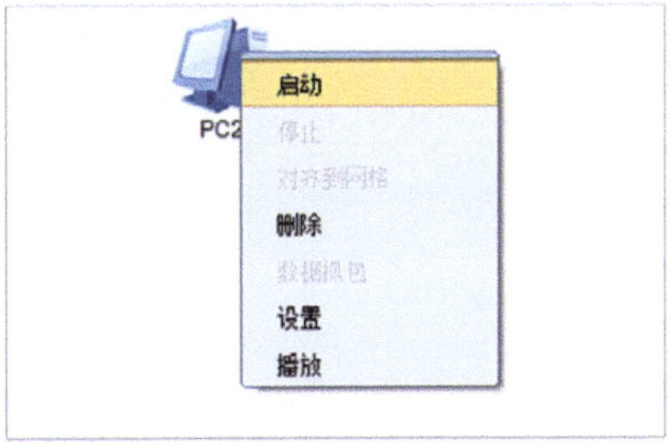

qǐdòng suǒ xū wǎngluò shèbèi

启动　所　需　网络　设备

Start the Required Network Equipment

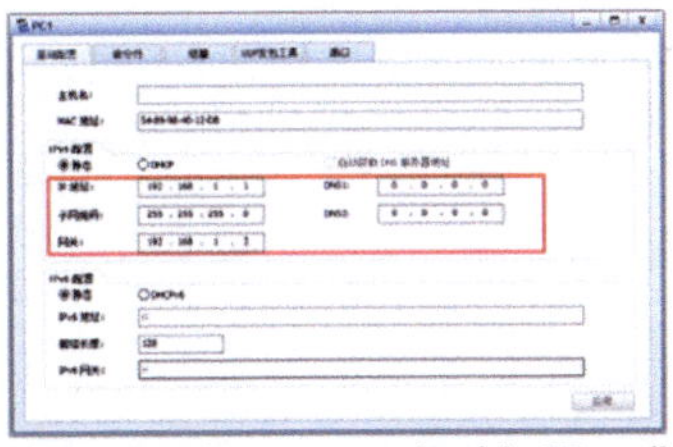

dǎkāi　jìsuànjī,　　pèizhì　IP　dìzhǐ,

打开计算机，配置 IP 地址，

zǐwǎng yǎnmǎ　hé wǎngguān

子网　掩码　和　网关

Turn on the Computer, Configure the IP Address, Subnet Mask and Gateway

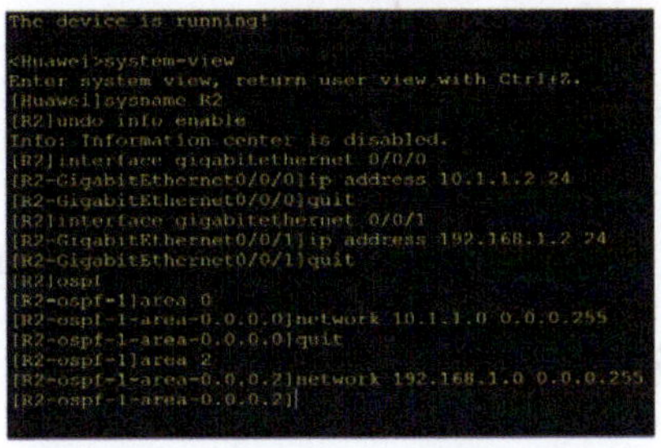

měi tái　lùyóuqì　dōu pèizhì　OSPF dòngtài lùyóu　xiéyì

每台路由器都配置 OSPF 动态路由协议

Configure the OSPF Dynamic Routing Protocol on Each Router

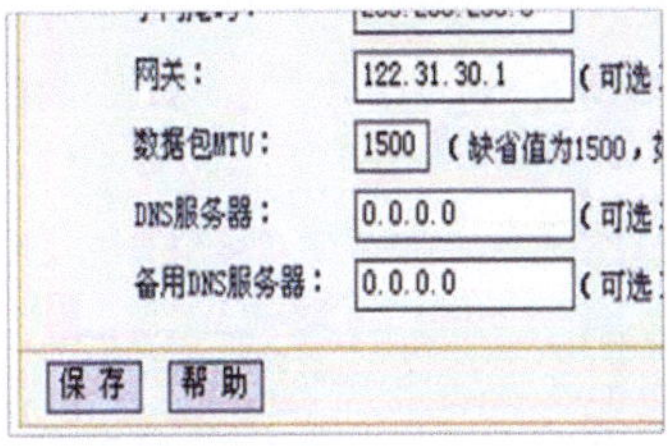

bǎocún pèizhì,　cèshì měi tái　PC

保存　配置，测试每台 PC

zhījiān néng hùxiāng　ping tōng

之间　能　互相 ping 通

Save the Configuration and Test that Each PC Can Ping Each Other

题解　Introduction

1. 学习内容：OSPF 动态路由协议组建网络的基本流程、OSPF 路由协议和 RIP 协议的区别，以及 OSPF 路由配置的基本步骤和作业要求。
   Learning content: The basic process of networking with the OSPF dynamic routing protocol, the differences between the OSPF routing protocol and the RIP protocol, and the basic steps and working requirements of OSPF routing configuration
2. 知识目标：掌握 OSPF 动态路由协议组建网络的关键词语，了解汉字的偏旁“氵”“讠”“艹”“辶”，学写相关汉字。
   Knowledge objectives: To master the keywords for OSPF dynamic routing protocol networking, understand the Chinese radicals “氵”, “讠”, “艹”, “辶”, and learn to write the related Chinese characters
3. 技能目标：学会 OSPF 路由的配置，让计算机之间可以互通。
   Skill objective: To master OSPF routing configuration and enable computers to communicate with each other

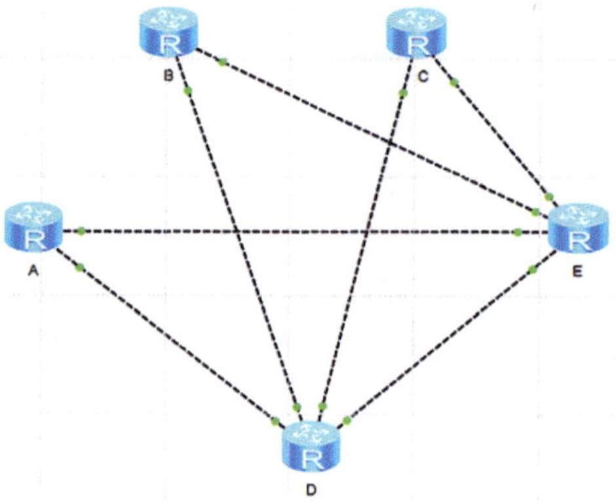

第一部分　Part 1

课文　Texts

一、热身　rèshēn　Warm-up

1. 给词语选择对应的图片。　**Choose the corresponding pictures for the words.**

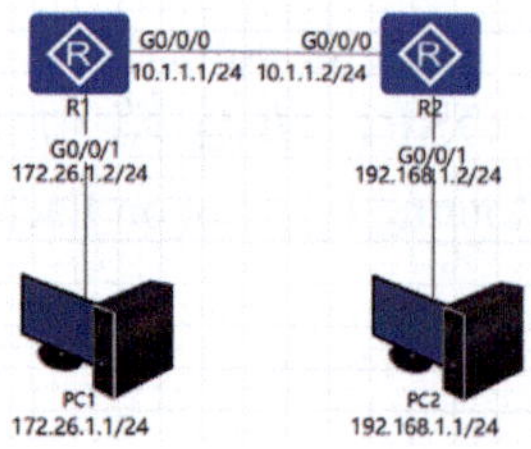

A.

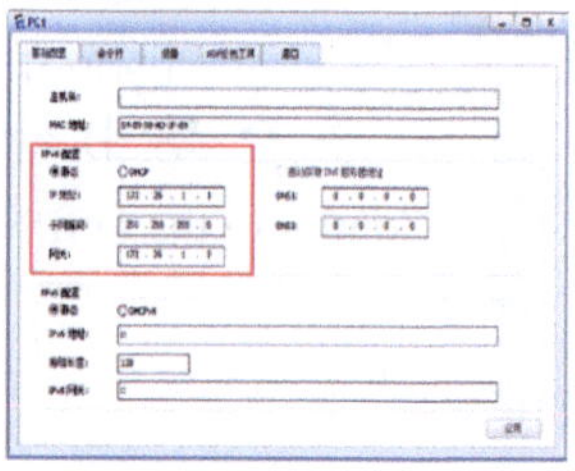

B.

C.

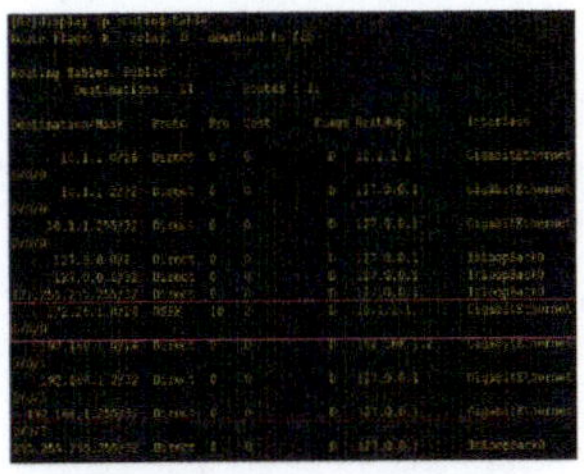

D.

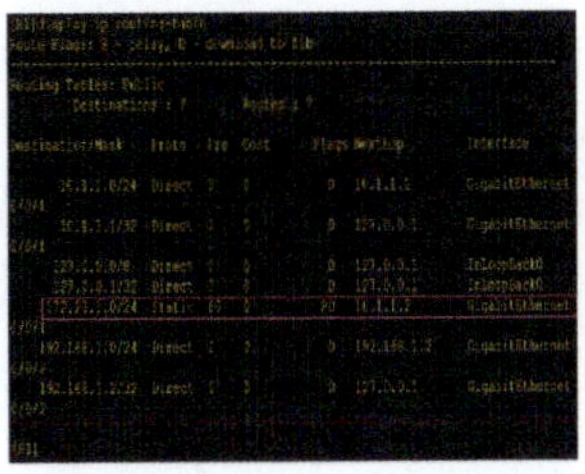

E.

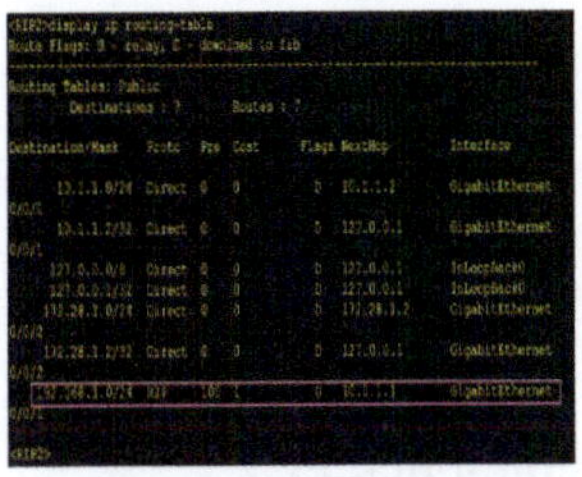

F.

RIP lùyóu tiáomù
① RIP 路由条目 ______________
RIP routing entry

jìngtài lùyóu tiáomù
② 静态路由条目 ______________
static routing entry

IP dìzhǐ
③ IP 地址 ______________
IP address

OSPF lùyóu tiáomù
④ OSPF 路由条目 ______________
OSPF routing entry

wǎngluò tuòpūtú
⑤ 网络拓扑图 ______________
network topology diagram

eNSP jièmiàn tú
⑥ eNSP 界面图 ______________
eNSP interface diagram

2. 观看介绍 OSPF 协议的视频，配置设备地址，将正确的步骤内容连线。

Watch the video introducing the OSPF protocol, configure the device address, and match the right steps.

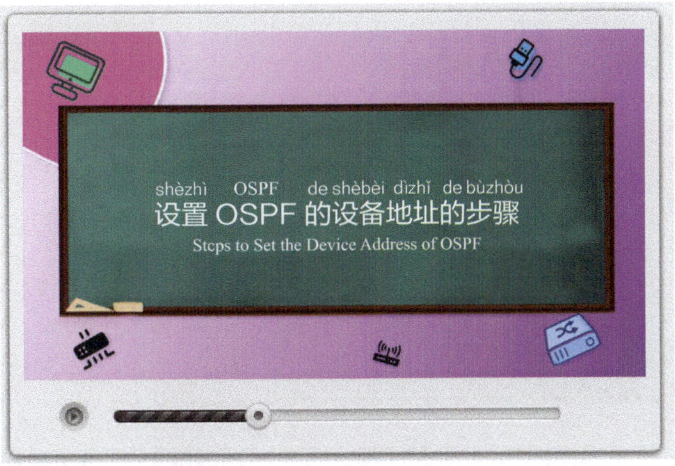

xuǎnzhòng suǒyǒu de
① 选中 所有的
Select all

shuāngjī PC1
② 双击 PC1
Double-click PC1

chóngfù dì-èr bù cāozuò
A. 重复第二步操作
Repeat Step 2

pèizhì R2 de OSPF dòngtài lùyóu
B. 配置 R2 的 OSPF 动态路由
Configure R2's OSPF dynamic routing

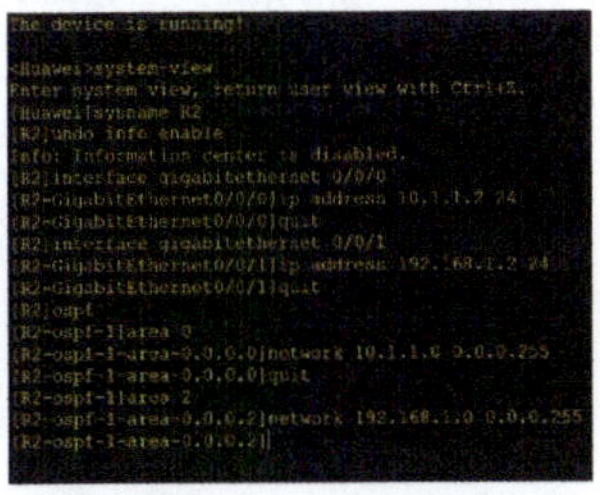

shuāngjī PC2
③ 双击 PC2
Double-click PC2

shuāngjī R1
④ 双击 R1
Double-click R1

shuāngjī R2
⑤ 双击 R2
Double-click R2

shèzhì IP dìzhǐ, zǐwǎng yǎnmǎ hé wǎngguān, diǎnjī "yìngyòng" ànniǔ
C. 设置IP地址，子网掩码和网关，点击"应用"按钮
Set the IP address, subnet mask and gateway, and click the "Apply" button

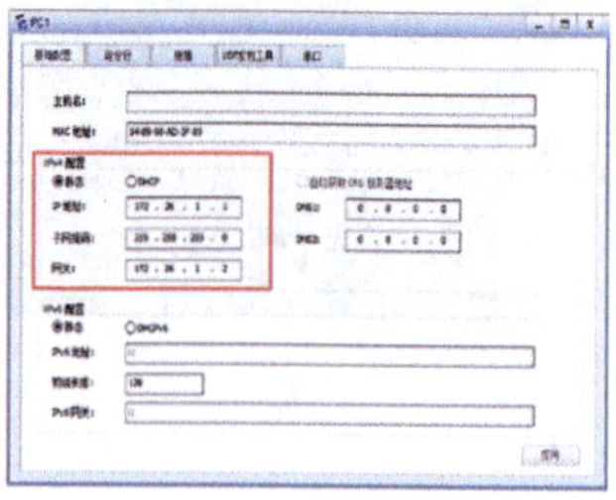

eNSP de shèbèi, bìng qǐdòng
D. eNSP 的设备，并启动
eNSP devices and start them

pèizhì R1 de OSPF dòngtài lùyóu
E. 配置 R1 的 OSPF 动态路由
Configure R1's OSPF dynamic routing

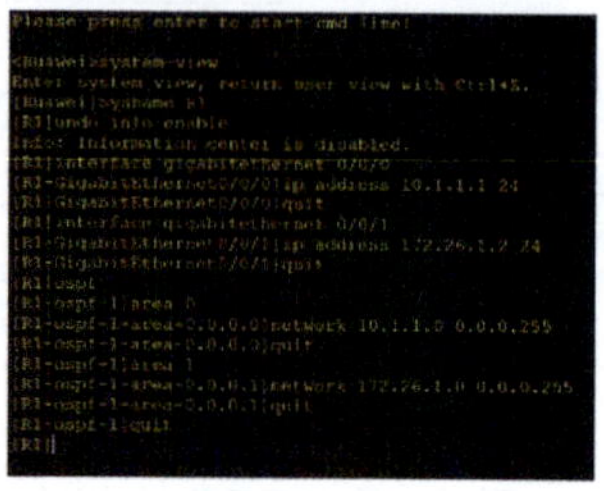

二、课文 kèwén Texts

A 02-01

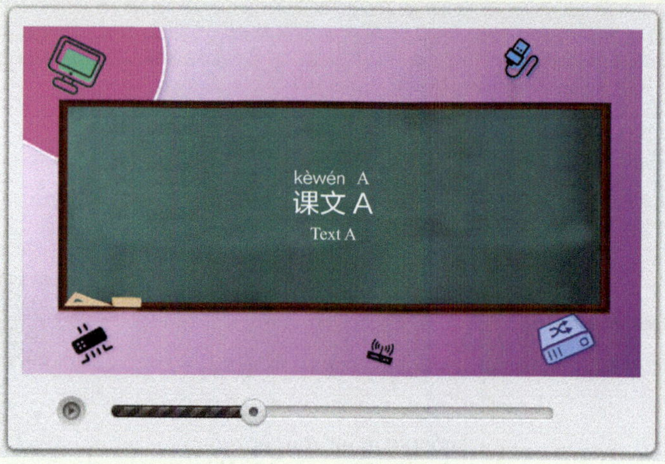

túdì: Shīfu, shénme shì dòngtài lùyóu?
徒弟：师傅，什么是动态路由？

shīfu: Dòngtài lùyóu shì zhǐ lùyóuqì nénggòu zìdòng de jiànlì zìjǐ de lùyóubiǎo, bìngqiě nénggòu gēnjù shíjì qíngkuàng de biànhuà shìdàng de jìnxíng tiáozhěng.
师傅：动态路由是指路由器能够自动地建立自己的路由表，并且能够根据实际情况的变化适当地进行调整。

túdì: OSPF dòngtài lùyóu zhōng yǒu nǎxiē lèixíng de liànlù zhuàngtài shùjùbāo ne?
徒弟：OSPF 动态路由中有哪些类型的链路状态数据包呢？

shīfu: OSPF yǒu wǔ zhǒng bù tóng lèixíng de liànlù zhuàngtài shùjùbāo, tāmen fēnbié shì Hello shùjùbāo、DBD shùjùbāo、LSR shùjùbāo、LSU shùjùbāo hé LSAck shùjùbāo.
师傅：OSPF 有五种不同类型的链路状态数据包，它们分别是 Hello 数据包、DBD 数据包、LSR 数据包、LSU 数据包和 LSAck 数据包。

túdì: Dòngtài lùyóu hé jìngtài lùyóu yǒu shénme qūbié?
徒弟：动态路由和静态路由有什么区别？

shīfu: Dòngtài lùyóu shì yǔ jìngtài lùyóu xiāngduì de yí gè gàiniàn, jìngtài lùyóu de lùyóu tiáomù shì bú huì gǎibiàn de, ér dòngtài lùyóu de lùyóu tiáomù shì huì búduàn biànhuà de.
师傅：动态路由是与静态路由相对的一个概念，静态路由的路由条目是不会改变的，而动态路由的路由条目是会不断变化的。

```
[R1]ip route-static 172.28.1.1 255.255.255.0 10.1.1.2
Info: The destination address and mask of the configured static route mismatched
, and the static route 172.28.1.0/24 was generated.
[R1]
```

pèizhì jìngtài lùyóu
配置静态路由
Configuration of static routing

```
The device is running!

<Huawei>system-view
Enter system view, return user view with Ctrl+Z.
[Huawei]sysname R2
[R2]undo info enable
Info: Information center is disabled.
[R2]interface gigabitethernet 0/0/0
[R2-GigabitEthernet0/0/0]ip address 10.1.1.2 24
[R2-GigabitEthernet0/0/0]quit
[R2]interface gigabitethernet 0/0/1
[R2-GigabitEthernet0/0/1]ip address 192.168.1.2 24
[R2-GigabitEthernet0/0/1]quit
[R2]ospf
[R2-ospf-1]area 0
[R2-ospf-1-area-0.0.0.0]network 10.1.1.0 0.0.0.255
[R2-ospf-1-area-0.0.0.0]quit
[R2-ospf-1]area 2
[R2-ospf-1-area-0.0.0.2]network 192.168.1.0 0.0.0.255
[R2-ospf-1-area-0.0.0.2]
```

pèizhì OSPF dòngtài lùyóu
配置 OSPF 动态路由
Configuration of OSPF dynamic routing

```
[R1]display this
#
sysname R1
#
undo info-center enable
#
ip route-static 172.28.1.0 255.255.255.0 10.1.1.2
#
return
[R1]
```

xiǎnshì jìngtài lùyóu tiáomù
显示静态路由条目
Indication of static routing entries

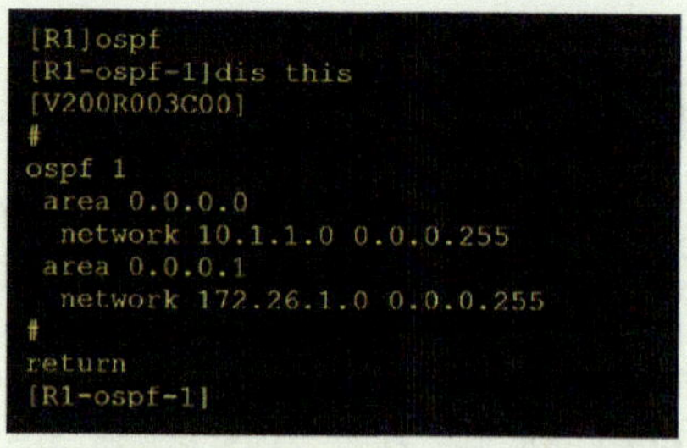

xiǎnshì dòngtài lùyóu tiáomù
显示动态路由条目
Indication of dynamic routing entries

译文 yìwén Text in English

Apprentice: What is dynamic routing, Master?

Master: It means that the router can automatically establish its own routing table and adjust it appropriately according to the changes in actual situations.

Apprentice: What types of link state packets are there in OSPF dynamic routing?

Master: OSPF has five different types of link state packets: Hello packet, DBD packet, LSR packet, LSU packet and LSAck packet respectively.

Apprentice: What's the difference between dynamic routing and static routing?

Master: Dynamic routing is a concept relative to static routing. The routing entries of static routing do not change, while the routing entries of dynamic routing change constantly.

普通词语 pǔtōng cíyǔ General Vocabulary

02-02

1.	指	zhǐ	v.	refer to
2.	自动	zìdòng	adv.	automatically
3.	建立	jiànlì	v.	establish
4.	并且	bìngqiě	conj.	and
5.	适当	shìdàng	adj.	appropriate
6.	调整	tiáozhěng	v.	adjust
7.	分别	fēnbié	adv.	respectively
8.	相对	xiāngduì	adj.	relative
9.	概念	gàiniàn	n.	concept
10.	会	huì	aux.	can, be able to
11.	改变	gǎibiàn	v.	change
12.	而	ér	conj.	*used to show a contrast*
13.	不断	búduàn	adv.	constantly

专业词语 zhuānyè cíyǔ Specialized Vocabulary

02-03

1.	OSPF			Open Shortest Path First
2.	路由器	lùyóuqì	n.	router
3.	链路	liànlù	n.	link
4.	数据包	shùjùbāo	n.	data packet
5.	路由条目	lùyóu tiáomù	phr.	routing entry

B 02-04

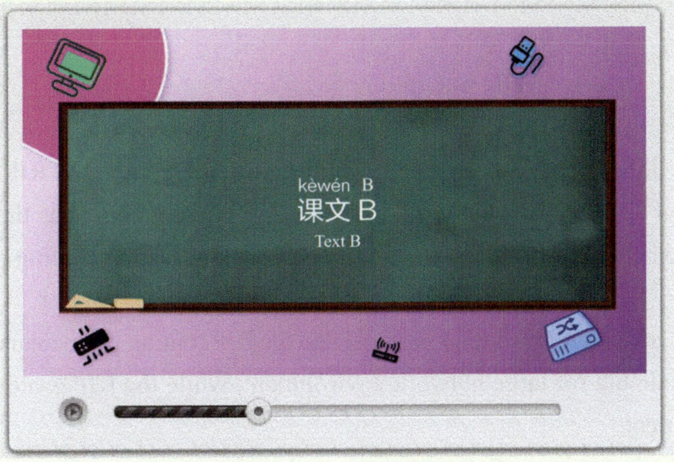

túdì: Shīfu, OSPF lùyóu xiéyì hé RIP lùyóu xiéyì yǒu hé qūbié?
徒弟：师傅，OSPF 路由协议和 RIP 路由协议有何区别？

shīfu: RIP shì yì zhǒng jīyú jùlí shǐliàng de lùyóu xiéyì, yǐ lùyóu tiàoshù zuòwéi jìshù dānwèi; ér OSPF shì liànlù zhuàngtài lùyóu xiéyì de yì zhǒng shíxiàn, gēnjù liànlù zhuàngtài de biànhuà tiáozhěng lùyóu tiáomù.
师傅：RIP 是一种基于距离矢量的路由协议，以路由跳数作为计数单位；而 OSPF 是链路状态路由协议的一种实现，根据链路状态的变化调整路由条目。

túdì: Nà OSPF lùyóu xiéyì hé RIP lùyóu xiéyì fēnbié yòngyú shénme huánjìng zhōng?
徒弟：那 OSPF 路由协议和 RIP 路由协议分别用于什么环境中？

shīfu: OSPF xiéyì shìhé yòngyú dàxíng de wǎngluò huánjìng, RIP xiéyì shìhé yòngyú xiǎoxíng de wǎngluò huánjìng.
师傅：OSPF 协议适合用于大型的网络环境，RIP 协议适合用于小型的网络环境。

túdì: Cháng jiàn de dòngtài lùyóu xiéyì hái yǒu nǎxiē?
徒弟：常见的动态路由协议还有哪些？

shīfu: IS-IS、BGP.
师傅：IS-IS、BGP。

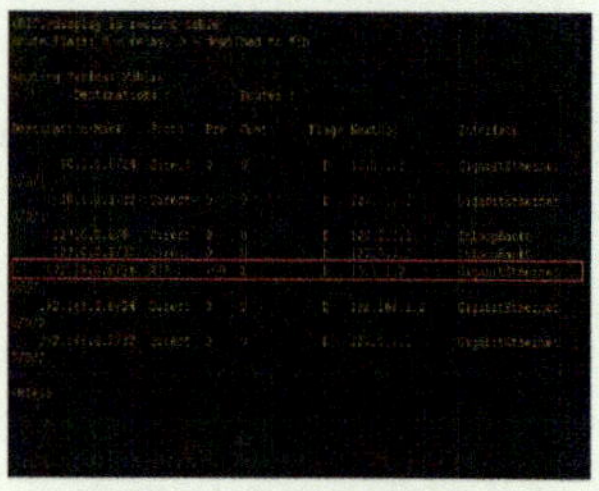

RIP lùyóu xiéyì
RIP 路由协议
RIP routing protocol

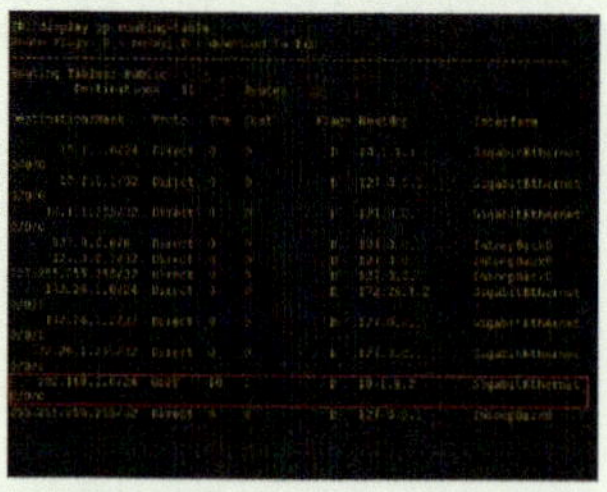

OSPF lùyóu xiéyì
OSPF 路由协议
OSPF routing protocol

译文 yìwén Text in English

Apprentice: Master, what is the difference between the OSPF routing protocol and the RIP routing protocol?

Master: RIP is a routing protocol based on distance vector, taking routing hop counts as the counting unit, while OSPF is an implementation of link state routing protocol, adjusting routing entries according to changes in link states.

Apprentice: What environments are the OSPF routing protocol and the RIP routing protocol used in respectively?

Master: The OSPF protocol is suitable for large network environment, while the RIP protocol is suitable for small network environment.

Apprentice: What other common dynamic routing protocols are there?

Master: IS-IS (Intermediate System-to-Intermediate System) and BGP (Border Gateway Protocol).

普通词语 pǔtōng cíyǔ General Vocabulary

02-05

1.	何	hé	pron.	what
2.	环境	huánjìng	n.	environment
3.	大型	dàxíng	adj.	large, large-scale
4.	常见	cháng jiàn	phr.	common
	常	cháng	adv.	frequently
	见	jiàn	v.	meet
5.	还	hái	adv.	still

专业词语 zhuānyè cíyǔ Specialized Vocabulary

02-06

1.	IS-IS	Intermediate System-to-Intermediate System
2.	BGP	Border Gateway Protocol

三、视听说 shì-tīng-shuō Viewing, Listening, and Speaking

1. 观看介绍使用 OSPF 动态路由协议组建网络的流程的视频，根据安装流程选择填空。

Watch the video introducing the process of network construction using the OSPF dynamic routing protocol, and fill in the blanks according to the installation process.

OSPF dòngtài lùyóu xiéyì
A. OSPF 动态路由协议
OSPF dynamic routing protocol

měi tái PC zhījiān néng hùxiāng ping tōng
B. 每台 PC 之间 能 互相 ping 通
each PC can ping each other

suǒyǒu duānkǒu de IP dìzhǐ
C. 所有 端 口的 IP 地址
the IP addresses of all the ports

suǒyǒu wǎngluò shèbèi
D. 所有 网 络 设备
all the network equipment

wǎngluò tuòpūtú
E. 网 络 拓扑图
network topology diagram

1 huìzhì
绘制 draw ________ 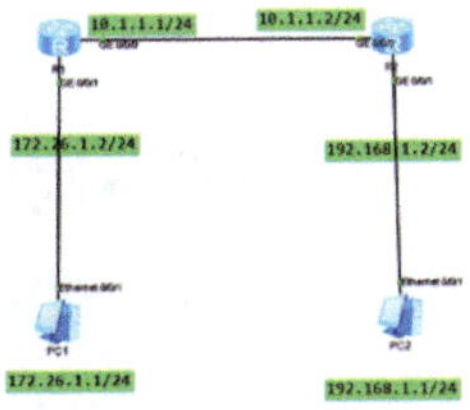

(　　)

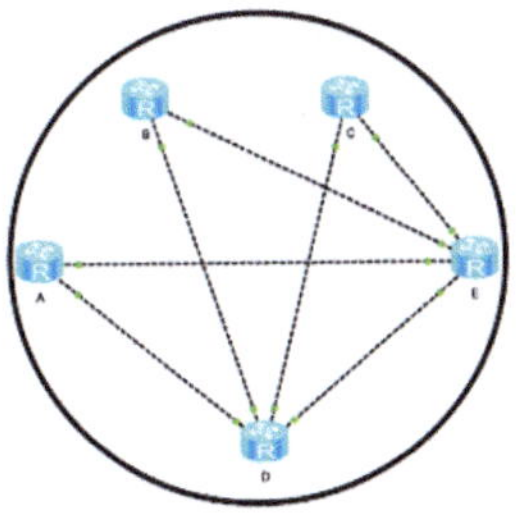

2 qǐdòng
启动 start ________ 
(　　)

3 pèizhì
配置 configure

(　　)

4 pèizhì
配置 configure
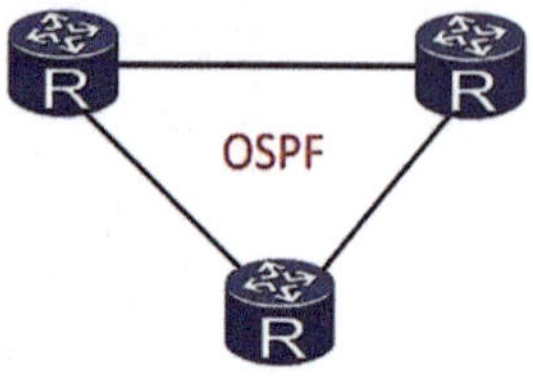

(　　)

5 cèshì
测试 test
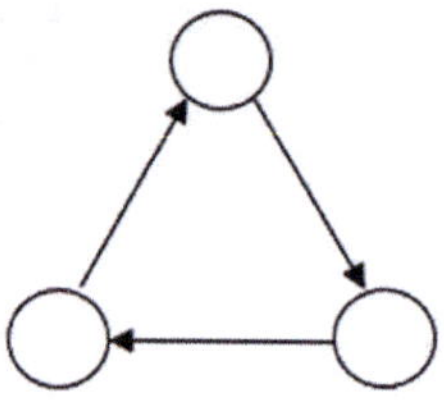
(　　)

2. 说一说　Let's talk

说一说 OSPF 路由配置的安装流程。

Talk about the installation process of OSPF routing configuration.

四、学以致用　xuéyǐzhìyòng　Practicing What You Have Learnt

观看介绍 RIP 协议与 OSPF 协议在实际运用中的特点与环境的视频，并将协议与相应的选项连线。

Watch the video introducing the characteristics and environment of the RIP protocol and OSPF protocol in practical applications, and match the protocols with the corresponding options.

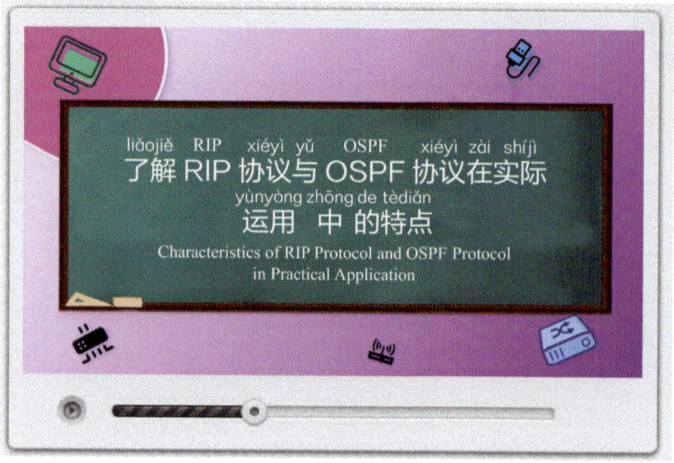

RIP xiéyì
① RIP 协议
RIP protocol

OSPF xiéyì
② OSPF 协议
OSPF protocol

liànlù zhuàngtài xiéyì
A. 链路 状态 协议
Link state protocol

jùlí shǐliàng xiéyì
B. 距离矢量协议
Distance-vector protocol

shìhé yòngyú xiǎoxíng de wǎngluò huánjìng
C. 适合用于 小型 的 网 络 环 境
Suitable for small network environment

shìhé yòngyú dàxíng de wǎngluò huánjìng
D. 适合用于 大型的 网 络 环 境
Suitable for large network environment

bù zhīchí qūyù huàfēn
E. 不支持区域划分
Area division is not supported

zhīchí duō qūyù huàfēn
F. 支持多区域划分
Multi-area division is supported

五、小知识 xiǎo zhīshi Tips

OSPF lùyóu xiéyì
OSPF 路由协议

Kāifàngshì zuì duǎn lùjìng yōuxiān (Open Shortest Path First, OSPF) shì guǎng-
开放式最 短 路径优先（Open Shortest Path First，OSPF）是 广

fàn shǐyòng de yì zhǒng dòngtài lùyóu xiéyì. Tā shǔyú liànlù zhuàngtài lùyóu xiéyì, jùyǒu lù-
泛使用 的一 种 动态路由协议。它属于链路 状态 路由协议，具有路

yóu biànhuà shōuliǎn sùdù kuài、 wú lùyóu huánlù、 zhīchí kě biàn cháng zǐwǎng yǎnmǎ (VLSM)
由 变化 收敛速度快、无路由环路、支持可变 长 子网 掩码（VLSM）

hé huìzǒng、 céngcì qūyù huàfēn děng yōudiǎn. Zài wǎngluò zhōng shǐyòng OSPF xiéyì hòu,
和汇总、层次区域划分 等 优点。在 网络 中 使用 OSPF 协议后，

dà bùfen lùyóu jiāng yóu OSPF xiéyì zìxíng jìsuàn hé shēngchéng, wúxū wǎngluò guǎnlǐyuán
大部分路由将由OSPF协议自行计算和生成，无须网络管理员

réngōng pèizhì. Dāng wǎngluò tuòpū fāshēng biànhuà shí, xiéyì kěyǐ zìdòng jìsuàn、gēngzhèng
人工配置。当网络拓扑发生变化时，协议可以自动计算、更正

lùyóu, jí dà de fāngbiàn le wǎngluò guǎnlǐ.
路由，极大地方便了网络管理。

OSPF Routing Protocol

As a widely used dynamic routing protocol, the Open Shortest Path First (OSPF) falls under link state routing protocols, with the advantages of high convergence speed of routing change, no routing loops, support for variable length subnet mask (VLSM) and summary, hierarchical area division and so on. After using the OSPF protocol in the network, most routes will be automatically calculated and generated by the OSPF protocol, requiring no manual configuration by a network administrator. When the network topology changes, the protocol can automatically calculate and correct routes, greatly facilitating network management.

补充专业词语 bǔchōng zhuānyè cíyǔ Supplementary Specialized Vocabulary

02-07

1.	静态路由表	jìngtài lùyóubiǎo	phr.	static routing table
2.	动态路由表	dòngtài lùyóubiǎo	phr.	dynamic routing table
3.	路由环路	lùyóu huánlù	phr.	routing loop
4.	区域划分	qūyù huàfēn	phr.	area division

第二部分 Part 2

汉字 Chinese Characters

一、汉字知识 Hànzì zhīshi Knowledge about Chinese Characters

汉字的偏旁（2）**Radicals of Chinese characters (2)**

偏旁 Radicals	例字 Examples	部件组合 Combinations	结构图示 Illustrations
氵	汽	氵+气	⿰
	法	氵+去	⿰
	汉	氵+又	⿰
	洗	氵+先	⿰
	澡	氵+喿	⿰
	没	氵+殳	⿰

（续表）

偏旁 Radicals	例字 Examples	部件组合 Combinations	结构图示 Illustrations
讠	语	讠＋吾	⿰
	课	讠＋果	⿰
讠	请	讠＋青	⿰
	谢	讠＋射	⿰
	词	讠＋司	⿰
	谁	讠＋隹	⿰
	认	讠＋人	⿰
	识	讠＋只	⿰
艹	节	艹＋卩	⿱
	英	艹＋央	⿱
	花	艹＋化	⿱
	苹	艹＋平	⿱
	蕉	艹＋焦	⿱
辶	远	辶＋元	⿺
	这	辶＋文	⿺
	运	辶＋云	⿺
	道	辶＋首	⿺
	边	辶＋力	⿺
	选	辶＋先	⿺
	还	辶＋不	⿺

二、汉字认读与书写 Hànzì rèndú yǔ shūxiě The Recognition and Writing of Chinese Characters

认读下列词语，并试着读写构成词语的汉字。**Recognize the following words, and try to read and write the Chinese characters forming these words.**

测试　　认证协议　　若干　　通信

测				试				认				证			
协				议				若				干			
通				信											

第三部分 Part 3

日常用语 Daily Expressions

1. 你一个人来吗？ Nǐ yí gè rén lái ma? Are you by yourself？
2. 你没有问题吧？ Nǐ méiyǒu wèntí ba? Is it all right with you?
3. 你在跟我开玩笑吧？ Nǐ zài gēn wǒ kāi wánxiào ba? Are you kidding me?

第四部分 Part 4

单元实训 Unit Practical Training

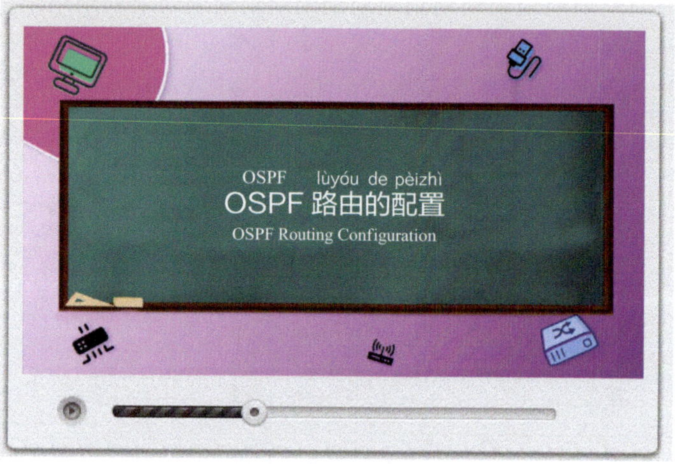

OSPF 路由的配置 OSPF lùyóu de pèizhì

OSPF Routing Configuration

实训目的 Training purpose

掌握 OSPF 路由配置的步骤，并能独立完成配置，让计算机之间可以互通。

To master the steps of OSPF routing configuration, and be able to complete the configuration independently to enable the computers to communicate with each other.

实训组织 Training organization

每组 4 人，选出一个组长。

Each group consists of four people, and a group leader is selected.

实训内容 Training content

OSPF 路由的配置。

Configuration of OSPF routing.

实训步骤 Training steps

1. 将参加人员分成若干小组，每组 4 人。

   Divide the trainees into groups of 4.

② 第一个人安装 eNSP APP。

The first person installs the eNSP App.

③ 第二个人绘制拓扑图，准备配置 OSPF 路由。

The second person draws the topology diagram and prepares to configure OSPF routing.

④ 第三个人启动设备并配置 OSPF 路由和 PC 机地址。

The third person starts the device and configures OSPF routing and PC address.

⑤ 第四个人测试计算机连通性。

The fourth person tests the connectivity between computers.

⑥ 实训结束，教师总结评价。

The training ends. The teacher makes a summary and an evaluation.

第五部分 Part 5

单元小结 Unit Summary

cíyǔ
词语
Vocabulary

普通词语 General Vocabulary

1.	指	zhǐ	v.	refer to
2.	自动	zìdòng	adv.	automatically
3.	建立	jiànlì	v.	establish
4.	并且	bìngqiě	conj.	and
5.	适当	shìdàng	adj.	appropriate
6.	调整	tiáozhěng	v.	adjust
7.	分别	fēnbié	adv.	respectively
8.	相对	xiāngduì	adj.	relative
9.	概念	gàiniàn	n.	concept
10.	会	huì	aux.	can, be able to
11.	改变	gǎibiàn	v.	change
12.	而	ér	conj.	*used to show a contrast*
13.	不断	búduàn	adv.	constantly
14.	何	hé	pron.	what
15.	环境	huánjìng	n.	environment
16.	大型	dàxíng	adj.	large, large-scale
17.	常见	cháng jiàn	phr.	common
	常	cháng	adv.	frequently
	见	jiàn	v.	meet
18.	还	hái	adv.	still

cíyǔ
词语
Vocabulary

专业词语 Specialized Vocabulary

1.	OSPF			Open Shortest Path First
2.	路由器	lùyóuqì	n.	router
3.	链路	liànlù	n.	link
4.	数据包	shùjùbāo	n.	data packet
5.	路由条目	lùyóu tiáomù	phr.	routing entry
6.	IS-IS			Intermediate System-to-Intermediate System
7.	BGP			Border Gateway Protocol

补充专业词语 Supplementary Specialized Vocabulary

1.	静态路由表	jìngtài lùyóubiǎo	phr.	static routing table
2.	动态路由表	dòngtài lùyóubiǎo	phr.	dynamic routing table
3.	路由环路	lùyóu huánlù	phr.	routing loop
4.	区域划分	qūyù huàfēn	phr.	area division

jùzi
句子
Sentences

1. 动态路由是指路由器能够自动地建立自己的路由表，并且能够根据实际情况的变化适当地进行调整。路由器启动后，双击路由器图标，进入路由器的命令行配置界面。
2. 动态路由是与静态路由相对的一个概念，静态路由的路由条目是不会改变的，而动态路由的路由条目是会不断变化的。
3. RIP是一种基于距离矢量的路由协议，以路由跳数作为计数单位；而OSPF是链路状态路由协议的一种实现，根据链路状态的变化调整路由条目。
4. OSPF 协议适合用于大型的网络环境，RIP 协议适合用于小型的网络环境。

3 Dòngtài xūnǐ júyùwǎng
动态虚拟局域网
Dynamic VLAN

huìzhì rúxià tuòpū, bìng xuéxí GVRP de jùtǐ pèizhì
绘制如下拓扑，并学习 GVRP 的具体配置
Draw the Following Topology and Learn the Specific Configuration of GVRP

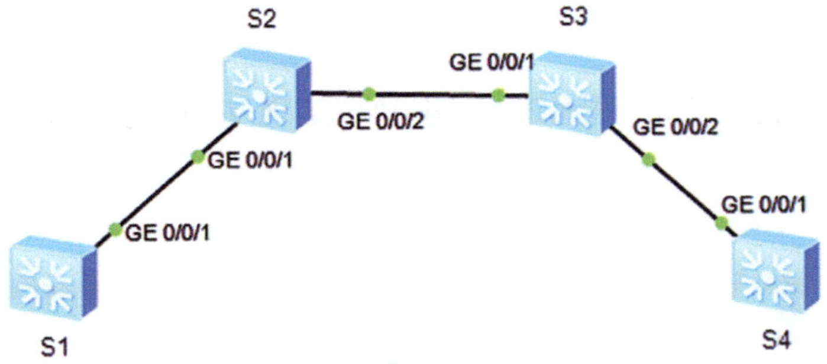


```
[S1]gvrp
```

duì jiāohuànjī S1 jìnxíng pèizhì, quánjú shǐnéng GVRP
对交换机 S1 进行配置，全局 使能 GVRP
Configure Switch S1 and Enable GVRP Globally

```
[S1]vlan batch 10 to 20
Info: This operation may take a few seconds. Please wait for a moment...done.
[S1]interface gigabitethernet 0/0/1
[S1-GigabitEthernet0/0/1]port link-type trunk
[S1-GigabitEthernet0/0/1]port trunk allow-pass vlan all
[S1-GigabitEthernet0/0/1]gvrp
[S1-GigabitEthernet0/0/1] User interface con0 is available
```

chuàngjiàn VLAN, shèzhì GE0/0/1 duānkǒu lèixíng Trunk, yǔnxǔ
创建 VLAN，设置 GE0/0/1 端口 类型 Trunk，允许
suǒyǒu de VLAN tōngguò, bìng zài cǐ duānkǒu xià shǐnéng GVRP
所有的 VLAN 通过，并在此 端口 下 使能 GVRP
Create a VLAN, Set the GE0/0/1 Port Type to Trunk, Allow All VLANs to Pass through, and Enable GVRP under This Port

```
[S2]gvrp
[S2]interface gigabitethernet 0/0/1
[S2-GigabitEthernet0/0/1]port link-type trunk
[S2-GigabitEthernet0/0/1]port trunk allow-pass vlan all
[S2-GigabitEthernet0/0/1]gvrp
[S2-GigabitEthernet0/0/1]quit
[S2]interface gigabitethernet 0/0/2
[S2-GigabitEthernet0/0/2]port link-type trunk
[S2-GigabitEthernet0/0/2]port trunk allow-pass vlan all
[S2-GigabitEthernet0/0/2]gvrp
[S2-GigabitEthernet0/0/2]quit
```

pèizhì S2, shèzhì GE0/0/1 hé GE0/0/2 duānkǒu
配置 S2，设置 GE0/0/1 和 GE0/0/2 端口
lèixíng wéi Trunk, yǔnxǔ suǒyǒu de VLAN tōngguò,
类型为 Trunk，允许 所有的 VLAN 通过，
bìng zài shàngshù duānkǒu xià shǐnéng GVRP
并在 上述 端口 下 使能 GVRP
Configure S2, Set the Port Type of GE0/0/1 and GE0/0/2 to Trunk, Allow All VLANs to Pass through, and Enable GVRP under the above Ports

pèizhì S3 yǔ S2 lèisì
配置 S3，与 S2 类似
Configure S3, Similar to S2

```
[S4]gvrp
[S4]interface gigabitethernet 0/0/1
[S4-GigabitEthernet0/0/1]port link-type trunk
[S4-GigabitEthernet0/0/1]port trunk allow-pass vlan all
[S4-GigabitEthernet0/0/1]gvrp
[S4-GigabitEthernet0/0/1]quit
```

pèizhì S4, shèzhì GE0/0/1 duānkǒu lèixíng wéi Trunk,
配置 S4，设置 GE0/0/1 端口 类型 为 Trunk，
yǔnxǔ suǒyǒu de VLAN tōngguò, bìng zài cǐ duānkǒu
允许 所有 的 VLAN 通过， 并 在此 端口
xià shǐnéng GVRP
下 使能 GVRP
Configure S4, Set the GE0/0/1 Port Type to Trunk, Allow All VLANs to Pass through, and Enable GVRP under This Port

```
[S4]display vlan summary
static vlan:
Total 1 static vlan.
  1

dynamic vlan:
Total 0 dynamic vlan.

reserved vlan:
Total 0 reserved vlan.
```

```
[S4]display vlan summary
static vlan:
Total 1 static vlan.
  1

dynamic vlan:
Total 11 dynamic vlan.
  10 to 20

reserved vlan:
Total 0 reserved vlan.
```

zài jiāohuànjī S4 shang chákàn VLAN huìzǒng xìnxī, duìbǐ
在 交换机 S4 上 查看 VLAN 汇总信息， 对比
yànzhèng shíyàn jiéguǒ
验证 实验 结果
View VLAN Summary Information on Switch S4 and Compare and Verify the Results

题解　Introduction

1. 学习内容：GVRP 的注册模式，GVRP 的使用，VLAN 信息指令的查看。
   Learning content: The registration mode of GVRP, the use of GVRP, and the view of VLAN information instructions
2. 知识目标：掌握与动态虚拟局域网相关的关键词语，了解汉字的偏旁“扌”“木”“纟”“心”“⻊”，学写相关汉字。
   Knowledge objectives: To master the keywords for dynamic VLAN, understand the Chinese radicals “扌”, “木”, “纟”, “心”, “⻊”, and learn to write the related Chinese characters
3. 技能目标：学会设置动态 VLAN，并通过 GVRP 协议实现 VLAN 的自动创建和注册。
   Skill objective: To learn to set up dynamic VLANs and realize the automatic creation and registration of VLANs through the GVRP protocol

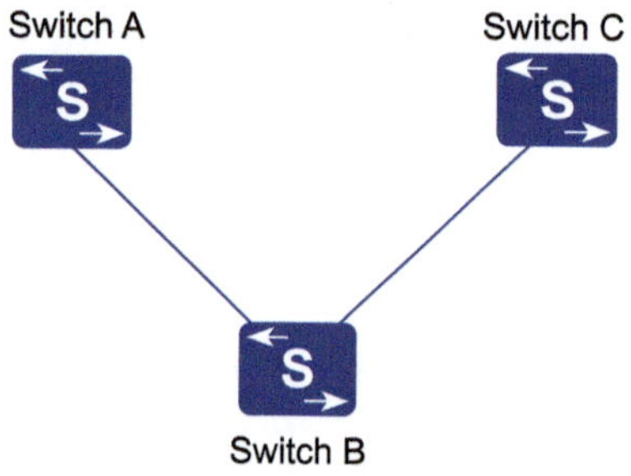

第一部分　Part 1

课文　Texts

一、热身　rèshēn　Warm-up

1. 根据图片内容，选择对应的指令功能。
   Choose the corresponding command functions according to the pictures.

```
[Huawei]gvrp
```

A.

```
[Huawei-GigabitEthernet0/0/2]gvrp
```

B.

```
[Huawei-GigabitEthernet0/0/2]port link-type trunk
[Huawei-GigabitEthernet0/0/2]port trunk allow-pass vlan all
```

C.

```
[Huawei-GigabitEthernet0/0/2]display vlan summary
static vlan:
Total 1 static vlan.
  1

dynamic vlan:
Total 0 dynamic vlan.
```

D.

```
[Huawei]display gvrp status
 Info: GVRP is enabled
```

E.

```
[Huawei-GigabitEthernet0/0/1]display gvrp statistics
```

F.

quánjú shǐnéng GVRP gōngnéng
① 全局使能 GVRP 功能
enable the GVRP function globally

duānkǒu shang GVRP gōngnéng de shǐnéng
② 端口上 GVRP 功能的使能
enable the GVRP function on the port

pèizhì xiāngyìng de duānkǒu wéi Trunk duānkǒu, bìng yǔnxǔ xiāngyìng de VLAN zhēn tōngguò
③ 配置相应的端口为 Trunk 端口，并允许相应的 VLAN 帧通过
configure the corresponding port as a trunk port and allow the corresponding VLAN frame to pass through

chákàn VLAN de xìnxī
④ 查看 VLAN 的信息
view the VLAN information

chákàn quánjú GVRP de shǐnéng qíngkuàng
⑤ 查看全局 GVRP 的使能情况
view the global GVRP enabling status

chákàn duānkǒu de GVRP tǒngjì xìnxī
⑥ 查看端口的 GVRP 统计信息
view the GVRP summary of the port

2. 观看介绍 GVRP 的视频，并根据其注册特点选择所对应的模式。

Watch the video introducing GVRP, and select the corresponding modes according to the registration characteristics.

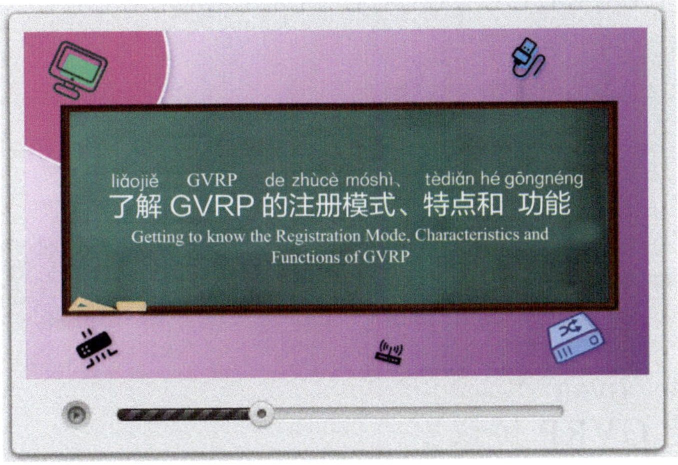

Yǔnxǔ jiēkǒu dòngtài zhùcè、zhùxiāo VLAN、
① 允许接口动态注册、注销 VLAN、
chuánbō dòngtài VLAN jí jìngtài VLAN.
传播动态 VLAN 及静态 VLAN。
Allow the interface to dynamically register and unregister VLANs, and propagate dynamic VLANs and static VLANs.

Forbidden móshì
A. Forbidden 模式
Forbidden mode

Bù néng dòngtài zhùcè huò zhùxiāo VLAN, zhǐ néng fāsòng jìngtài VLAN zhùcè xìnxī.
② 不能动态注册或注销 VLAN，只能发送静态 VLAN 注册信息。
VLANs cannot be dynamically registered or unregistered. Only static VLAN registration information can be sent.

Normal móshì
B. Normal 模式
Normal mode

Bù néng dòngtài zhùcè huò zhùxiāo VLAN, zhǐ bǎoliú VLAN1 de xìnxī.
③ 不能动态注册或注销 VLAN，只保留 VLAN1 的信息。
VLANs cannot be dynamically registered or unregistered, and only VLAN1 information is retained.

Fixed móshì
C. Fixed 模式
Fixed mode

二、课文 kèwén Texts

A 03-01

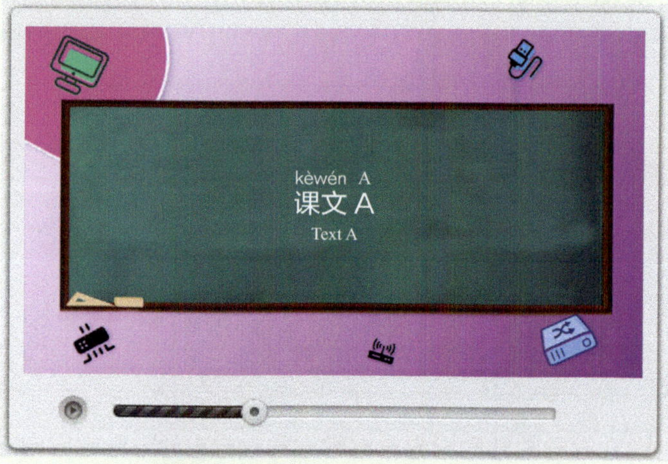

túdì: Shīfu, shénme shì GVRP xiéyì?
徒弟：师傅，什么是 GVRP 协议？

shīfu: GVRP de Zhōngwén quánchēng shì tōngyòng VLAN zhùcè xiéyì.
师傅：GVRP 的中文全称是通用 VLAN 注册协议。

túdì: Shénme qíngkuàng xià kǎolǜ shǐyòng zhège xiéyì ne?
徒弟：什么情况下考虑使用这个协议呢？

shīfu: Zài duì jiāohuànjī jìnxíng VLAN pèizhì de shíhou, xūyào zài měi yì tái jiāohuànjī shang shǒugōng chuàngjiàn gāi jiāohuànjī xūyào shèjí de suǒyǒu VLAN, bìngqiě
师傅：在对交换机进行 VLAN 配置的时候，需要在每一台交换机上手工创建该交换机需要涉及的所有 VLAN，并且

xūyào shǒugōng jiāng jiāohuànjī shang de gègè duānkǒu jiārù dào xiāngyìng de VLAN
需要手工将交换机上的各个端口加入到相应的VLAN

zhōng qù. Rúguǒ jiāohuànjī hé VLAN de shùliàng tài duō, tèbié shì VLAN de
中去。如果交换机和VLAN的数量太多，特别是VLAN的

shùliàng yòu jīngcháng biànhuà shí, zé zhè zhǒng shǒugōng pèizhì fāngshì jì hàofèi shíjiān
数量又经常变化时，则这种手工配置方式既耗费时间

yòu hàofèi jīnglì, qiě fēicháng róngyì chū cuò.
又耗费精力，且非常容易出错。

túdì: Nándào GVRP nénggòu jiějué zhège wèntí?
徒弟：难道GVRP能够解决这个问题？

shīfu: Shìde, GVRP nénggòu zìdòng shíxiàn VLAN xìnxī zài jiāohuànjī shang de dòngtài
师傅：是的，GVRP能够自动实现VLAN信息在交换机上的动态

zhùcè guòchéng hé zhùxiāo guòchéng, cóng'ér dàdà jiǎnshǎole VLAN pèizhì guòchéng
注册过程和注销过程，从而大大减少了VLAN配置过程

zhōng de shǒugōng gōngzuò.
中的手工工作。

译文 yìwén Text in English

Apprentice: Master, what is the GVRP protocol?

Master: The full name of GVRP in Chinese is GARP VLAN 注册协议 (GARP VLAN Registration Protocol).

Apprentice: Under what circumstances should we consider using this protocol?

Master: When configuring VLANs for switches, we need to manually create on each switch all the VLANs involved in this switch, and we need to manually add each port on the switch to the corresponding VLAN. If the number of switches and VLANs is too large, especially when the number of VLANs changes frequently, this manual configuration method is time-consuming and energy-consuming, and is very error-prone.

Apprentice: Can GVRP solve this problem?

Master: Yes. GVRP can automatically realize the dynamic registration process and unregistration process of VLAN information on the switch, thus greatly reducing the manual work in the VLAN configuration process.

普通词语 pǔtōng cíyǔ General Vocabulary

03-02

1.	中文	Zhōngwén	n.	Chinese (language)
2.	全称	quánchēng	n.	full name
3.	考虑	kǎolǜ	v.	consider
4.	该	gāi	pron.	the, this
5.	涉及	shèjí	v.	involve
6.	各个	gègè	pron.	each

7.	加入	jiārù	v.	join
8.	数量	shùliàng	n.	number
9.	太	tài	adv.	too
10.	特别	tèbié	adv.	especially
11.	经常	jīngcháng	adv.	frequently
12.	则	zé	conj.	then
13.	既	jì	conj.	(to be echoed by 且，又，也，etc.) both...and...
14.	耗费	hàofèi	v.	consume
15.	精力	jīnglì	n.	energy
16.	且	qiě	conj.	and
17.	非常	fēicháng	adv.	very
18.	容易	róngyì	adj.	easy
19.	出错	chū cuò	phr.	make a mistake
20.	难道	nándào	adv.	*used in a rhetorical question for emphasis*
21.	解决	jiějué	v.	solve
22.	问题	wèntí	n.	problem
23.	大大	dàdà	adv.	greatly
24.	减少	jiǎnshǎo	v.	reduce
25.	工作	gōngzuò	n.	work

专业词语 zhuānyè cíyǔ Specialized Vocabulary

03-03

1.	GVRP			GARP VLAN Registration Protocol
2.	注册	zhù//cè	v.	register
3.	注销	zhùxiāo	v.	logout, unregister

B 03-04

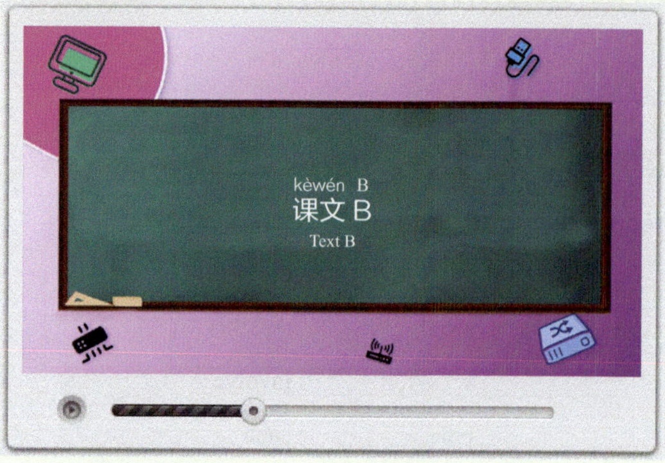

túdì: Shīfu, qǐngwèn GVRP xiéyì zěnme shǐyòng?
徒弟：师傅，请问 GVRP 协议怎么使用？

shīfu: Zài shǐnéng (kāiqǐ) duānkǒu de GVRP gōngnéng zhīqián, xūyào xiān quánjú shǐnéng GVRP gōngnéng.
师傅：在使能（开启）端口的 GVRP 功能之前，需要先全局使能 GVRP 功能。

túdì: Hái yǒu qítā xūyào zhùyì de ma?
徒弟：还有其他需要注意的吗？

shīfu: GVRP gōngnéng zhǐ néng pèizhì zài Trunk lèixíng de duānkǒu shang.
师傅：GVRP 功能只能配置在 Trunk 类型的端口上。

túdì: Kěshì mòrèn de duānkǒu lèixíng bú shì Trunk lèixíng a!
徒弟：可是默认的端口类型不是 Trunk 类型啊！

shīfu: Suǒyǐ xūyào pèizhì xiāngguān de duānkǒu wéi Trunk, bìng yǔnxǔ xiāngyìng de VLAN tōngguò.
师傅：所以需要配置相关的端口为 Trunk，并允许相应的 VLAN 通过。

译文 yìwén Text in English

Apprentice: Master, how can I use the GVRP protocol?

Master: Before enabling (starting) the GVRP function of the port, you need to enable the GVRP function globally.

Apprentice: Is there anything else I need to pay attention to?

Master: The GVRP function can only be configured on Trunk-type ports.

Apprentice: But the default port type is not Trunk.

Master: So you need to configure the relevant port as Trunk and allow the corresponding VLANs to pass through.

普通词语 pǔtōng cíyǔ General Vocabulary

03-05

1.	开启	kāiqǐ	v.	start
2.	之前	zhīqián	n.	before
3.	注意	zhùyì	v.	pay attention to
4.	可是	kěshì	conj.	but
5.	默认	mòrèn	v.	do by default
6.	相关	xiāngguān	v.	relate
7.	允许	yǔnxǔ	v.	allow

专业词语 zhuānyè cíyǔ Specialized Vocabulary

03-06

1.	使能	shǐnéng	v.	enable
2.	全局	quánjú	n.	being global

三、视听说 shì-tīng-shuō Viewing, Listening, and Speaking

1. 观看介绍 GVRP 的配置思路及查看配置结果的视频，并根据图片所示，判断交换机是否有了动态注册的 VLAN。如果有，请写出动态 VLAN 的数量。

Watch the video introducing the configuration idea of GVRP and the view of the configuration results. Tell whether the switch has dynamically registered VLANs according to the picture. If so, write the number of dynamic VLANs.

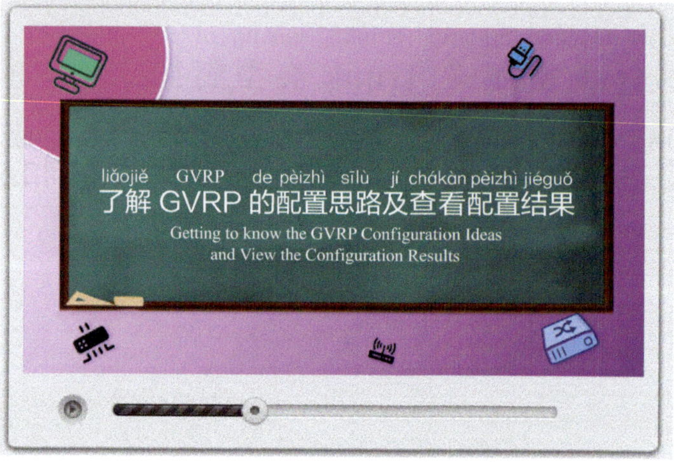

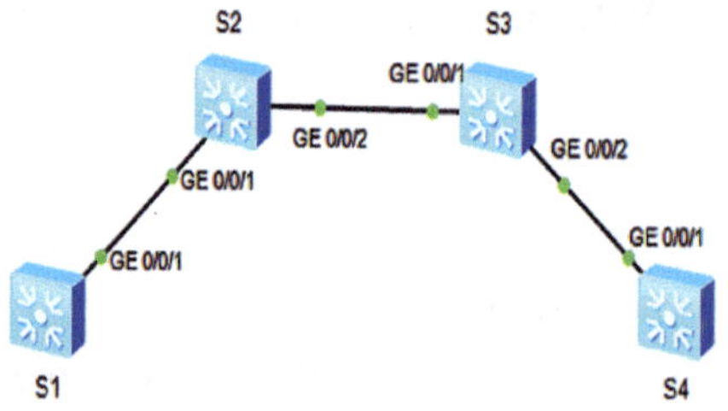

Zài suǒyǒu de jiāohuànjī shang quánjú shǐnéng GVRP, yǐ S1 wéi lì.

（1）在所有的交换机上全局使能 GVRP，以 S1 为例。

Enable GVRP globally on all switches. Take S1 as an example.

```
[S1]gvrp
```

Zài trunk duānkǒu xià shǐnéng GVRP, yǐ S1 de GE0/0/1 duānkǒu wéi lì.

（2）在 trunk 端口下使能 GVRP，以 S1 的 GE0/0/1 端口为例。

Enable GVRP under trunk port. Take the GE0/0/1 port of S1 as an example.

```
[S1-GigabitEthernet0/0/1]gvrp
```

Chákàn jiāohuànjī shang suǒyǒu VLAN de huìzǒng xìnxī, yǐ S3 wéi lì.

（3）查看交换机上所有 VLAN 的汇总信息，以 S3 为例。

View the summary information of all VLANs on the switch. Take S3 as an example.

```
[S3]display vlan summary
static vlan:
Total 1 static vlan.
  1

dynamic vlan:
Total 1 dynamic vlan.
  10

reserved vlan:
Total 0 reserved vlan.
```

①
```
[S4]display vlan summary
static vlan:
Total 1 static vlan.
  1

dynamic vlan:
Total 0 dynamic vlan.

reserved vlan:
Total 0 reserved vlan.
```

②
```
[S4]display vlan summary
static vlan:
Total 1 static vlan.
  1

dynamic vlan:
Total 11 dynamic vlan.
  10 to 20

reserved vlan:
Total 0 reserved vlan.
```

2. 说一说　Let's talk

说一说 GVRP 的主要配置思路、如何查看配置结果，以及如图所示配置结果的含义。

Talk about the main configuration idea of GVRP, how to view the configuration results, and the meaning of the configuration results as shown in the picture.

```
[S3]display vlan summary
static vlan:
Total 1 static vlan.
  1

dynamic vlan:
Total 1 dynamic vlan.
  10

reserved vlan:
Total 0 reserved vlan.
```

四、学以致用　xuéyǐzhìyòng　Practicing What You Have Learnt

观看视频，绘制如下拓扑图，按要求完成 GVRP 的具体配置，并将下列指令与其含义匹配，答案写在横线上。

Watch the video, draw the following topology diagram, complete the specific configuration of GVRP as required, match the following instructions with their meanings, and write the answers on the lines.

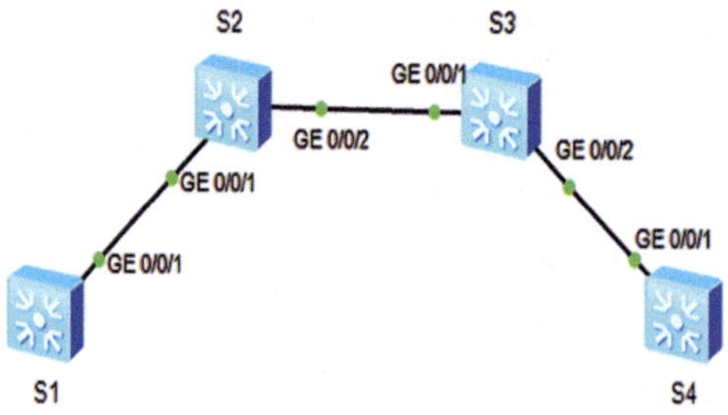

huìzhì tuòpūtú

（1）绘制拓扑图

Draw the topology diagram

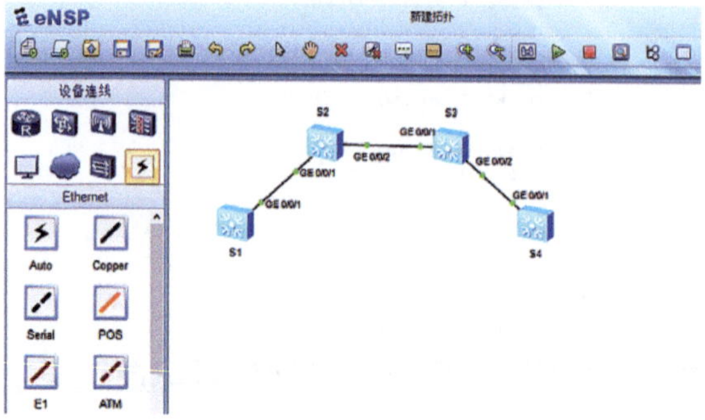

duì jiāohuànjī S1 jìnxíng pèizhì

（2）对交换机S1进行配置

Configure switch S1

```
[Huawei]sysname S1
[S1]gvrp
[S1]vlan batch 10 to 20
Info: This operation may take a few seconds. Please wait for a moment...done.
[S1]interface gigabitethernet 0/0/1
[S1-GigabitEthernet0/0/1]port link-type trunk
[S1-GigabitEthernet0/0/1]port trunk allow-pass vlan all
[S1-GigabitEthernet0/0/1]gvrp
[S1-GigabitEthernet0/0/1] User interface con0 is available
```

duì jiāohuànjī S2 jìnxíng pèizhì

（3）对交换机S2进行配置

Configure switch S2

```
[Huawei]sysname S2
[S2]gvrp
[S2]interface gigabitethernet 0/0/1
[S2-GigabitEthernet0/0/1]port link-type trunk
[S2-GigabitEthernet0/0/1]port trunk allow-pass vlan all
[S2-GigabitEthernet0/0/1]gvrp
[S2-GigabitEthernet0/0/1]quit
[S2]interface gigabitethernet 0/0/2
[S2-GigabitEthernet0/0/2]port link-type trunk
[S2-GigabitEthernet0/0/2]port trunk allow-pass vlan all
[S2-GigabitEthernet0/0/2]gvrp
[S2-GigabitEthernet0/0/2]quit
```

duì jiāohuànjī S3 jìnxíng pèizhì

（4）对交换机S3进行配置

Configure switch S3

```
[Huawei]sysname S3
[S3]gvrp
[S3]interface gigabitethernet 0/0/1
[S3-GigabitEthernet0/0/1]port link-type trunk
[S3-GigabitEthernet0/0/1]port trunk allow-pass vlan all
[S3-GigabitEthernet0/0/1]gvrp
[S3-GigabitEthernet0/0/1]quit
[S3]interface gigabitethernet 0/0/2
[S3-GigabitEthernet0/0/2]port link-type trunk
[S3-GigabitEthernet0/0/2]port trunk allow-pass vlan all
[S3-GigabitEthernet0/0/2]gvrp
[S3-GigabitEthernet0/0/2]quit
```

duì jiāohuànjī S4 jìnxíng pèizhì
（5）对交换机 S4 进行配置
Configure switch S4

```
[Huawei]sysname S4
[S4]gvrp
[S4]interface gigabitethernet 0/0/1
[S4-GigabitEthernet0/0/1]port link-type trunk
[S4-GigabitEthernet0/0/1]port trunk allow-pass vlan all
[S4-GigabitEthernet0/0/1]gvrp
[S4-GigabitEthernet0/0/1]quit
```

① [S1]gvrp //全局使能GVRP

② [S1]vlan batch 10 to 20 //创建连续的，10-20，一共11个vlan

③ [S1-GigabitEthernet0/0/1]port link-type trunk //设置端口类型为trunk

④ [S1]interface GigabitEthernet 0/0/1 //进入G0/0/1端口

⑤ [S1-GigabitEthernet0/0/1]port trunk allow-pass vlan all//允许所有vlan通过

⑥ [S1-GigabitEthernet0/0/1]gvrp//端口使能GVRP

⑦ [Huawei]sysname S1 //将设备命名为S1

jìnrù G0/0/1 duānkǒu
A. 进入 G0/0/1 端口
Enter the G0/0/1 Port

shèzhì duānkǒu lèixíng wéi trunk
B. 设置端口类型为 trunk
Set the port type to trunk

chuàngjiàn liánxù de VLAN10~VLAN20 (yígòng 11 gè VLAN)
C. 创建连续的 VLAN10~VLAN20（一共 11 个 VLAN）
Create consecutive VLANs 10-20 (with a total of 11 VLANs)

yǔnxǔ suǒyǒu VLAN tōngguò
D. 允许所有 VLAN 通过
Allow all the VLANs to pass through

quánjú shǐnéng GVRP
E. 全局使能 GVRP
Enable GVRP globally

jiāng shèbèi mìngmíng wéi S1
F. 将设备命名为 S1
Name the device S1

duānkǒu shǐnéng GVRP
G. 端口使能 GVRP
Enable GVRP on the port

① ________ ② ________ ③ ________ ④ ________
⑤ ________ ⑥ ________ ⑦ ________

五、小知识 xiǎo zhīshi Tips

GARP

IEEE Zhìdìngle yí gè míng wéi GARP (tōngyòng shǔxìng zhùcè xiéyì) de kuàngjià xié-
IEEE 制定了一个名为 GARP（通用属性注册协议）的框架协
yì, gāi kuàngjià xiéyì bāokuò liǎng gè jùtǐ de xiéyì: GMRP (zǔbō zhùcè xiéyì) hé
议，该框架协议包括两个具体的协议：GMRP（组播注册协议）和
GVRP (tōngyòng VLAN zhùcè xiéyì). Jiāohuànjī shang bùshǔle GVRP xiéyì hòu,
GVRP（通用 VLAN 注册协议）。交换机上部署了 GVRP 协议后，
yònghù zhǐ xūyào duì shǎoliàng de jiāohuànjī jìnxíng jìngtài VLAN pèizhì, biàn kě jiāng zhèxiē
用户只需要对少量的交换机进行静态 VLAN 配置，便可将这些
VLAN pèizhì xìnxī chuándì bìng yìngyòng dào qítā de jiāohuànjī shang.
VLAN 配置信息传递并应用到其他的交换机上。

GARP

IEEE has developed a framework protocol called GARP (Generic Attribute Registration Protocol), which includes two specific protocols: GMRP (GARP Multicast Registration Protocol) and GVRP (GARP VLAN Registration Protocol). After the GVRP protocol is deployed on the switch, users only need to configure static VLAN for a small number of switches to transmit and apply these VLAN configuration information to other switches.

补充专业词语 bǔchōng zhuānyè cíyǔ Supplementary Specialized Vocabulary

03-07

1.	属性	shǔxìng	n.	attribute
2.	GARP			Generic Attribute Registration Protocol

第二部分 Part 2

汉字 Chinese Characters

一、汉字知识 Hànzì zhīshi Knowledge about Chinese Characters

汉字的偏旁（3） **Radicals of Chinese Characters (3)**

偏旁 Radicals	例字 Examples	部件组合 Combinations	结构图示 Illustrations
扌	打	扌+丁	
	拾	扌+合	

（续表）

偏旁 Radicals	例字 Examples	部件组合 Combinations	结构图示 Illustrations
扌	报	扌＋艮	⿰
	找	扌＋戈	⿰
	排	扌＋非	⿰
	搬	扌＋般	⿰
木	树	木＋对	⿰
	机	木＋几	⿰
	极	木＋及	⿰
	杯	木＋不	⿰
	校	木＋交	⿰
	样	木＋羊	⿰
纟	经	纟＋𢀖	⿰
	红	纟＋工	⿰
	绿	纟＋录	⿰
	绒	纟＋戎	⿰
心	怎	乍＋心	⿱
	想	相＋心	⿱
	态	太＋心	⿱
	感	咸＋心	⿱
	您	你＋心	⿱
⻊	路	⻊＋各	⿰
	跟	⻊＋艮	⿰
	踢	⻊＋易	⿰
	跑	⻊＋包	⿰

二、汉字认读与书写 Hànzì rèndú yǔ shūxiě The Recognition and Writing of Chinese Characters

认读下列词语，并试着读写构成词语的汉字。

Recognize the following words, and try to read and write the Chinese characters forming these words.

根据　双绞线　光纤跳线　路由信息

根				据				双				绞			

线				光				纤				跳			
线				路				由				信			
息															

第三部分　Part 3

日常用语 *Daily Expressions*

1. 如果你们方便的话，我想现在讨论一下儿日程安排的问题。Rúguǒ nǐmen fāngbiàn dehuà, wǒ xiǎng xiànzài tǎolùn yíxiàr rìchéng ānpái de wèntí. If it's convenient for you, I would like to discuss the schedule now.
2. 哪一天都可以？ Nǎ yì tiān dōu kěyǐ? Any day will do?

第四部分　Part 4

单元实训 *Unit Practical Training*

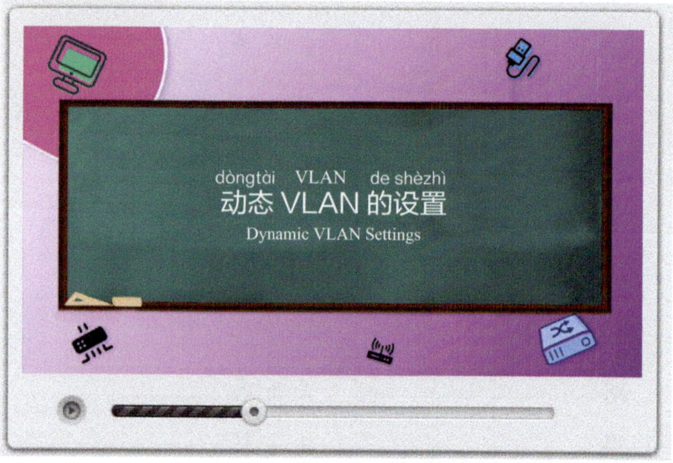

动态 VLAN 的设置　dòngtài VLAN de shèzhì

Dynamic VLAN Settings

实训目的 Training purpose

用 GVRP 实现 VLAN。

To use GVRP to realize VLAN.

实训组织 Training organization

每组 3 人，选出一个组长。

Each group consists of three people, and a group leader is selected.

实训内容 Training content

根据拓扑图，在交换机 S1 上创建 VLANs 10~20，使用 GVRP 协议，使其他交换机也能动态注册 VLAN，然后出现 VLANs 10~20（共 11 个 VLAN）。

Based on the topology diagram, create VLANs 10–20 on switch S1, and use the GVRP protocol to enable other switches to dynamically register VLANs. Then there are 11 VLANs from VLANs 10–20 in total.

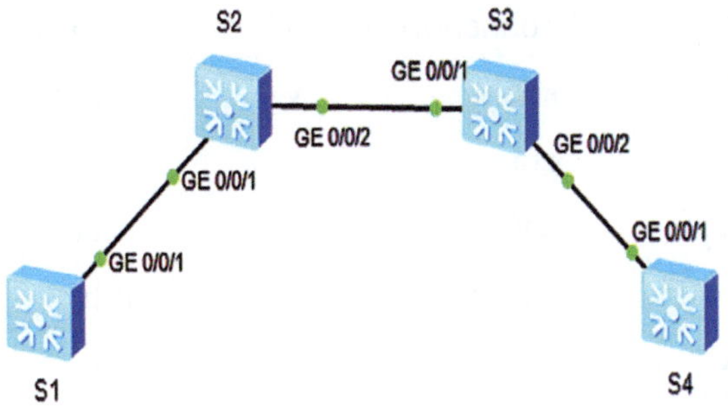

实训步骤 Training steps

① 绘制拓扑图。

Draw the topology diagram.

② 配置 S1，全局使能 GVRP，创建连续的 VLANs10～20（一共 11 个 VLAN），设置 GE0/0/1 端口类型为 trunk, 允许所有的 VLAN 通过，并在此端口下使能 GVRP。

Configure S1, enable GVRP globally, create consecutive VLANs 10–20 (with a total of 11 VLANs), set the GE0/0/1 port type to trunk, allow all the VLANs to pass through, and enable GVRP under this port.

③ 配置 S2，设置 GE0/0/1 和 GE0/0/2 端口类型为 trunk，允许所有的 VLAN 通过，并在上述端口下使能 GVRP。

Configure S2, set the port type of GE0/0/1 and GE0/0/2 to trunk, allow all the VLANs to pass through, and enable GVRP under the above ports.

④ 配置 S3，与 S2 类似。

Configure S3, which is similar to S2.

⑤ 配置 S4，设置 GE0/0/1 端口类型为 trunk，允许所有的 VLAN 通过，并在此端口下使能 GVRP。

Configure S4, set the GE0/0/1 port type to trunk, allow all the VLANs to pass through, and enable GVRP under this port.

⑥ 在交换机上查看所有 VLAN 汇总信息，判断是否达到了实验目的。

View the summary information of all the VLANs on the switch to tell whether the experimental purpose has been achieved.

⑦ 实训结束，教师总结评价。

The training ends. The teacher makes a summary and an evaluation.

第五部分 Part 5

单元小结 Unit Summary

cíyǔ
词语
Vocabulary

普通词语 General Vocabulary

1.	中文	Zhōngwén	n.	Chinese (language)
2.	全称	quánchēng	n.	full name
3.	考虑	kǎolǜ	v.	consider
4.	该	gāi	pron.	the, this
5.	涉及	shèjí	v.	involve
6.	各个	gègè	pron.	each
7.	加入	jiārù	v.	join
8.	数量	shùliàng	n.	number
9.	太	tài	adv.	too
10.	特别	tèbié	adv.	especially
11.	经常	jīngcháng	adv.	frequently
12.	则	zé	conj.	then
13.	既	jì	conj.	(to be echoed by 且，又，也，etc.) both... and...
14.	耗费	hàofèi	v.	consume
15.	精力	jīnglì	n.	energy
16.	且	qiě	conj.	and
17.	非常	fēicháng	adv.	very
18.	容易	róngyì	adj.	easy
19.	出错	chū cuò	phr.	make a mistake
20.	难道	nándào	adv.	*used in a rhetorical question for emphasis*
21.	解决	jiějué	v.	solve
22.	问题	wèntí	n.	problem
23.	大大	dàdà	adv.	greatly
24.	减少	jiǎnshǎo	v.	reduce
25.	工作	gōngzuò	n.	work
26.	开启	kāiqǐ	v.	start
27.	之前	zhīqián	n.	before
28.	注意	zhùyì	v.	pay attention to
29.	可是	kěshì	conj.	but
30.	默认	mòrèn	v.	do by default
31.	相关	xiāngguān	v.	relate
32.	允许	yǔnxǔ	v.	allow

cíyǔ
词语
Vocabulary

专业词语 Specialized Vocabulary

1.	GVRP			GARP VLAN Registration Protocol
2.	注册	zhù//cè	v.	register
3.	注销	zhùxiāo	v.	logout, unregister
4.	使能	shǐnéng	v.	enable
5.	全局	quánjú	n.	being global

补充专业词语 Supplementary Specialized Vocabulary

1.	属性	shǔxìng	n.	attribute
2.	GARP			Generic Attribute Registration Protocol

jùzi
句子
Sentences

1. GVRP 的中文全称是通用 VLAN 注册协议。
2. 在对交换机进行 VLAN 配置的时候，需要在每一台交换机上手工创建该交换机需要涉及的所有 VLAN，并且需要手工将交换机上的各个端口加入到相应的 VLAN 中去。
3. 如果交换机和 VLAN 的数量太多，特别是 VLAN 的数量又经常变化时，则这种手工配置方式既耗费时间又耗费精力，且非常容易出错。
4. GVRP 能够自动实现 VLAN 信息在交换机上的动态注册过程和注销过程，从而大大减少了 VLAN 配置过程中的手工工作。
5. 在使能（开启）端口的 GVRP 功能之前，需要先全局使能 GVRP 功能。
6. GVRP 功能只能配置在 Trunk 类型的端口上，所以需要配置相关的端口为 Trunk，并允许相应的 VLAN 通过。

4

VLAN jiān lùyóu

VLAN 间路由

Inter-VLAN Routing

sāncéng jiāohuànjī VLAN lùyóu de bùzhòu

三 层 交换机 VLAN 路由的步骤

Steps of VLAN Routing on a Layer 3 Switch

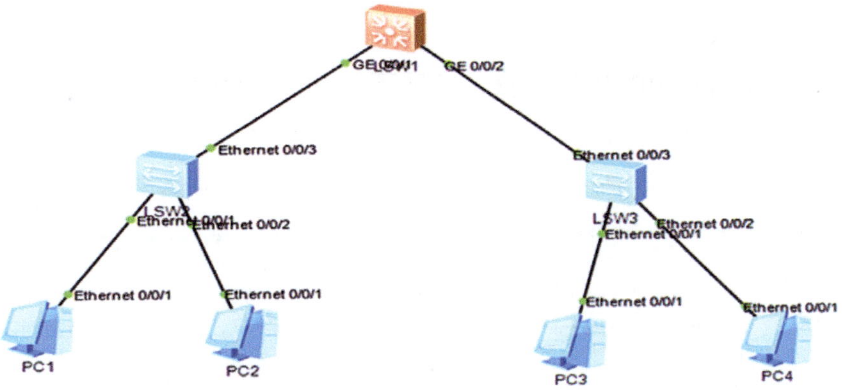


```
<Huawei>sys
Enter system view, return user view with Ctrl+Z
[Huawei]vlan batch 2 3
Info: This operation may take a few seconds. Please wait for a moment. done
Mar 16 2022 13:55:43-08:00 Huawei DS/4/DATASYNC_CFGCHANGE:OID 1.3.6.1.4.1.2011.5
.25.191.3.1 configurations have been changed. The current change number is 4, th
e change loop count is 0, and the maximum number of records is 4096.
```

chuàngjiàn VLAN2 hé VLAN3

创建 VLAN2 和 VLAN3

Create VLAN 2 and VLAN 3

```
[Huawei]int g0/0/1
[Huawei-GigabitEthernet0/0/1]port link-type access
[Huawei-GigabitEthernet0/0/1]port link-type access
[Huawei-GigabitEthernet0/0/1]port default vlan 2
[Huawei-GigabitEthernet0/0/1]int g0/0/2
[Huawei-GigabitEthernet0/0/2]port link-type access
[Huawei-GigabitEthernet0/0/2]port default vlan 3
```

jiāng jiēkǒu GE0/0/1 hé jiēkǒu GE0/0/2 fēnbié jiārù VLAN2 hé VLAN3

将 接口 GE0/0/1 和接口 GE0/0/2 分别加入 VLAN2 和 VLAN3

Join Interface GE0/0/1 and Interface GE0/0/2 to VLAN 2 and VLAN 3 Respectively

```
[Huawei]interface Vlanif 2
[Huawei]interface Vlanif 3
```

chuàngjiàn VLANIF jiēkǒu

创建 VLANIF 接口

Create the VLANIF Interface

```
[Huawei-Vlanif2]ip address 192.168.1.254 24
[Huawei-Vlanif3]ip address 192.168.2.254 24
```

zài VLANIF jiēkǒu xià pèizhì IP dìzhǐ

在 VLANIF 接口 下 配置 IP 地址

Configure IP Addresses under the VLANIF Interface

```
PC>ping 192.168.1.1

Ping 192.168.1.1: 32 data bytes, Press Ctrl_C to break
From 192.168.1.1: bytes=32 seq=1 ttl=128 time<1 ms
From 192.168.1.1: bytes=32 seq=2 ttl=128 time<1 ms
From 192.168.1.1: bytes=32 seq=3 ttl=128 time<1 ms
From 192.168.1.1: bytes=32 seq=4 ttl=128 time<1 ms
From 192.168.1.1: bytes=32 seq=5 ttl=128 time<1 ms

--- 192.168.1.1 ping statistics ---
  5 packet(s) transmitted
  5 packet(s) received
  0.00% packet loss
  round-trip min/avg/max = 0/0/0 ms
```

yànzhèng zhǔjī A yǔ zhǔjī B néngfǒu zhèngcháng tōngxìn

验证 主机 A 与主机 B 能否 正常 通信

Verify Whether Host A and Host B Can Communicate Normally

题解　Introduction

1. 学习内容：VLAN 间路由及三层交换机的概念，以及实现 VLAN 间路由的操作步骤。
   Learning content: The concepts of inter-VLAN routing and layer 3 switches, as well as the operation steps for implementing inter-VLAN routing
2. 知识目标：掌握 VLAN 间路由相关的关键词语，了解汉字的偏旁"阝(左)""宀""又""月""钅""王"，学写相关汉字。
   Knowledge objectives: To master the keywords for inter-VLAN routing, understand the Chinese radicals "阝(left)", "宀", "又", "月", "钅", "王", and learn to write the related Chinese characters
3. 技能目标：学会 VLAN 间路由的操作步骤，实现不同 VLAN 间的设备通信。
   Skill objective: To master the operation steps of inter-VLAN routing to realize device communication between different VLANs

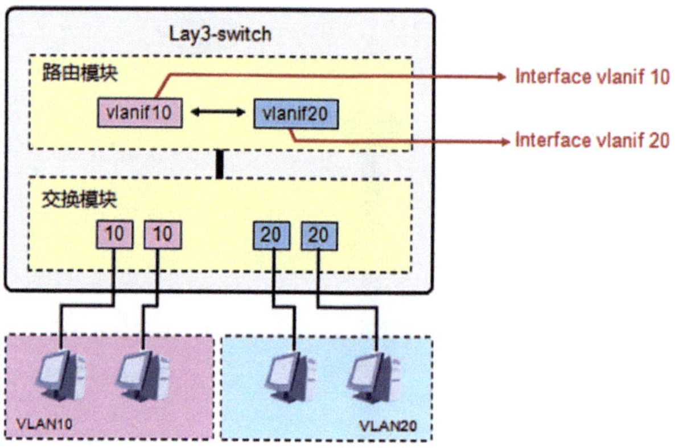

第一部分　Part 1

课文　Texts

一、热身　rèshēn　Warm-up

1. 给下面的操作选择对应的图片。　Choose the corresponding pictures for the following operations.

A. `[Huawei]vlan batch`

B. `[Huawei]interface vlanif`

C. `[Huawei]display interface vlanif`

D. `[Huawei]undo interface vlanif`

E. `[Huawei-GigabitEthernet0/0/1]port link-type`

F. `[Huawei-GigabitEthernet0/0/1]port default vlan`

pīliàng chuàngjiàn VLAN
① 批量 创建 VLAN ________________
create VLANs in batches

chákàn VLANIF jiēkǒu
② 查看 VLANIF 接口 ________________
view the VLANIF interface

shèzhì duānkǒu mòrèn suǒshǔ de VLAN
③ 设置 端口 默认 所属的 VLAN ________________
set the default VLAN of the port

shānchú VLANIF jiēkǒu
④ 删除 VLANIF 接口 ________________
delete the VLANIF interface

shèzhì duānkǒu liànlù lèixíng
⑤ 设置 端口 链路类型 ________________
set the link type of the port

chuàngjiàn VLANIF jiēkǒu
⑥ 创建 VLANIF 接口 ________________
create the VLANIF interface

2. 观看介绍三层交换机部署 VLAN 间路由的拓扑图的视频，将下列词语填入对应空格中。

Watch the video introducing the topology diagram of inter-VLAN routing deployed by a layer 3 switch, and fill in the corresponding blanks with the following words.

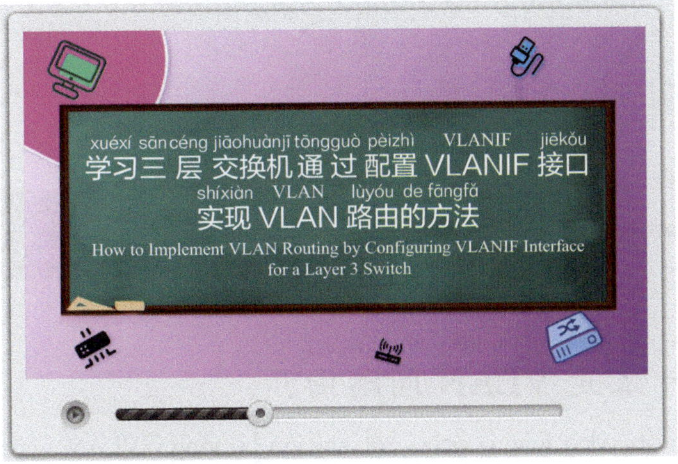

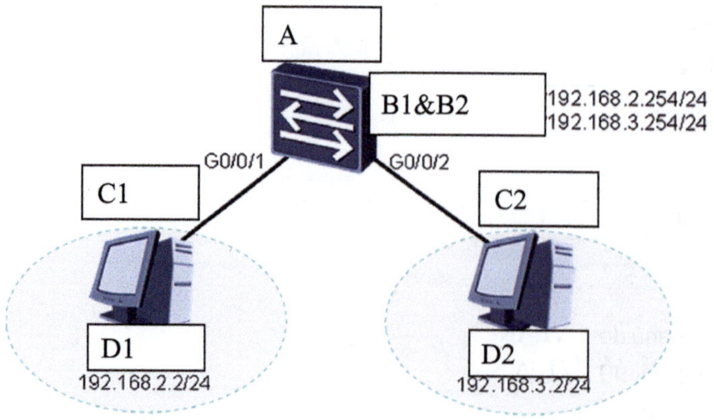

① VLAN (VLAN)
Virtual Local Area Network

② 三层交换机 (sān céng jiāohuànjī)
Layer 3 Switch

③ 主机 (zhǔjī)
Host

④ VLANIF (VLANIF)
Virtual Local Area Network Interface

二、课文 kèwén Texts

A 04-01

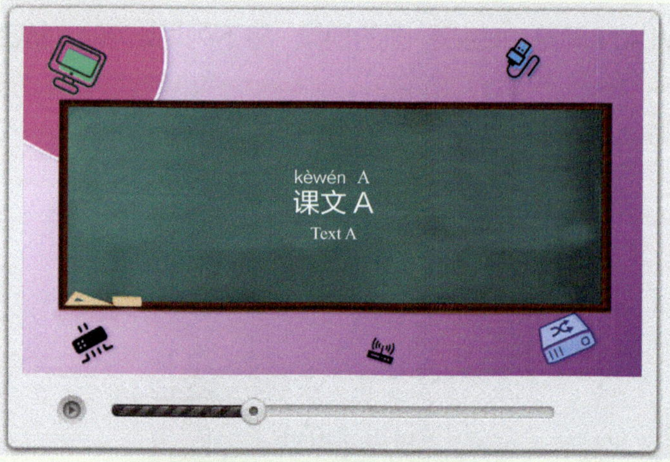

túdì: Shīfu, qǐngwèn shénme shì VLAN jiān lùyóu?
徒弟：师傅，请问什么是VLAN间路由？

shīfu: VLAN jiān lùyóu shì yòng lùyóu jìshù lái shíxiàn bù tóng VLAN jiān de shèbèi tōngxìn.
师傅：VLAN间路由是用路由技术来实现不同VLAN间的设备通信。

túdì: VLAN de zuòyòng shì shénme?
徒弟：VLAN的作用是什么？

shīfu: VLAN de zuòyòng shì gélí shùjù liànlùcéng de tōngxìn, gélí guǎngbōyù,
师傅：VLAN 的作用是隔离数据链路层的通信，隔离广播域，

fángzhǐ guǎngbō fēngbào, bǎohù xìnxī ānquán.
防止广播风暴，保护信息安全。

túdì: Zěnme shíxiàn VLAN jiān lùyóu ne?
徒弟：怎么实现 VLAN 间路由呢？

shīfu: Xūyào tōngguò wǎngluòcéng lùyóu shíxiàn. Kěyǐ tōngguò èr céng jiāohuànjī pèihé
师傅：需要通过网络层路由实现。可以通过二层交换机配合

lùyóuqì lái shíxiàn, yě kěyǐ tōngguò sān céng jiāohuànjī lái shíxiàn.
路由器来实现，也可以通过三层交换机来实现。

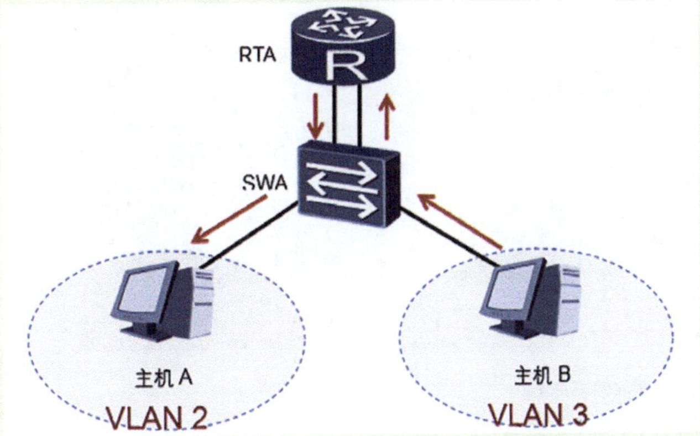

译文 yìwén Text in English

Apprentice: Master, what is inter-VLAN routing?

Master: It uses routing technology to realize device communication between different VLANs.

Apprentice: What is the function of VLAN?

Master: It is used to isolate the communication of data link layer, isolate broadcast domain, prevent broadcast storm and protect information security.

Apprentice: How can we implement inter-VLAN routing?

Master: It needs to be implemented through routing at the network layer. It can be implemented by using a layer 2 switch in conjunction with a router or using a layer 3 switch.

普通词语 pǔtōng cíyǔ General Vocabulary

04-02

1.	隔离	gélí	v.	isolate
2.	防止	fángzhǐ	v.	prevent
3.	保护	bǎohù	v.	protect
4.	安全	ānquán	n.	security
5.	配合	pèihé	v.	(be) in conjunction with

专业词语 zhuānyè cíyǔ Specialized Vocabulary

04-03

1.	链路层	liànlùcéng	n.	link layer
	层	céng	n.	layer
2.	广播域	guǎngbōyù	phr.	broadcast domain
3.	广播风暴	guǎngbō fēngbào	phr.	broadcast storm
	风暴	fēngbào	n.	storm
4.	网络层	wǎngluòcéng	n.	network layer

B 04-04

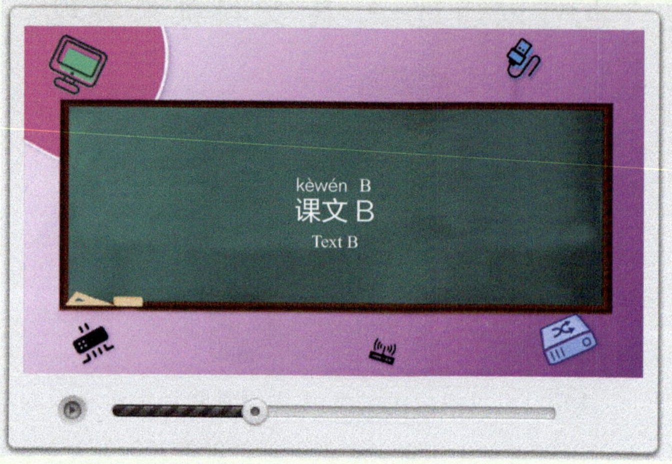

túdì: Shīfu, bù tóng VLAN de yònghù zhījiān kěyǐ jìnxíng èr céng tōngxìn ma?
徒弟：师傅，不同 VLAN 的用户之间可以进行二层通信吗？

shīfu: Bù kěyǐ. Yīnwèi VLAN gélíle èr céng guǎngbōyù, yě gélíle VLAN zhījiān de èr céng liúliàng. Bìxū tōngguò sān céng lùyóu cái néng jiāng bàowén cóng yí gè VLAN zhuǎnfā dào lìngwài yí gè VLAN.
师傅：不可以。因为 VLAN 隔离了二层广播域，也隔离了 VLAN 之间的二层流量。必须通过三层路由才能将报文从一个 VLAN 转发到另外一个 VLAN。

túdì: Mùqián, zuì cháng yòng shénme lái shíxiàn VLAN lùyóu?
徒弟：目前，最常用什么来实现 VLAN 路由？

shīfu: Yòng sān céng jiāohuànjī, tā jùyǒu sān céng gōngnéng.
师傅：用三层交换机，它具有三层功能。

túdì: Shì tōngguò zài sān céng jiāohuànjī shang pèizhì VLANIF jiēkǒu lái shíxiàn VLAN jiān lùyóu ma?
徒弟：是通过在三层交换机上配置 VLANIF 接口来实现 VLAN 间路由吗？

shīfu: Shìde. Rúguǒ wǎngluò shang yǒu duō gè VLAN, jiù xūyào wèi měi gè VLAN pèizhì yí gè VLANIF jiēkǒu, bìng gěi měi gè VLANIF jiēkǒu pèizhì yí gè IP dìzhǐ. Yònghù shèzhì de quēshěng wǎngguān jiù shì sān céng jiāohuànjī zhōng VLANIF jiēkǒu de IP dìzhǐ.

师傅：是的。如果网络上有多个VLAN，就需要为每个VLAN配置一个VLANIF接口，并给每个VLANIF接口配置一个IP地址。用户设置的缺省网关就是三层交换机中VLANIF接口的IP地址。

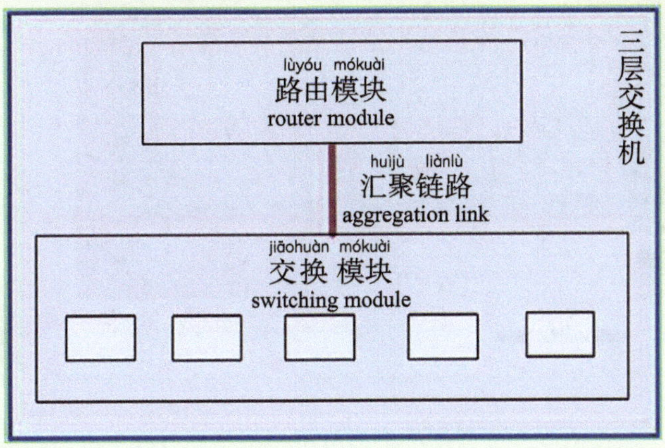

译文 yìwén Text in English

Apprentice: Master, is it possible to carry out layer 2 communication between users of different VLANs?

Master: No. Because the VLAN isolates layer 2 broadcast domains as well as layer 2 traffic between VLANs. Messages must be forwarded from one VLAN to another through layer 3 routing.

Apprentice: At present, what is the most commonly used to implement VLAN routing?

Master: A layer 3 switch, which has three layers of functionality.

Apprentice: Is inter-VLAN routing implemented by configuring VLANIF interfaces on a layer 3 switch?

Master: Yes. If there are several VLANs on the network, you need to configure a VLANIF interface for each VLAN, and configure an IP address for each VLANIF interface. The default gateway set by the user is the IP address of the VLANIF interface in the layer 3 switch.

普通词语 pǔtōng cíyǔ General Vocabulary

04-05

1.	必须	bìxū	adv.	must
2.	转发	zhuǎnfā	v.	forward
3.	另外	lìngwài	pron.	other, another
4.	目前	mùqián	n.	the present
5.	具有	jùyǒu	v.	have

专业词语 zhuānyè cíyǔ Specialized Vocabulary 04-06

报文	bàowén	n.	message

三、视听说 shì-tīng-shuō Viewing, Listening, and Speaking

1\. 观看介绍单臂路由实现 VLAN 间路由的配置的视频，将配置操作与其中文含义连线。

Watch the video introducing how to configure single-arm routing to implement inter-VLAN routing, and match the configuration operations with the corresponding Chinese meanings.

① [SWA-GigabitEthernet0/0/1] port link-type trunk

② [SWA-GigabitEthernet0/0/1] port trunk allow-pass vlan 2 3

③ [RTA] interface GigabitEthernet0/0/1.1

④ [RTA-GigabitEthernet0/0/1.1] dot1q termination vid 2

⑤ [RTA-GigabitEthernet0/0/1.1] arp broadcast enable

chuàngjiàn bìng jìnrù lùyóuqì zǐ jiēkǒu shìtú
A. 创建 并 进入路由器子接口视图
create and enter router sub-interface view

shǐnéng ARP guǎngbō gōngnéng
B. 使能 ARP 广播 功能
enable ARP broadcast function

shèzhì trunk jiēkǒu yǔnxǔ tōngguò de VLAN ID
C. 设置 trunk 接口允许通过的 VLAN ID
set the VLAN ID allowed to pass through the trunk interface

pèizhì jiēkǒu wéi trunk lèixíng jiēkǒu
D. 配置接口为 trunk 类型接口
configure the interface as a trunk-type interface

pèizhì gāi zǐ jiēkǒu dot1q zhōngjié de dān céng VLAN ID
E. 配置该子接口 dot1q 终结的单 层 VLAN ID
configure single-layer VLAN ID terminated by the sub-interface dot1q

2. 说一说　Let's talk

说一说单臂路由实现 VLAN 间路由的配置步骤。

Talk about the configuration steps for single-arm routing to implement inter-VLAN routing.

四、学以致用　xuéyǐzhìyòng　Practicing What You Have Learnt

观看三层交换机配置 VLAN 路由的视频，并对以下步骤进行排序。

Watch the video about the VLAN routing deployed by a layer 3 switch and put the following steps in order.

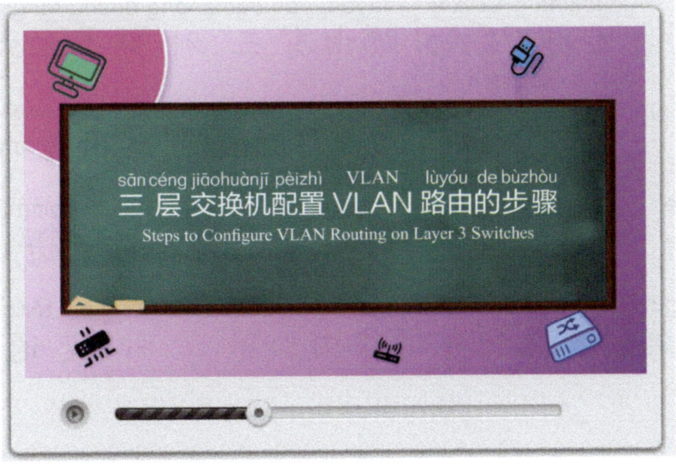

chuàngjiàn VLANIF jiēkǒu
A. 创建 VLANIF 接口
Create the VLANIF interface

pīliàng chuàngjiàn VLAN2 hé VLAN3
B. 批量创建 VLAN 2 和 VLAN 3
Create VLAN 2 and VLAN 3 in batches

zài VLANIF jiēkǒu xià pèizhì IP dìzhǐ
C. 在 VLANIF 接口下配置 IP 地址
Configure the IP address under the VLANIF interface

yànzhèng zhǔjī A yǔ zhǔjī B néngfǒu zhèngcháng tōngxìn
D. 验证主机 A 与主机 B 能否正常通信
Verify whether Host A and Host B can communicate with each other normally

jiāng jiēkǒu GE0/0/1 hé jiēkǒu GE0/0/2 fēnbié jiārù VLAN2 hé VLAN3
E. 将接口 GE0/0/1 和接口 GE0/0/2 分别加入 VLAN 2 和 VLAN 3
Join port GE0/0/1 and port GE0/0/2 to VLAN 2 and VLAN 3 respectively

① ______ → ② ______ → ③ ______ → ④ ______ → ⑤ ______

五、小知识 xiǎo zhīshi Tips

VLAN jiān lùyóu

VLAN 间路由

VLAN huàfēnle guǎngbōyù, yīncǐ, VLAN zhījiān mòrèn bù néng jìnxíng tōngxìn.
VLAN 划分了广播域，因此，VLAN 之间默认不能进行通信。
Bù tóng VLAN zhījiān xūyào gòngxiǎng zīyuán tōngxìn, shíxiàn VLAN tōngxìn de fāngfǎ bèi
不同 VLAN 之间需要共享资源通信，实现 VLAN 通信的方法被
chēngwéi VLAN jiān lùyóu. Shíxiàn VLAN lùyóu yǒu sān zhǒng bùshǔ fāngshì: dì-yì zhǒng
称为 VLAN 间路由。实现 VLAN 路由有三种部署方式：第一种
shì měi gè VLAN shǐyòng yì tiáo dúzhàn de wùlǐ liànlù liánjiē dào lùyóuqì de yí gè jiēkǒu
是每个 VLAN 使用一条独占的物理链路连接到路由器的一个接口
shang; dì-èr zhǒng shì duō gè VLAN gòngxiǎng tóng yì tiáo wùlǐ liànlù, bìng liánjiē dào lùyóu-
上；第二种是多个 VLAN 共享同一条物理链路，并连接到路由
qì de yí gè jiēkǒu shang, gāi fāngshì yě jiào dānbì lùyóu; dì-sān zhǒng shì tōngguò sān céng jiāo-
器的一个接口上，该方式也叫单臂路由；第三种是通过三层交
huànjī shíxiàn.
换机实现。

Inter-VLAN Routing

VLANs are divided into broadcast domains. Therefore, communication between VLANs cannot be carried out by default. Different VLANs need to communicate by sharing resources, and the method of implementing VLAN communication is called inter-VLAN routing. There are three deployment methods to implement VLAN routing. The first method is that each VLAN is connected to an interface of the router using an exclusive physical link. The second method is that multiple VLANs share the same physical link and are connected to an interface of the router, which is called single-arm routing. The third method is using a layer 3 switch.

补充专业词语 bǔchōng zhuānyè cíyǔ Supplementary Specialized Vocabulary

04-07

1.	VLANIF			Virtual Local Area Network Interface
2.	ARP			Address Resolution Protocol
3.	广播功能	guǎngbō gōngnéng	phr.	broadcast function
4.	批量创建	pīliàng chuàngjiàn	phr.	create...in batches
5.	物理链路	wùlǐ liànlù	phr.	physical link
6.	单臂路由	dānbì lùyóu	phr.	single-arm routing, router-on-a-stick routing

第二部分 Part 2

汉字 Chinese Characters

一、汉字知识 Hànzì zhīshi Knowledge about Chinese Characters

汉字的偏旁（4） Radicals of Chinese characters (4)

偏旁 Radicals	例字 Examples	部件组合 Combinations	结构图示 Illustrations
阝(左)	阿	阝＋可	⿰
	院	阝＋完	⿰
	陪	阝＋音	⿰
宀	宿	宀＋佰	⿱
	家	宀＋豕	⿱
	安	宀＋女	⿱
	室	宀＋至	⿱
	客	宀＋各	⿱
	字	宀＋子	⿱
	定	宀＋𤴓	⿱
又	对	又＋寸	⿰
	难	又＋隹	⿰
	欢	又＋欠	⿰
	友	𠂇＋又	⿸
月	朋	月＋月	⿰
	服	月＋𠬝	⿰
	脑	月＋𡿺	⿰
	期	其＋月	⿰
钅	银	钅＋艮	⿰
	错	钅＋昔	⿰
	钱	钅＋戋	⿰
	钟	钅＋中	⿰
王	玩	王＋元	⿰
	现	王＋见	⿰
	球	王＋求	⿰
	班	王＋丿＋王	⿲

二、汉字认读与书写 Hànzì rèndú yǔ shūxiě The Recognition and Writing of Chinese Characters

认读下列词语，并试着读写构成词语的汉字。

Recognize the following words, and try to read and write the Chinese characters forming these words.

隔离　　安全　　报文　　电脑　　现在　　链路层

隔				离				安				全			
报				文				电				脑			
现				在				链				路			
层															

第三部分 Part 3

日常用语 *Daily Expressions*

① 尽可能快！ Jǐn kěnéng kuài! As soon as possible!

② 信不信由你！ Xìn bu xìn yóu nǐ! Believe it or not!

③ 下次会更好！ Xià cì huì gèng hǎo! Better luck next time!

第四部分 Part 4

单元实训 *Unit Practical Training*

配置 VLAN 间路由 pèizhì VLAN jiān lùyóu

Configuring inter-VLAN Routing

实训目的 Training purpose

掌握三层交换机上配置 VLAN 间路由的方法和步骤。

To master the methods and steps of configuring inter-VLAN routing on layer 3 switches.

实训组织 Training organization

每组 3 人，选出一个组长。

Each group consists of three people, and a group leader is selected.

实训内容 Training content

三层交换机上配置 VLAN 间路由。

Configuring inter-VLAN routing on layer 3 switches

实训步骤 Training steps

1. 将参加实训的人员分成若干小组，每组 3 人，轮流上机操作与实践。
   Divide the trainees into groups of 3. The students take turns to operate and practice.
2. 运行 eNSP 软件，新建拓扑图如图所示。
   Run the eNSP software to create a new topology diagram as shown in the figure.
3. 创建 VLAN，主机 A 和主机 B 分别加入 VLAN 2 和 VLAN 3。
   Create VLANs, and join Host A and Host B to VLAN 2 and VLAN 3 respectively.
4. 配置三层交换机，实现主机 A 和主机 B 互通。
   Configure the layer 3 switch to implement the intercommunication between Host A and Host B.
5. 实训结束，教师总结评价。
   The training ends. The teacher makes a summary and an evaluation.

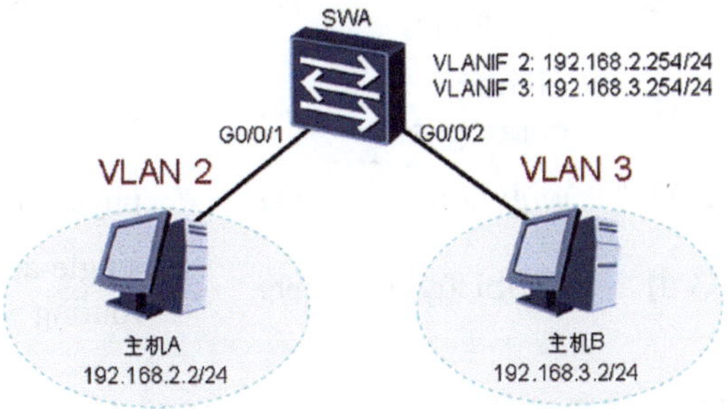

第五部分 Part 5

单元小结 *Unit Summary*

cíyǔ
词语
Vocabulary

普通词语 General Vocabulary

1.	隔离	gélí	v.	isolate
2.	防止	fángzhǐ	v.	prevent

cíyǔ
词语
Vocabulary

3.	保护	bǎohù	v.	protect
4.	安全	ānquán	n.	security
5.	配合	pèihé	v.	(be) in conjunction with
6.	必须	bìxū	adv.	must
7.	转发	zhuǎnfā	v.	forward
8.	另外	lìngwài	pron.	other, another
9.	目前	mùqián	n.	the present
10.	具有	jùyǒu	v.	have

专业词语 Specialized Vocabulary

1.	链路层	liànlùcéng	n.	link layer
	层	céng	n.	layer
2.	广播域	guǎngbōyù	phr.	broadcast domain
3.	广播风暴	guǎngbō fēngbào	phr.	broadcast storm
	风暴	fēngbào	n.	storm
4.	网络层	wǎngluòcéng	n.	network layer
5.	报文	bàowén	n.	message

补充专业词语 Supplementary Specialized Vocabulary

1.	VLANIF			Virtual Local Area Network Interface
2.	ARP			Address Resolution Protocol
3.	广播功能	guǎngbō gōngnéng	phr.	broadcast function
4.	批量创建	pīliàng chuàngjiàn	phr.	create...in batches
5.	物理链路	wùlǐ liànlù	phr.	physical link
6.	单臂路由	dānbì lùyóu	phr.	single-arm routing, router-on-a-stick routing

jùzi
句子
Sentences

1. VLAN 间路由是用路由技术来实现不同 VLAN 间的设备通信。
2. VLAN 的作用是隔离数据链路层的通信，隔离广播域，防止广播风暴，保护信息安全。
3. VLAN 间路由需要通过网络层路由实现。可以通过二层交换机配合路由器来实现，也可以通过三层交换机来实现。
4. 如果网络上有多个 VLAN，就需要为每个 VLAN 配置一个 VLANIF 接口，并给每个 VLANIF 接口配置一个 IP 地址。用户设置的缺省网关就是三层交换机中 VLANIF 接口的 IP 地址。

5

DHCP zhōngjì dàilǐ pèizhì

DHCP 中继代理配置

DHCP Relay Agent Configuration

DHCP Relay jiēkǒu pèizhì cāozuò bùzhòu

DHCP Relay 接口 配置 操作 步骤

Operation Steps of DHCP Relay Interface configuration

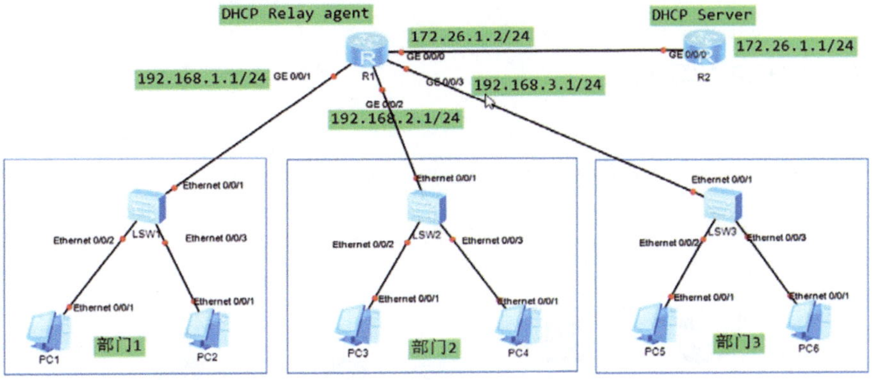


```
<Huawei>system-view
Enter system view, return user view with Ctrl+Z.
```

zhíxíng mìnglìng system-view, jìnrù xìtǒng shìtú

执行 命令 system-view，进入 系统 视图

Execute the Command *system-view* to Enter the System View

```
<Huawei>system-view
Enter system view, return user view with Ctrl+Z.
[Huawei]dhcp enable
```

zhíxíng mìnglìng dhcp enable, kāiqǐ DHCP fúwù

执行 命令 dhcp enable，开启 DHCP 服务

Execute the Command *dhcp enable* to Start the DHCP Service

```
<Huawei>system-view
Enter system view, return user view with Ctrl+Z.
[Huawei]dhcp enable
[Huawei]interface gigabitethernet0/0/1
```

zhíxíng mìnglìng interface, jìnrù DHCP Relay jiēkǒu shìtú

执行 命令 interface，进入 DHCP Relay 接口 视图

Execute the Command *interface* to Enter the DHCP Relay Interface View

```
<Huawei>system-view
Enter system view, return user view with Ctrl+Z.
[Huawei]dhcp enable
[Huawei]interface gigabitethernet0/0/1
[Huawei-GigabitEthernet0/0/1]dhcp relay server-ip 172.26.1.1
```

zhíxíng mìnglìng ip relay address, zài DHCP Relay

执行 命令 ip relay address，在 DHCP Relay

jiēkǒu shang zhǐdìng DHCP Server de IP dìzhǐ

接口 上 指定 DHCP Server 的 IP 地址

Execute the Command *ip relay address* to Specify the IP Address of the DHCP Server on the DHCP Relay Interface

```
<Huawei>system-view
Enter system view, return user view with Ctrl+Z.
[Huawei]dhcp enable
[Huawei]interface gigabitethernet0/0/1
[Huawei-GigabitEthernet0/0/1]dhcp relay server-ip 172.26.1.1
[Huawei-GigabitEthernet0/0/1]dhcp select relay
```

zhíxíng mìnglìng dhcp select relay, jiāng DHCP Relay jiēkǒu shang

执行 命令 dhcp select relay，将 DHCP Relay 接口 上

de pèizhì xìnxī yìngyòng dào dāngqián jiēkǒu

的配置信息 应用 到 当前 接口

Execute the Command *dhcp select relay* to Apply the Configuration Information on the DHCP Relay Interface to the Current Interface

```
<Huawei>system-view
Enter system view, return user view with Ctrl+Z.
[Huawei]dhcp enable
[Huawei]interface gigabitethernet0/0/1
[Huawei-GigabitEthernet0/0/1]dhcp relay server-ip 172.26.1.1
[Huawei-GigabitEthernet0/0/1]dhcp select relay
[Huawei-GigabitEthernet0/0/1]
```

zhíxíng mìnglìng dhcp relay source-ip agent-ip, jiāng DHCP qǐngqiú bàowén

执行 命令 dhcp relay source-ip agent-ip，将 DHCP 请求 报文

de yuán IP dìzhǐ shèzhì wéi pèizhìle DHCP zhōngjì de jiēkǒu IP dìzhǐ

的 源 IP 地址 设置 为 配置了 DHCP 中继 的 接口 IP 地址

Execute the Command *dhcp relay source-ip agent-ip* to Set the Source IP Address of the DHCP Request Message to the IP Address of the Interface Configured with DHCP Relay

题解 Introduction

1. 学习内容：DHCP 中继代理的基本概念、作用和配置方法。
   Learning content: The basic concepts, functions and configuration methods of DHCP relay agent
2. 知识目标：掌握 DHCP 配置相关的关键词语，了解汉字的偏旁“巾”“广”“小”“⺌”“八”“刂”，学写相关汉字。
   Knowledge objectives: To master the keywords for DHCP configuration, understand the Chinese radicals “巾”, “广”, “小”, “⺌”, “八”, “刂”, and learn to write the related Chinese characters
3. 技能目标：学会 DHCP 的配置。
   Skill objective: To master DHCP configuration

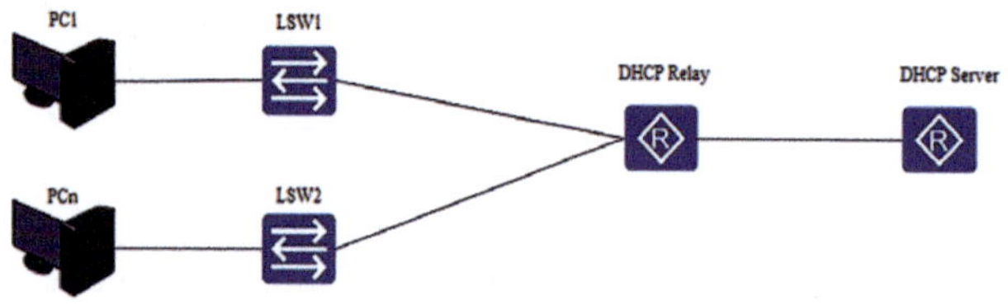

第一部分 Part 1

课文 Texts

一、热身 rèshēn Warm-up

1. 给词语选择对应的图片。 **Choose the corresponding pictures for the words.**

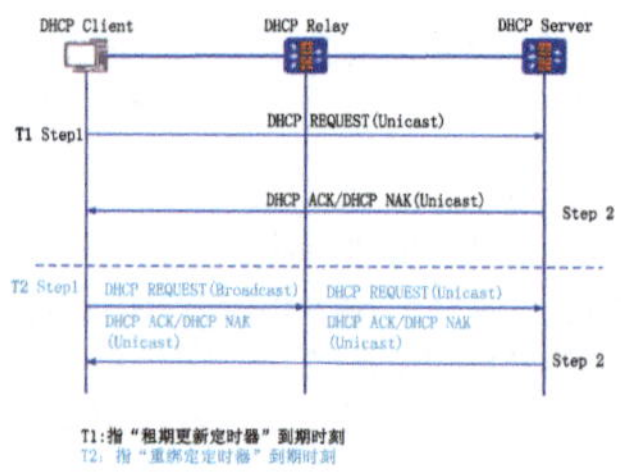

A.

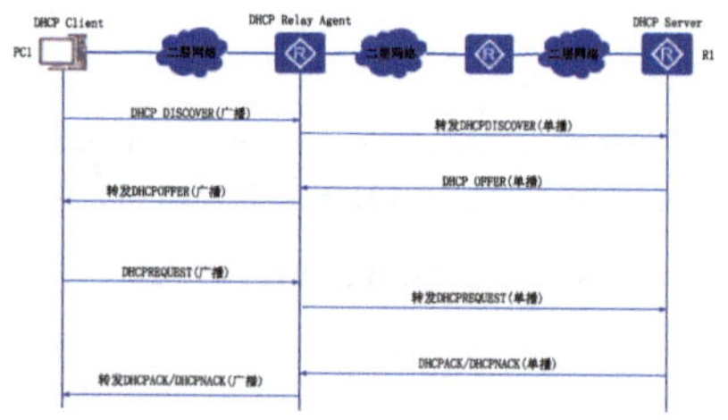

B.

C.

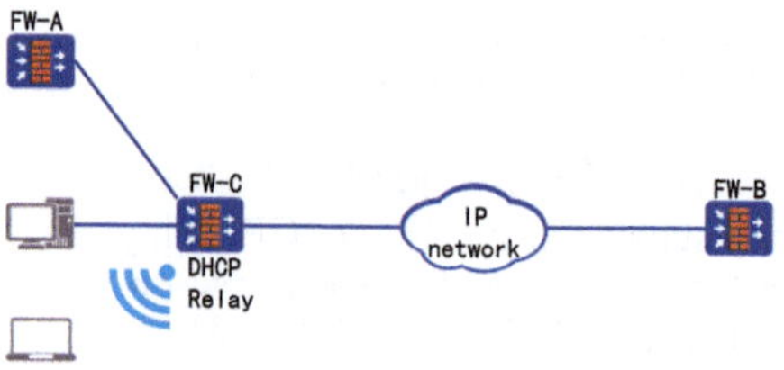

D.

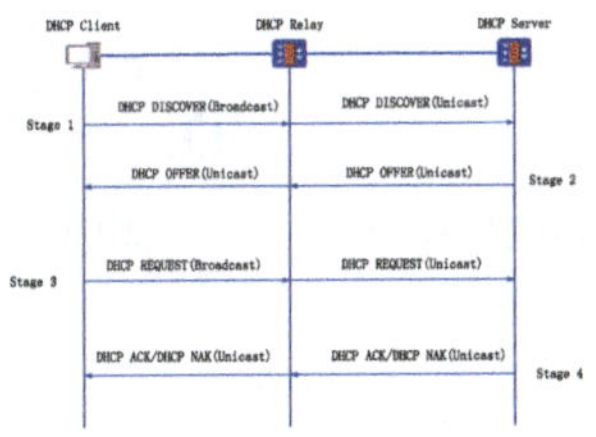

E.

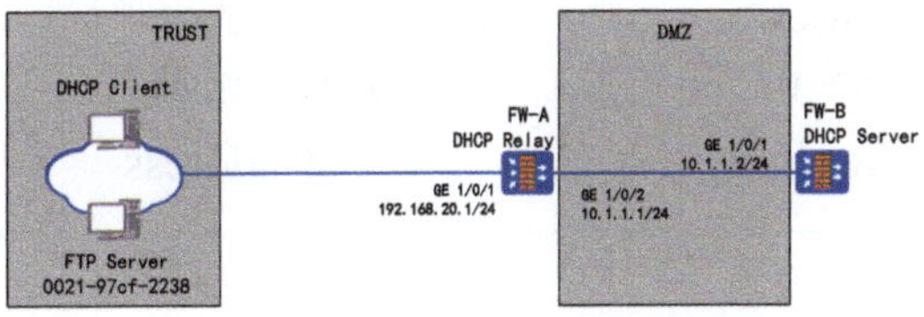

F.

DHCP diǎnxíng zǔwǎng
❶ DHCP 典型 组网 ________________
typical DHCP networking

DHCP zhōngjì dàilǐ
❷ DHCP 中继代理________________
DHCP relay agent

DHCP Client tōngguò DHCP Relay shǒucì shēnqǐng IP dìzhǐ guòchéngtú
❸ DHCP Client 通过 DHCP Relay 首次 申请 IP 地址 过程图 ________________
process diagram of DHCP Client applying for an IP address for the first time through DHCP Relay

DHCP Client tōngguò DHCP Relay gēngxīn zūqī shìyìtú
❹ DHCP Client 通过 DHCP Relay 更新租期示意图________________
schematic diagram of DHCP Client updating lease term through DHCP Relay

pèizhì DHCP Relay zǔwǎngtú
❺ 配置 DHCP Relay 组网图 ________________
diagram of configuring DHCP Relay networking

DHCP xìtǒng zǔchéng
❻ DHCP 系统 组成 ________________
components of DHCP system

2. 观看介绍 DHCP Relay 配置的前提条件的视频，根据视频内容填空。

Watch the video introducing the prerequisites for DHCP relay configuration, and fill in the blanks according to the video.

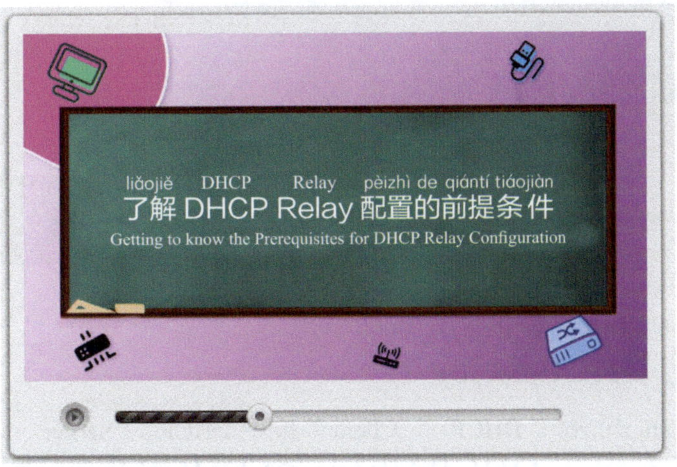

lùyóu A. 路由 routing	IP dìzhǐ B. IP 地址 IP address	wǎngduàn C. 网段 network segment	quánjú dìzhǐchí D. 全局地址池 global address pool

前提条件 qiántí tiáojiàn Prerequisites

wánchéng jīyú de DHCP Server pèizhì;
① 完成基于（ ）的 DHCP Server 配置；
The DHCP Server configuration based on ( ) is completed;

DHCP Server yǔ DHCP Relay jiēkǒu zhījiān kě dá;
② DHCP Server 与 DHCP Relay 接口之间（ ）可达；
The ( ) between DHCP Server and DHCP Relay interface is reachable;

DHCP Relay jiēkǒu yǔ DHCP Client zài tóng yī
③ DHCP Relay 接口与 DHCP Client 在同一（ ）；
DHCP Relay interface and DHCP Client are in the same ( );

DHCP Client de quēshěng wǎngguān dìzhǐ yīng wéi DHCP Relay jiēkǒu de
④ DHCP Client 的缺省网关地址应为 DHCP Relay 接口的（ ）。
The default gateway address of DHCP Client should be the ( ) of DHCP Relay interface.

二、课文 kèwén Texts

A 05-01

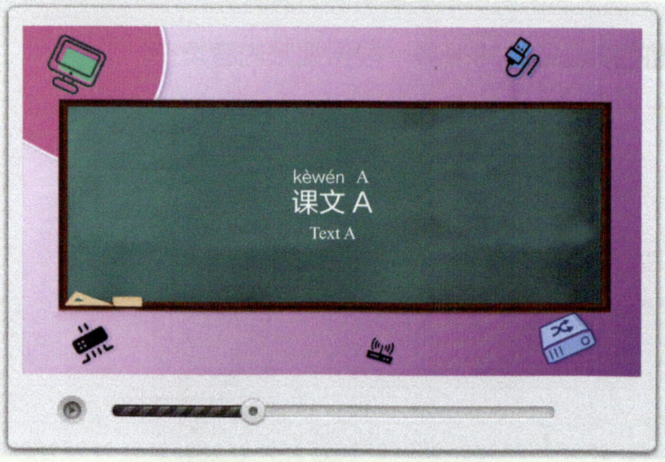

túdì: Shīfu, shénme shì DHCP Relay?
徒弟：师傅，什么是 DHCP Relay？

shīfu: DHCP Relay shì zhǐ zài DHCP Client hé DHCP Server zhījiān shíxiàn DHCP xiāoxi zhōngzhuǎn gōngnéng de shèbèi.
师傅：DHCP Relay 是指在 DHCP Client 和 DHCP Server 之间实现 DHCP 消息中转功能的设备。

túdì: Pèizhì shèbèi zuòwéi DHCP Relay de zuòyòng shì shénme?
徒弟：配置设备作为 DHCP Relay 的作用是什么？

shīfu: DHCP Client kěyǐ tōngguò DHCP Relay qítā wǎngduàn de DHCP Server tōngxìn, zuìzhōng huòqǔ IP dìzhǐ.
师傅：DHCP Client 可以通过 DHCP Relay 其他网段的 DHCP Server 通信，最终获取 IP 地址。

túdì: DHCP Relay yǒu shénme yōudiǎn?
徒弟：DHCP Relay 有什么优点？

shīfu: Zài qǐyè wǎngluò zhōng, bùshǔ DHCP Relay, kěyǐ shǐ bù tóng wǎngduàn de zhōngduān gòng yòng yí gè DHCP Server, jiéshěngle fúwùqì zīyuán, yě fāngbiàn tǒngyī guǎnlǐ.
师傅：在企业网络中，部署 DHCP Relay，可以使不同网段的终端共用一个 DHCP Server，节省了服务器资源，也方便统一管理。

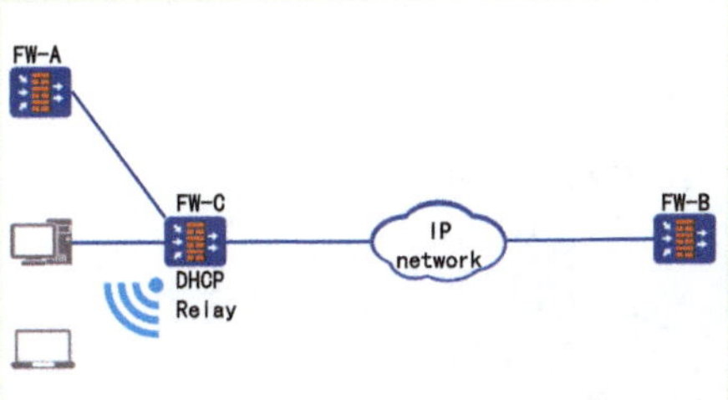

DHCP diǎnxíng zǔwǎng
DHCP 典型组网
Typical DHCP networking

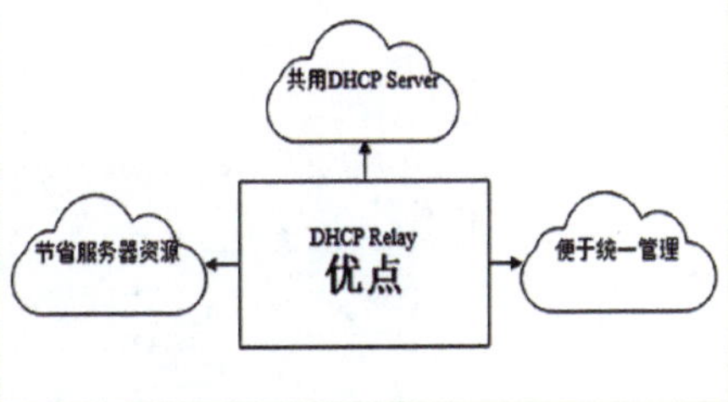

DHCP Relay yōudiǎn
DHCP Relay 优点
Advantages of DHCP Relay

译文 yìwén Text in English

Apprentice: Master, what is DHCP Relay?

Master: It refers to the device that realizes the DHCP message transfer function between DHCP Client and DHCP Server.

Apprentice: What is the role of configuring the device as a DHCP Relay?

Master: DHCP Client can communicate through DHCP Server of other network segments of DHCP Relay, and finally obtain the IP address.

Apprentice: What are the advantages of DHCP Relay?

Master: If a DHCP Relay is deployed in the enterprise network, it enables the terminals of different network segments to share a DHCP Server, thus saving server resources and facilitating unified management.

普通词语 pǔtōng cíyǔ General Vocabulary

05-02

1.	最终	zuìzhōng	n.	finally
2.	企业	qǐyè	n.	enterprise
3.	终端	zhōngduān	n.	terminal
4.	共	gòng	adv.	together
5.	资源	zīyuán	n.	resource
6.	方便	fāngbiàn	v.	provide convenience for

专业词语 zhuānyè cíyǔ Specialized Vocabulary

05-03

1.	DHCP			Dynamic Host Configuration Protocol
2.	消息中转	xiāoxi zhōngzhuǎn	phr.	message transfer
3.	服务器	fúwùqì	n.	server

B 05-04

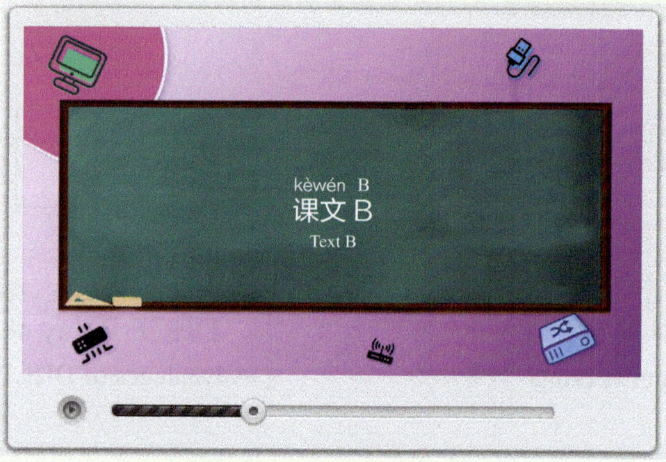

túdì: Shīfu, zài DHCP zǔwǎng zhōng, DHCP Relay de zuòyòng shì shénme?
徒弟：师傅，在 DHCP 组网 中，DHCP Relay 的作用是什么？

shīfu: DHCP Relay fùzé zhuǎnfā DHCP Server hé DHCP Client zhījiān de DHCP bàowén, xiézhù DHCP Server xiàng DHCP Client dòngtài fēnpèi wǎngluò cānshù.
师傅：DHCP Relay 负责转发 DHCP Server 和 DHCP Client 之间的 DHCP 报文，协助 DHCP Server 向 DHCP Client 动态分配网络参数。

túdì: Shénme qíngkuàng xià xūyào tōngguò DHCP Relay zhuǎnfā DHCP bàowén ne?
徒弟：什么情况下需要通过 DHCP Relay 转发 DHCP 报文呢？

shīfu: Rúguǒ DHCP Client yǔ DHCP Server bú zài tóng yí gè wǎngduàn, DHCP
师傅：如果 DHCP Client 与 DHCP Server 不在同一个网段，DHCP

Server wúfǎ jiēshōu láizì DHCP Client de qǐngqiú bàowén, cǐshí, xūyào
Server 无法接收来自 DHCP Client 的请求报文，此时，需要

tōngguò DHCP Relay lái zhuǎnfā DHCP bàowén.
通过 DHCP Relay 来转发 DHCP 报文。

túdì: Yǔ chuántǒng de IP bàowén zhuǎnfā yǒu shénme qūbié ne?
徒弟：与传统的 IP 报文转发有什么区别呢？

shīfu: Bù tóng yú chuántǒng de IP bàowén zhuǎnfā, DHCP Relay jiēshōu dào DHCP
师傅：不同于传统的 IP 报文转发，DHCP Relay 接收到 DHCP

qǐngqiú huò yìngdá bàowén hòu, huì chóngxīn xiūgǎi bàowén géshi bìng shēngchéng yí gè xīn
请求或应答报文后，会重新修改报文格式并生成一个新

de DHCP bàowén zài jìnxíng zhuǎnfā.
的 DHCP 报文再进行转发。

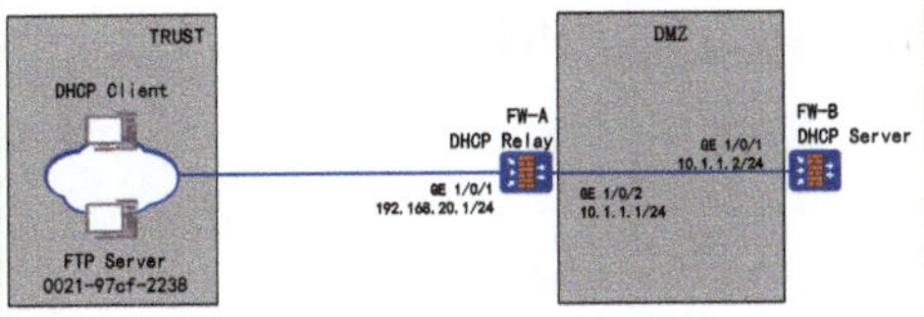

pèizhì DHCP Relay zǔwǎng
配置 DHCP Relay 组网
Configuring DHCP Relay networking

DHCP xìtǒng zǔchéng
DHCP 系统组成
Components of DHCP system

译文 yìwén Text in English

Apprentice: Master, what is the role of DHCP Relay in DHCP networking?

Master: DHCP Relay is responsible for forwarding DHCP messages between DHCP Server and DHCP Client, assisting DHCP Server to assign network parameters to DHCP Client dynamically.

Apprentice: Under what circumstances do we need to forward DHCP messages through DHCP Relay?

Master: If DHCP Client and DHCP Server are not in the same network segment, DHCP Server cannot receive the request message from DHCP Client. At this time, we need to forward the DHCP message through DHCP Relay.

Apprentice: How does it differ from the traditional IP message forwarding?

Master: Unlike the traditional IP message forwarding, after DHCP Relay receives the DHCP request or response message, it will modify the message format again and generate a new DHCP message for forwarding.

普通词语 pǔtōng cíyǔ General Vocabulary

05-05

1.	协助	xiézhù	v.	assist
2.	向	xiàng	prep.	to
3.	无法	wúfǎ	v.	cannot
4.	接收	jiēshōu	v.	receive
5.	此时	cǐshí	n.	this moment
6.	传统	chuántǒng	adj.	traditional
7.	应答	yìngdá	v.	respond
8.	修改	xiūgǎi	v.	modify
9.	生成	shēngchéng	v.	generate

专业词语 zhuānyè cíyǔ Specialized Vocabulary

05-06

DHCP 组网	DHCP zǔwǎng	phr.	DHCP networking

三、视听说 shì-tīng-shuō Viewing, Listening, and Speaking

1. 观看介绍 DHCP Relay 接口配置操作步骤的视频，选择合适的词语填空。

Watch the video introducing the operation steps of DHCP Relay interface configuration, and choose the right words to fill in the blanks.

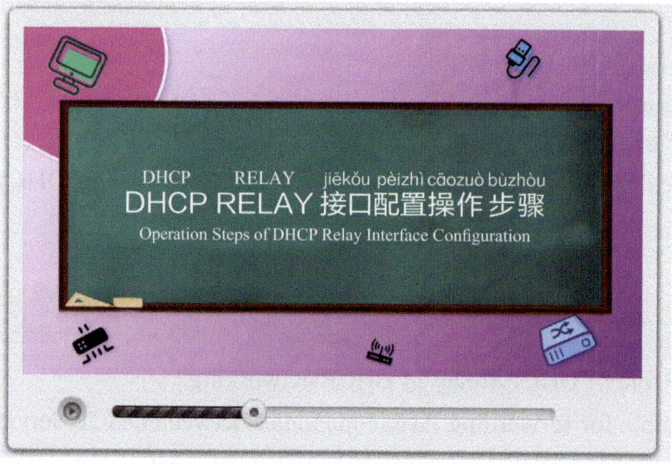

A. 接口视图 (jiēkǒu shìtú) interface view

B. IP 地址 (IP dìzhǐ) IP address

C. 当前 接口 (dāngqián jiēkǒu) current interface

D. 系统视图 (xìtǒng shìtú) system view

E. DHCP 中继 (DHCP zhōngjì) DHCP Relay

F. DHCP 服务 (DHCP fúwù) DHCP service

zhíxíng mìnglìng system view, jìnrù
① 执行命令 system view，进入 ________________

Execute the command *system view* to enter ________________

zhíxíng mìnglìng dhcp enable, kāiqǐ
② 执行命令 dhcp enable，开启 ________________

Execute the command *dhcp enable* to start ________________

zhíxíng mìnglìng interface, jìnrù
③ 执行命令 interface，进入 ________________

Execute the command *interface* to enter ________________

zhíxíng mìnglìng ip relay address, zhǐdìng
④ 执行命令 ip relay address，指定 ________________

Execute the command *ip relay address* to specify ________________

zhíxíng mìnglìng dhcp select relay,
⑤ 执行命令 dhcp select relay，
jiāng jiēkǒu shang pèizhì xìnxī yìngyòng dào
将接口上配置信息应用到 ________________

Execute the command *dhcp select relay* to apply the configuration information on the interface to ________________

zhíxíng mìnglìng dhcp relay source-ip
⑥ 执行命令 dhcp relay source-ip
agent-ip, shèzhì pèizhìle
agent-ip，设置配置了 ________________
de jiēkǒu IP dìzhǐ
的接口 IP 地址

Execute the command *dhcp relay source-ip agent-ip* to set the interface IP address configured with ________________

2. 说一说 Let's talk

说一说 DHCP Relay 接口配置操作步骤。

Talk about the operation steps of DHCP Relay interface configuration.

四、学以致用 xuéyǐzhìyòng Practicing What You Have Learnt

观看介绍实际操作过程中 DHCP Relay 组网配置思路的视频，将配置和相应的功能连线。

Watch the video introducing the idea of DHCP Relay networking configuration during the actual operation, and match the configuration with the corresponding functions.

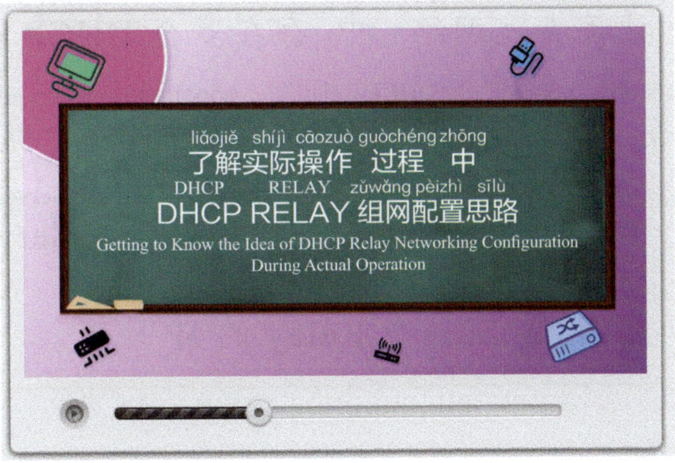

pèizhì quánjú dìzhǐchí
① 配置全局地址池
Configuring a global address pool

shíxiàn DHCP Client, néng zìdòng huòqǔ DHCP Server fēnpèi IP dìzhǐ jí qítā wǎngluò cānshù
A. 实现 DHCP Client，能自动获取 DHCP Server 分配 IP 地址及其他网络参数
To enable DHCP Client to obtain the IP address and other network parameters assigned by DHCP Server automatically

pèizhì DHCP Relay gōngnéng
② 配置 DHCP Relay 功能
Configuring DHCP Relay function

shíxiàn bù tóng wǎngduàn de DHCP Client hé DHCP Server néng xiānghù tōngxìn
B. 实现不同网段的DHCP Client和DHCP Server 能相互通信
To enable DHCP Client and DHCP Server of different network segments to communicate with each other

pèizhì DHCP Client de TCP/IP shǔxìng
③ 配置 DHCP Client 的 TCP/IP 属性
Configuring TCP / IP properties of DHCP Client

shíxiàn DHCP Server duì kuà wǎngduàn de DHCP Client fēnpèi IP dìzhǐ jí qítā wǎngluò cānshù
C. 实现 DHCP Server 对跨网段的 DHCP Client 分配 IP 地址及其他网络参数
To enable DHCP Server to assign IP addresses and other network parameters to DHCP Client across network segments

五、小知识 xiǎo zhīshi Tips

DHCP Relay

DHCP Server hé Client zhījiān de DHCP Relay bù néng chāoguò 4 cì,
DHCP Server 和 Client 之间的 DHCP Relay 不能超过 4 次，

fǒuzé DHCP bàowén jiāng bèi diūqì. Wǎngluò zhōng cúnzài duō gè DHCP Relay shí,
否则 DHCP 报文将被丢弃。网络中存在多个 DHCP Relay 时，

xūyào zài měi tái zhōngjì shèbèi shang pèizhì DHCP Relay gōngnéng, bìng quèbǎo bǐcǐ jiān
需要在每台中继设备上配置 DHCP Relay 功能，并确保彼此间

lùyóu kě dá, zài zuìhòu yì tái DHCP Relay shang zhǐdìng DHCP Server IP dìzhǐ,
路由可达，在最后一台 DHCP Relay 上指定 DHCP Server IP 地址，

zài qítā DHCP Relay shang zhǐdìng xià yí gè Relay de IP dìzhǐ.
在其他 DHCP Relay 上指定下一个 Relay 的 IP 地址。

DHCP Relay

DHCP Relay between DHCP Server and Client cannot exceed 4 times, otherwise DHCP messages will be discarded. When there are multiple DHCP Relays in the network, it is necessary to configure the DHCP relay function on each relay device and ensure that the routing between each other is reachable, with the DHCP Server IP address specified on the last DHCP Relay and the IP address of the next Relay specified on other DHCP Relays.

补充专业词语 bǔchōng zhuānyè cíyǔ Supplementary Specialized Vocabulary

05-07

1.	DHCP 典型组网	DHCP diǎnxíng zǔwǎng	phr.	typical DHCP networking
2.	DHCP 中继代理	DHCP zhōngjì dàilǐ	phr.	DHCP relay agent
3.	DHCP Relay 组网	DHCP Relay zǔwǎng	phr.	DHCP Relay networking

第二部分 Part 2

汉字 Chinese Characters

一、汉字知识 Hànzì zhīshi Knowledge about Chinese Characters

汉字的偏旁（5） **Radicals of Chinese characters (5)**

偏旁 Radicals	例字 Examples	部件组合 Combinations	结构图示 Illustrations
巾	帽	巾 + 冒	⿰
	帮	邦 + 巾	⿱
	带	龷 + 冖 + 巾	⿳
广	店	广 + 占	⿸
	床	广 + 木	⿸
	麻	广 + 林	⿸
	应	广 + 业	⿸
小	少	小 + 丿	⿱
	尘	小 + 土	⿱
	尖	小 + 大	⿱

（续表）

偏旁 Radicals	例字 Examples	部件组合 Combinations	结构图示 Illustrations
⺌	光	⺌＋兀	
	当	⺌＋彐	
	尝	⺌＋冖＋云	
八	分	八＋刀	
	公	八＋厶	
	共	龷＋八	
	兴	龸＋八	
	典	曲＋八	
刂	到	至＋刂	
	刻	亥＋刂	
	别	另＋刂	
	制	𠚤＋刂	

二、汉字认读与书写　Hànzì rèndú yǔ shūxiě　The Recognition and Writing of Chinese Characters

认读下列词语，并试着读写构成词语的汉字。

Recognize the following words, and try to read and write the Chinese characters forming these words.

宽带　　应用　　注销　　公共　　系列

宽				带				应				用			
注				销				公				共			
系				列											

第三部分　Part 3

日常用语　*Daily Expressions*

1. 别太拘束！　Bié tài jūshù!　Don't stand on ceremony!
2. 帮我一个忙！　Bāng wǒ yí gè máng!　Give me a hand!
3. 午餐我请你。Wǔcān wǒ qǐng nǐ.　I'll treat you to lunch.

第四部分　Part 4

单元实训　*Unit Practical Training*

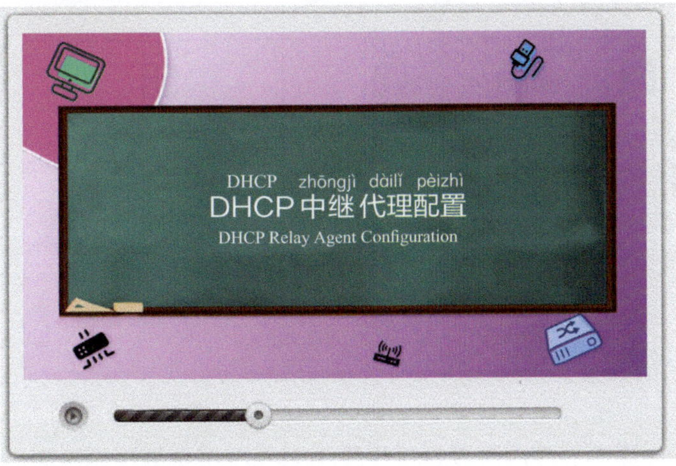

DHCP 中继代理配置　DHCP zhōngjì dàilǐ pèizhì　DHCP Relay Agent Configuration

实训目的 Training purpose

学会 DHCP 中继代理配置。

To master DHCP relay agent configuration.

实训组织 Training organization

每组 3 ～ 5 人，选出一个组长。

Each group consists of 3-5 people, and a group leader is selected.

实训内容 Training content

DHCP 中继代理配置。

DHCP relay agent configuration

实训步骤 Training steps

1. 如下图所示，在 eNSP 软件中绘制网络拓扑图。
   As shown in the figure below, draw the network topology diagram in the eNSP software.
2. 进入系统视图，然后执行命令 dhcp enable，使能 DHCP 功能。
   Enter the system view, and then execute the command *dhcp enable* to enable the DHCP function.
3. 在 R1 的各个接口使能 DHCP 中继功能。
   Enable the DHCP relay function on each interface of R1.
4. 验证 DHCP 中继配置。
   Verify the DHCP relay configuration.
5. 实训结束，教师评价。
   The training ends. The teacher makes a summary and an evaluation.

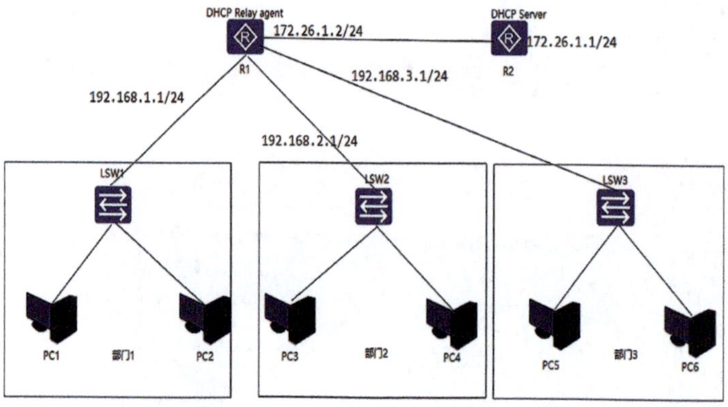

第五部分　Part 5

单元小结 Unit Summary

cíyǔ
词语
Vocabulary

普通词语　General Vocabulary

1.	最终	zuìzhōng	n.	finally
2.	企业	qǐyè	n.	enterprise
3.	终端	zhōngduān	n.	terminal
4.	共	gòng	adv.	together
5.	资源	zīyuán	n.	resource
6.	方便	fāngbiàn	v.	provide convenience for
7.	协助	xiézhù	v.	assist
8.	向	xiàng	prep.	to
9.	无法	wúfǎ	v.	cannot
10.	接收	jiēshōu	v.	receive
11.	此时	cǐshí	n.	this moment
12.	传统	chuántǒng	adj.	traditional
13.	应答	yìngdá	v.	respond
14.	修改	xiūgǎi	v.	modify
15.	生成	shēngchéng	v.	generate

专业词语　Specialized Vocabulary

1.	DHCP			Dynamic Host Configuration Protocol
2.	消息中转	xiāoxi zhōngzhuǎn	phr.	message transfer
3.	服务器	fúwùqì	n.	server
4.	DHCP 组网	DHCP zǔwǎng	phr.	DHCP networking

cíyǔ
词语
Vocabulary

补充专业词语 Supplementary Specialized Vocabulary

1.	DHCP 典型组网	DHCP diǎnxíng zǔwǎng	phr.	typical DHCP networking
2.	DHCP 中继代理	DHCP zhōngjì dàilǐ	phr.	DHCP relay agent
3.	DHCP Relay 组网	DHCP Relay zǔwǎng	phr.	DHCP Relay networking

jùzi
句子
Sentences

1. DHCP Relay 是指在 DHCP Client 和 DHCP Server 之间实现 DHCP 消息中转功能的设备。
2. 在企业网络中，部署 DHCP Relay，可以使不同网段的终端共用一个 DHCP Server，节省了服务器资源，也方便统一管理。
3. DHCP Relay 负责转发 DHCP Server 和 DHCP Client 之间的 DHCP 报文，协助 DHCP Server 向 DHCP Client 动态分配网络参数。
4. 如果 DHCP Client 与 DHCP Server 不在同一个网段，DHCP Server 无法接收来自 DHCP Client 的请求报文，此时，需要通过 DHCP Relay 来转发 DHCP 报文。
5. 不同于传统的 IP 报文转发，DHCP Relay 接收到 DHCP 请求或应答报文后，会重新修改报文格式并生成一个新的 DHCP 报文再进行转发。

6

liànlù jùhé
链路聚合
Link Aggregation

liànlù jùhé pèizhì de cāozuò mìnglìng jí jùtǐ cāozuò
链路聚合配置的操作命令及具体操作
Operation Commands and Specific Operations for Link Aggregation Configuration

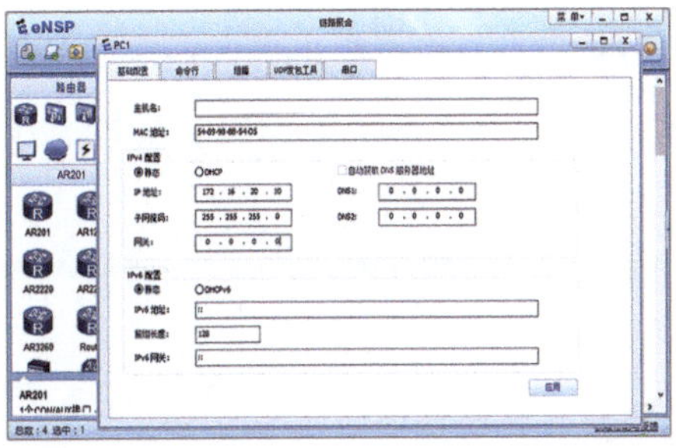

shèzhì liǎng tái jìsuànjī de IP dìzhǐ、zǐwǎng yǎnmǎ
设置两台计算机的IP地址、子网掩码

Set the IP Addresses and Subnet Masks of Two Computers

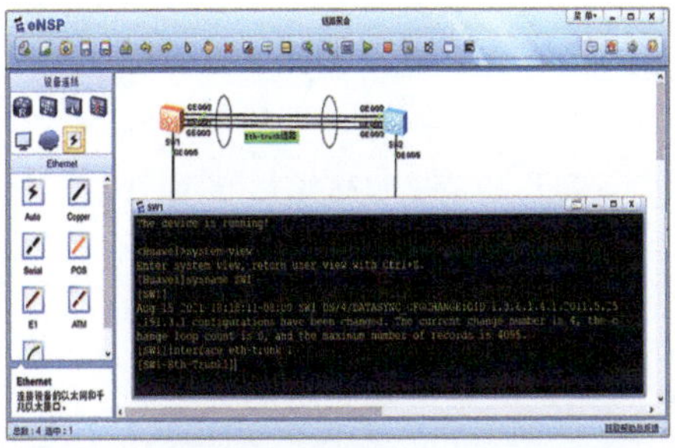

zài jiāohuànjī S1、S2 chuàngjiàn biānhào wéi 1 de Eth-trunk duānkǒu
在交换机S1、S2创建编号为1的Eth-trunk端口

Create Eth-trunk Ports Numbered 1 on Switches S1 and S2

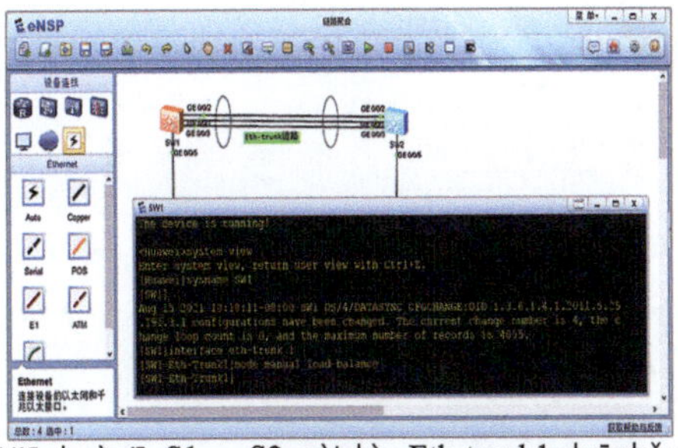

zài jiāohuànjī S1、S2 pèizhì Eth-trunk1 duānkǒu de gōngzuò móshì wéi shǒugōng fùzài fēndān móshì
在交换机S1、S2配置Eth-trunk1端口的工作模式为手工负载分担模式

Configure the Working Mode of Eth-trunk Port 1 as Manual Load-Balance Mode on Switches S1 and S2

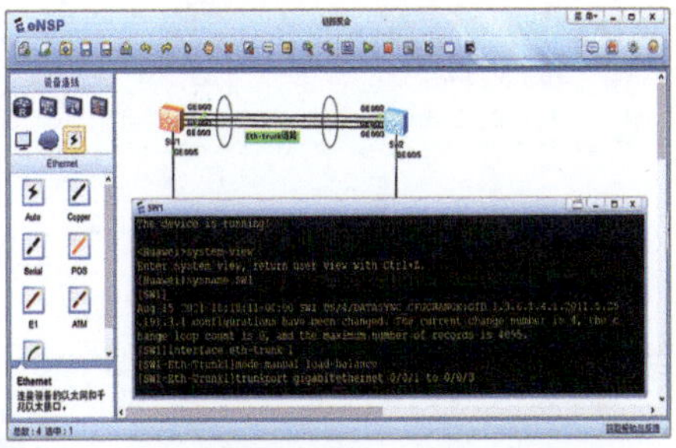

jiāng wùlǐ duānkǒu jiārù eth-trunk duānkǒu
将物理端口加入eth-trunk端口

Join the Physical Port to the Eth-trunk Port

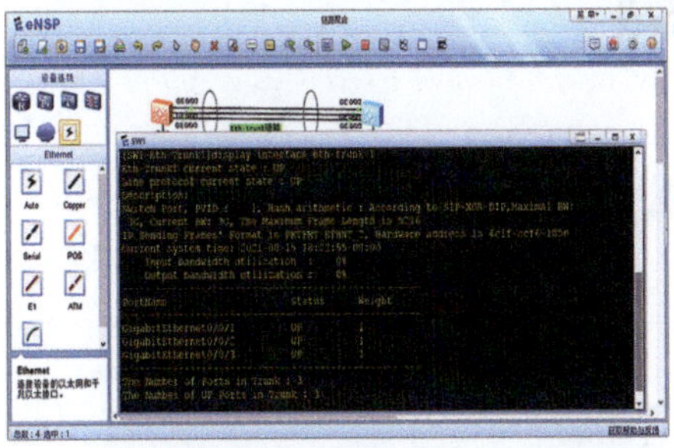

yòng mìnglìng chákàn jiāohuànjī S1、S2 de jiéguǒ
用命令查看交换机S1、S2的结果

Use the Command to View the Results on Switches S1 and S2

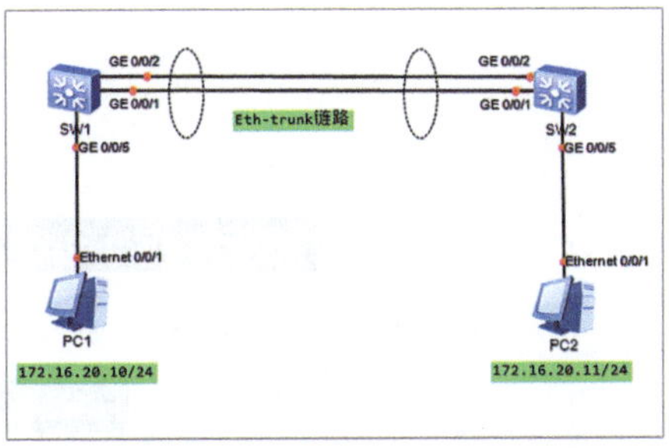

cèshì liǎng tái diànnǎo de liántōngxìng
测试两台电脑的连通性

Test the Connectivity of Two Computers

题解 Introduction

1. 学习内容：链路聚合的功能、配置方法和配置要求。
   Learning content: The functions, configuration methods and requirements of link aggregation
2. 知识目标：掌握与链路聚合配置相关的关键词语，了解汉字的偏旁“⺮”“⺌”“礻”“⻗”“土”，学写相关汉字。
   Knowledge objectives: To master the keywords for link aggregation configuration, understand the Chinese radicals “⺮”, “⺌”, “礻”, “⻗”, “土”, and learn to write the related Chinese characters
3. 技能目标：学会简单的链路聚合配置，实现链路的速率叠加。
   Skill objective: To master simple link aggregation configuration to realize link rate superposition

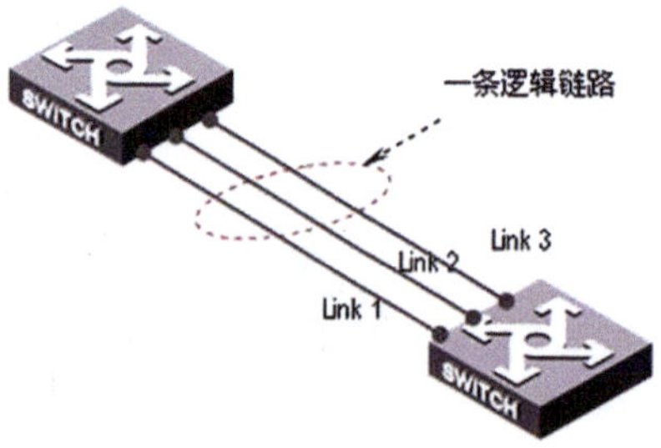

第一部分 Part 1

课文 Texts

一、热身 rèshēn Warm-up

1. 给词语选择对应的图片。 **Choose the corresponding pictures for the words.**

```
[SW1]interface eth-trunk 1
```

A.

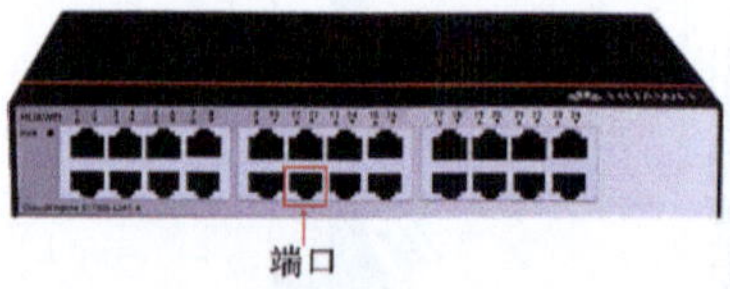

B.

```
[SW1-Eth-Trunk1]trunkport GigabitEthernet 0/0/1 to 0/0/3
```

C.

```
[SW1]display interface eth-trunk 1
```

D.

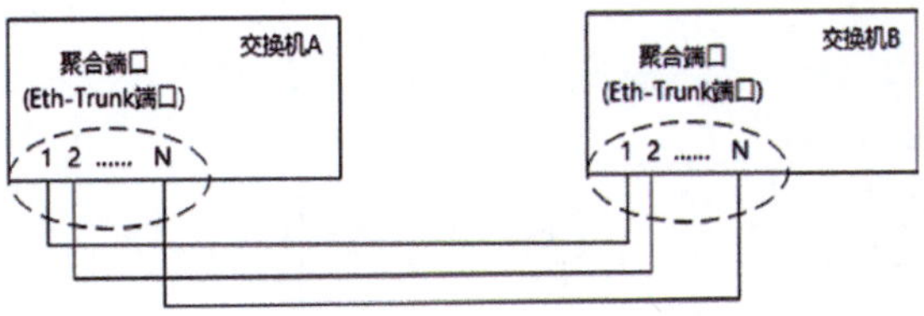

E.

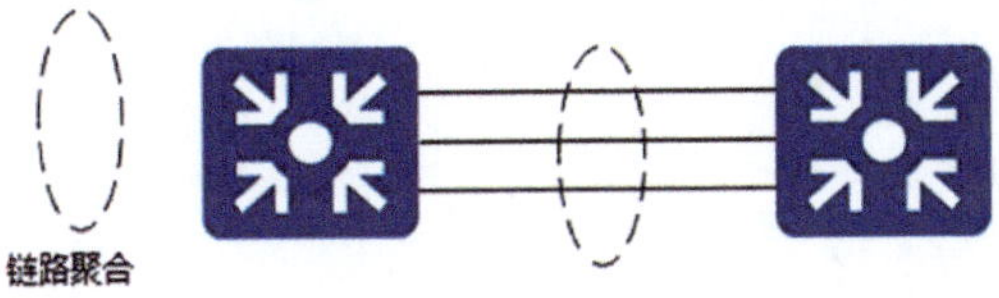

F.

① yǒu eth-trunk duānkǒu biānhào de shì
有 eth-trunk 端口 编号 的是____
with eth-trunk port number

② jiāng wùlǐ duānkǒu jiārù eth-trunk duānkǒu de shì
将物理端口加入 eth-trunk 端口 的是____
joining a physical port to eth-trunk port

③ kě chákàn eth-trunk duānkǒu xìnxī de shì
可查看 eth-trunk 端口信息的是____
being able to view eth-trunk port information

④ hányǒu duānkǒu de shì
含有 端口 的是____
with ports

⑤ yǒu jùhé duānkǒu de shì
有聚合 端口 的是____
with aggregation ports

⑥ yǒu jùhé liànlù de shì
有聚合链路的是____
with aggregation link

2. 观看介绍链路聚合配置的前期工作的视频，对操作步骤进行排序。

Watch the video introducing the preliminary work of link aggregation configuration, and put the operation steps in order.

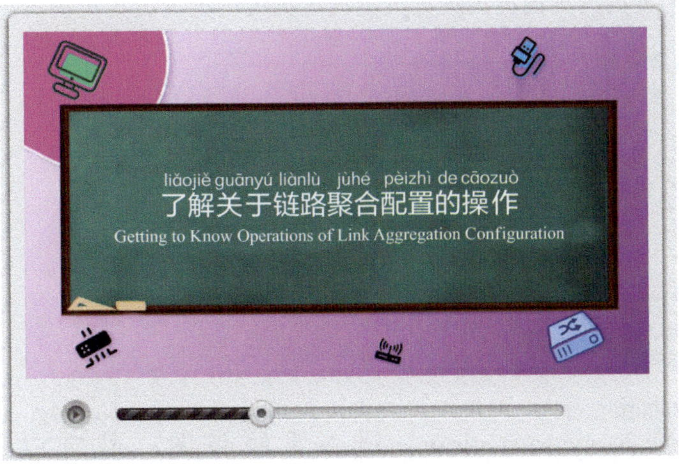

Liǎng tái jiāohuànjī de GE 0/0/1、GE 0/0/2、GE 0/0/3 jiēkǒu hùlián, PC1 yǔ SW1 liánjiē,
A. 两台交换机的 GE 0/0/1、GE 0/0/2、GE 0/0/3 接口互连，PC1 与 SW1 连接，
PC2 yǔ SW2 liánjiē.
PC2 与 SW2 连接。
Interconnect the GE0/0/1, GE0/0/2 and GE0/0/3 interfaces of two switches, and connect PC1 to SW1, and PC2 to SW2.

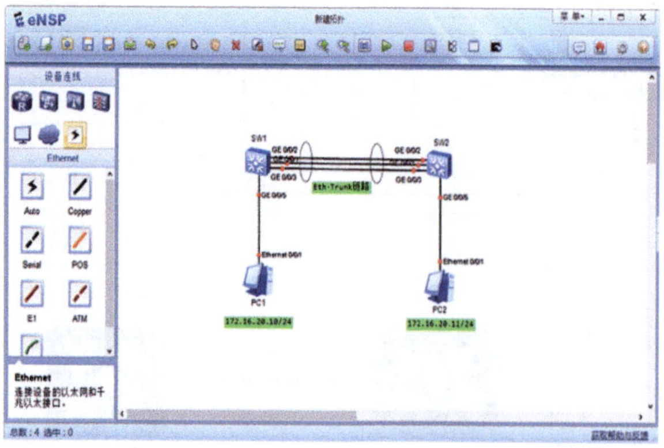

Suǒyǒu shèbèi qǐdòng hòu, shuāngjī jiāohuànjī SW1 túbiāo, jìnrù jiāohuànjī de mìnglìngháng jièmiàn.

B. 所有设备启动后，双击交换机SW1图标，进入交换机的命令行界面。

After starting all the devices, double-click the SW1 icon to enter the command line interface of the switch.

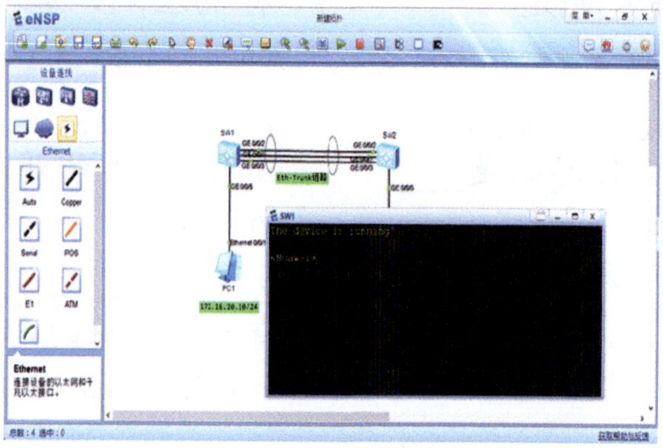

Xuǎnzhòng suǒyǒu shèbèi, qǐdòng suǒyǒu shèbèi.

C. 选中所有设备，启动所有设备。

Select all the devices and start them.

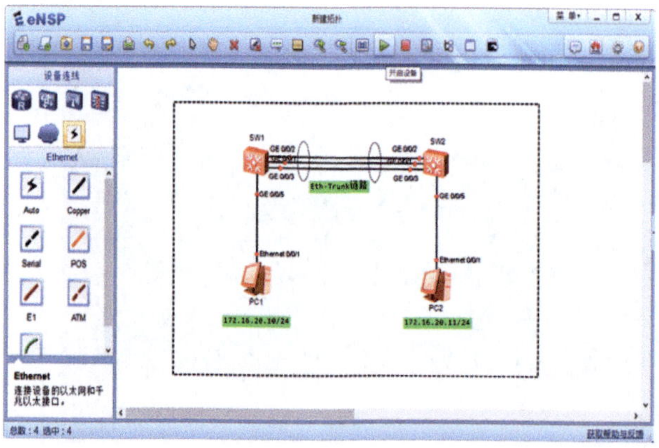

Zài mìnglìngháng jièmiàn, shūrù system-view, jìnrù xìtǒng shìtú, jiù kěyǐ kāishǐ liànlù jùhé de pèizhì le.

D. 在命令行界面，输入system-view，进入系统视图，就可以开始链路聚合的配置了。

In the command line interface, enter *system-view* to enter the system view and start the link aggregation configuration.

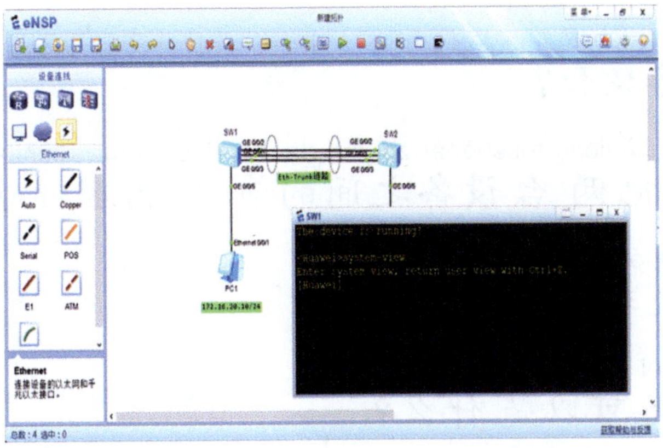

Zài eNSP fàngzhì 2 tái jiāohuànjī、 2 tái PC.
E. 在 eNSP 放置 2 台 交换机、2 台 PC。
Place two switches and two PCs in eNSP.

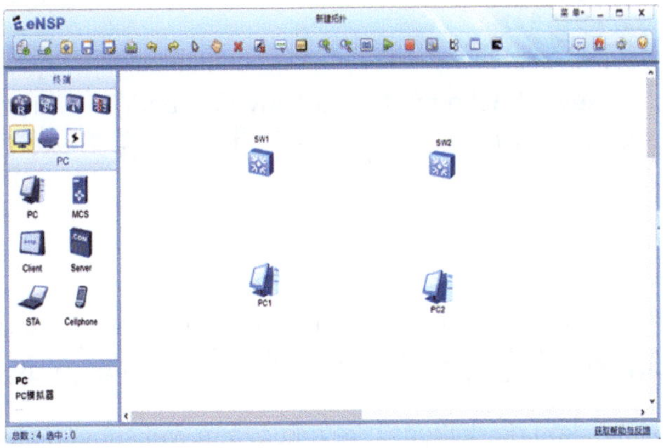

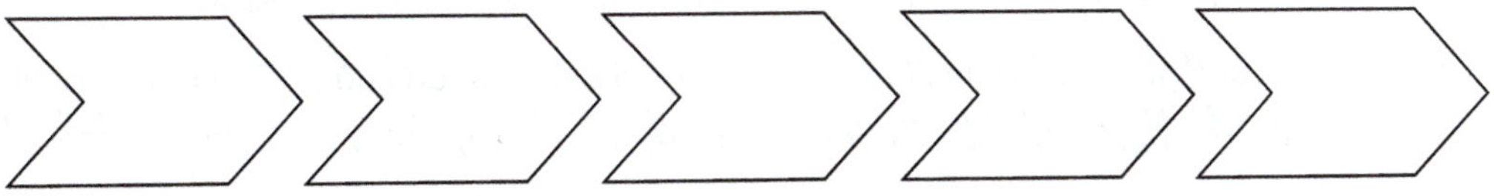

二、课文 kèwén Texts

A 06-01

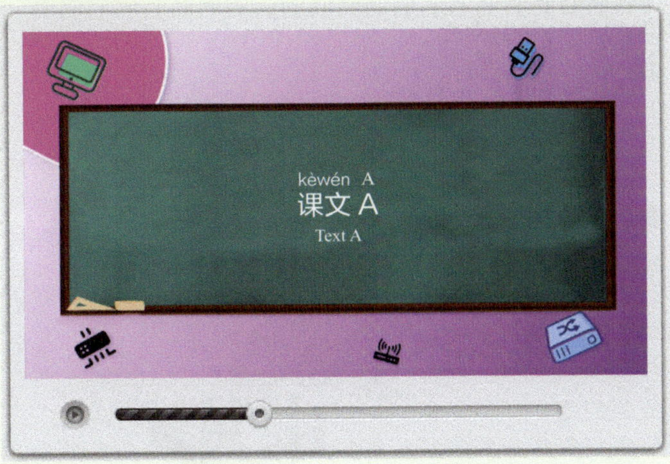

túdì: Shénme shì liànlù jùhé?
徒弟：什么 是链路聚合？

shīfu: Liànlù jùhé shì bǎ liǎng tái shèbèi zhījiān de duō tiáo wùlǐ liànlù jùhé zài yìqǐ, dàngzuò yì tiáo luójí liànlù lái shǐyòng.
师傅：链路聚合是把两 台设备之间的多 条 物理链路聚合在一起，当作 一条逻辑链路来使用。

túdì: Zhè liǎng tái shèbèi kěyǐ shì shénme?
徒弟：这 两 台设备可以是 什么？

shīfu: Zhè liǎng tái shèbèi kěyǐ shì yí duì lùyóuqì、yí duì jiāohuànjī, huòzhě shì yì tái lùyóuqì hé yì tái jiāohuànjī.
师傅：这 两 台设备可以是一对 路由器、一对交换机，或者是一台路由器和一台 交换机。

túdì: Yì tiáo jùhé liànlù kěyǐ bāohán jǐ tiáo chéngyuán liànlù? Liànlù jùhé yǒu shénme gōngnéng?
徒弟：一条聚合链路可以包含几条 成员 链路？链路聚合有 什么功能？

shīfu: Yì tiáo jùhé liànlù kěyǐ bāohán duō tiáo chéngyuán liànlù, tōngguò jùhé jǐ tiáo liànlù, yí gè jùhé kǒu de dàikuān kěyǐ kuòzhǎn wéi suǒyǒu chéngyuán kǒu dàikuān de zǒnghé, zhèyàng jiù yǒuxiào de zēngjiāle luójí liànlù de dàikuān. Dāng yì tiáo liànlù chūxiàn gùzhàng shí, liúliàng huì zìdòng zài shèngxia de liànlù jiān chóngxīn fēnpèi, bìngqiě zhè zhǒng gùzhàng qiēhuàn suǒ yòng de shíjiān shì háomiǎo jí de, duì dàbùfen yìngyòng dōu bú huì zàochéng yǐngxiǎng.
师傅：一条聚合链路可以包含 多 条 成员 链路，通过 聚合几条链路，一个聚合口的带宽可以扩展为所有 成员 口 带宽 的总和，这样就有效地增加了逻辑链路的带宽。当一条 链路出现 故障 时，流量会自动在 剩下的链路间 重新 分配，并且这 种 故障 切换 所 用 的时间是毫秒级的，对大部分应用 都不会 造成 影响。

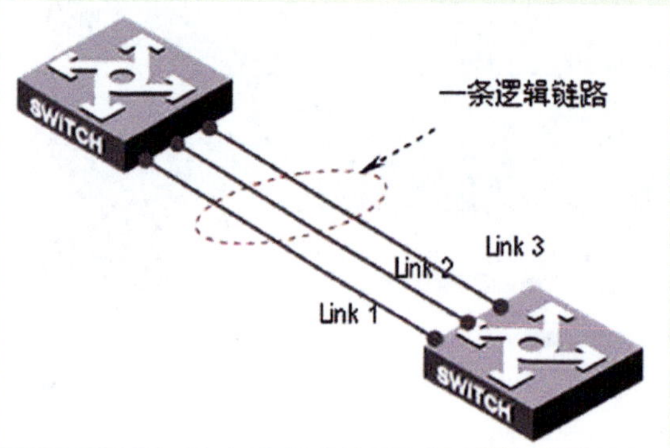

译文 yìwén Text in English

Apprentice: What is link aggregation?

Master: It is to aggregate multiple physical links between two devices and use them as a logical link.

Apprentice: What can these two devices be?

Master: They can be a pair of routers, a pair of switches, or a router and a switch.

Apprentice: How many member links can an aggregated link contain? What are the functions of link aggregation?

Master: An aggregated link can contain multiple member links. By aggregating several links, the bandwidth of an aggregation port can be expanded to the sum of the bandwidths of all the member ports, which effectively increases the bandwidth of the logical link. When a link fails, the traffic will be automatically redistributed among the remaining links, and the failover time is in milliseconds, which will not affect most applications.

普通词语 pǔtōng cíyǔ General Vocabulary

06-02

1.	当作	dàngzuò	v.	treat/regard...as...
2.	对	duì	m.	pair
3.	包含	bāohán	v.	contain
4.	成员	chéngyuán	n.	member
5.	总和	zǒnghé	n.	sum
6.	有效	yǒuxiào	v.	be effective
7.	增加	zēngjiā	v.	increase
8.	当	dāng	prep.	when
9.	出现	chūxiàn	v.	appear
10.	剩下	shèngxia	phr.	remaining
11.	大部分	dàbùfen	n.	most, the majority
12.	造成	zàochéng	v.	cause
13.	影响	yǐngxiǎng	n.	influence, effect

专业词语 zhuānyè cíyǔ Specialized Vocabulary

06-03

1.	链路聚合	liànlù jùhé	phr.	link aggregation
2.	带宽	dàikuān	n.	bandwidth
3.	故障	gùzhàng	n.	breakdown, fault
4.	毫秒	háomiǎo	m.	millisecond

B 06-04

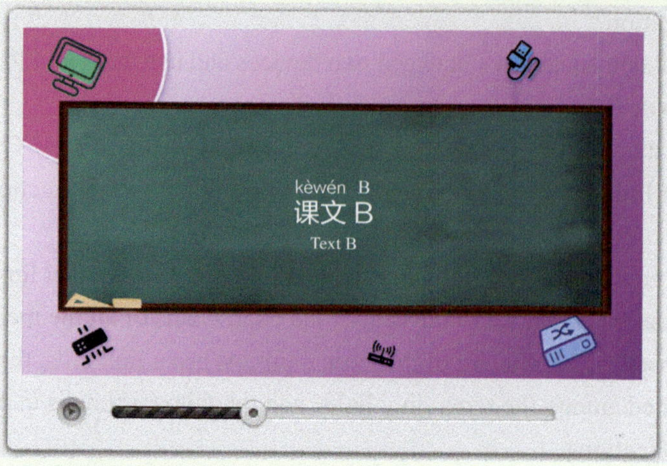

túdì: Jiāohuànjī SW1 liánjiēle 10 tái diànnǎo, měi tái diànnǎo de dàikuān shì 100M, 2 tái jiāohuànjī yòng 1G de liànlù, zhè zhǒng qíngkuàng xià wǎngluò liúliàng huì yōngsè ma?

徒弟：交换机 SW1 连接了 10 台电脑，每台电脑的带宽是 100M，2 台交换机用 1G 的链路，这种情况下网络流量会拥塞吗？

shīfu: Bú huì. Yīnwèi měi tái diànnǎo 100M, 10 tái diànnǎo de dàikuān zǒng xūqiú shì 1G.

师傅：不会。因为每台电脑 100M，10 台电脑的带宽总需求是 1G。

túdì: Rúguǒ SW1 liánjiē 20 tái diànnǎo, huì chūxiàn shénme qíngkuàng ne?

徒弟：如果 SW1 连接 20 台电脑，会出现什么情况呢？

shīfu: SW1 liánjiē 20 tái diànnǎo, dàikuān de zǒng xūqiú shì 2G, dàn SW1 hé SW2 zhījiān de liànlù zuì duō zhǐ néng tígōng 1G de dàikuān, suǒyǐ huì chūxiàn liúliàng yōngsè de xiànxiàng.

师傅：SW1 连接 20 台电脑，带宽的总需求是 2G，但 SW1 和 SW2 之间的链路最多只能提供 1G 的带宽，所以会出现流量拥塞的现象。

túdì: Nà rúhé jiějué ne?

徒弟：那如何解决呢？

shīfu: Kěyǐ zài SW1 hé SW2 zhījiān yòng 3 tiáo GE liànlù, shǐyòng liànlù jùhé jìshù, jiāng zhè 3 tiáo GE liànlù zhěnghé chéng yì tiáo zuì dà dàikuān kě dá 3G de luójí liànlù.

师傅：可以在 SW1 和 SW2 之间用 3 条 GE 链路，使用链路聚合技术，将这 3 条 GE 链路整合成一条最大带宽可达 3G 的逻辑链路。

译文 yìwén Text in English

Apprentice: 10 computers are connected to SW1 switch and the bandwidth of each computer is 100M. Two switches use a 1G link. Will the network traffic be congested in this situation?

Master: No. Because each computer is 100M, and the total bandwidth demand of 10 computers is 1G.

Apprentice: What will happen if SW1 is connected to 20 computers?

Master: If SW1 is connected to 20 computers, the total bandwidth demand is 2G, but the link between SW1 and SW2 can only provide 1G bandwidth at most, so traffic congestion will occur.

Apprentice: How can we solve it?

Master: Use three GE links between SW1 and SW2, and use link aggregation technology to integrate these three GE links into a logical link with a maximum bandwidth of 3G.

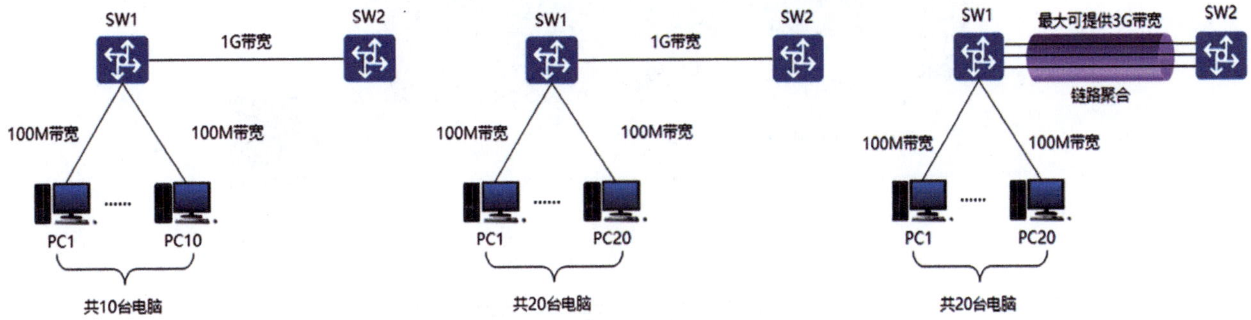

普通词语 pǔtōng cíyǔ General Vocabulary

06-05

1.	总	zǒng	adj.	total
2.	需求	xūqiú	n.	demand
3.	但	dàn	conj.	but
4.	所以	suǒyǐ	conj.	so
5.	现象	xiànxiàng	n.	phenomenon
6.	整合	zhěnghé	v.	integrate
7.	成	chéng	v.	become, turn into
8.	可	kě	aux.	can
9.	达	dá	v.	reach, achieve

专业词语 zhuānyè cíyǔ Specialized Vocabulary

06-06

1.	拥塞	yōngsè	v.	congest
2.	逻辑链路	luójí liànlù	phr.	logical link

三、视听说 shì-tīng-shuō Viewing, Listening, and Speaking

1. 观看介绍链路聚合配置的视频，将命令的中文含义与对应的命令配对。

Watch the video introducing link aggregation configuration and match the Chinese meanings of the commands with the corresponding commands.

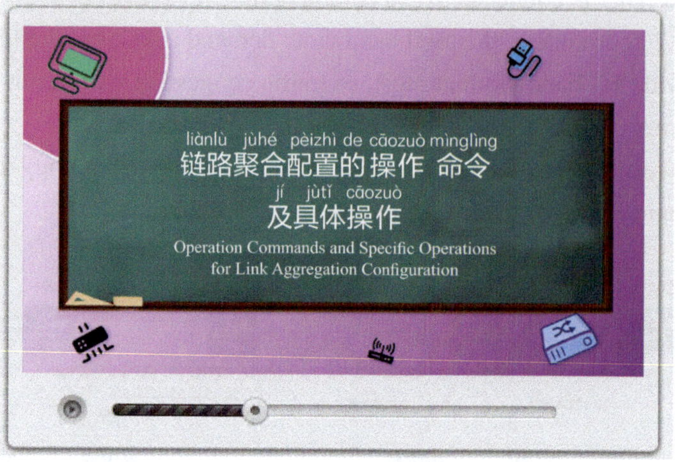

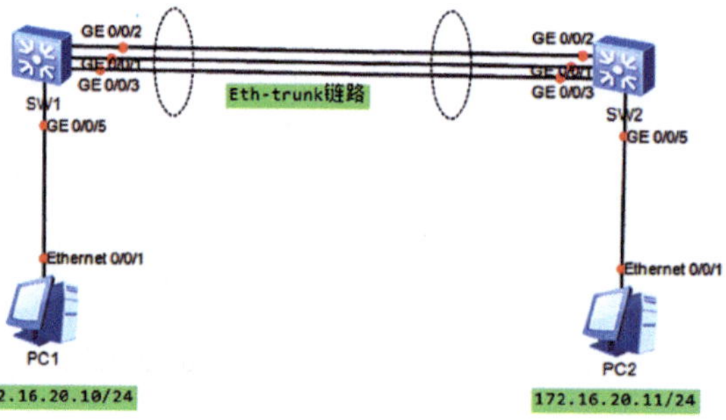

Shèzhì PC1 de IP dìzhǐ wéi 172.16.20.10, zǐwǎng yǎnmǎ wéi 255.255.255.0. Shèzhì PC2 de IP dìzhǐ wéi 172.16.20.11, zǐwǎng yǎnmǎ wéi 255.255.255.0.

（1）设置 PC1 的 IP 地址为 172.16.20.10，子网掩码为 255.255.255.0。设置 PC2 的 IP 地址为 172.16.20.11，子网掩码为 255.255.255.0。

Set the IP address of PC1 to 172.16.20.10 and the subnet mask to 255.255.255.0. Set the IP address of PC2 to 172.16.20.11 and the subnet mask to 255.255.255.0.

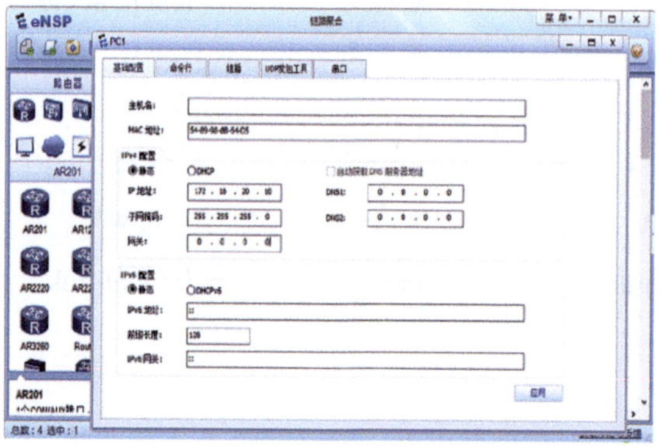

Shuāngjī jiāohuànjī SW1 túbiāo, shūrù mìnglìng interface eth-trunk 1, zài jiāohuànjī shang chuàngjiàn
(2) 双击交换机 SW1 图标，输入命令 interface eth-trunk 1，在交换机上创建
biānhào wéi 1 de eth-trunk duānkǒu.
编号为 1 的 eth-trunk 端口。

Double-click the SW1 icon, enter the command *interface eth-trunk 1* to create an eth-trunk port numbered 1 on the switch.

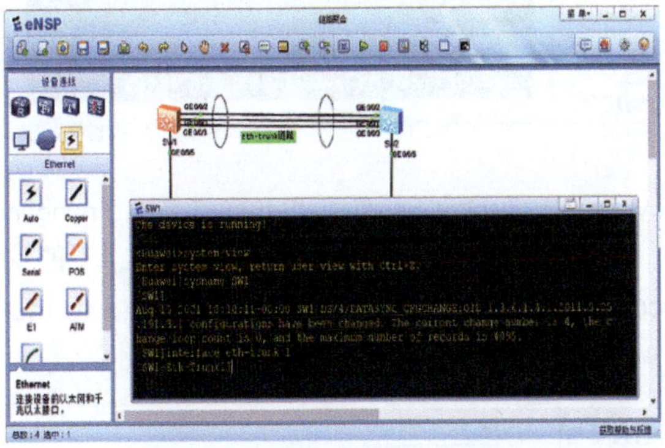

Zài jiāohuànjī SW1 zhōng, shūrù mode manual load-balance mìnglìng, pèizhì eth-trunk 1 duānkǒu de
(3) 在交换机 SW1 中，输入 mode manual load-balance 命令，配置 eth-trunk 1 端口的
gōngzuò móshì.
工作模式。

On switch SW1, enter the command *mode manual load-balance* to configure the working mode of eth-trunk port 1.

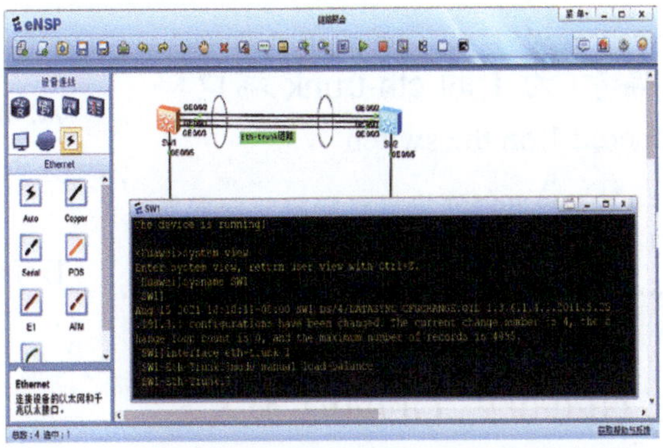

Zài jiāohuànjī SW1 zhōng, shūrù trunkport gigabitethernet 0/0/1 to 0/0/3 mìnglìng, jiāng wùlǐ
(4) 在交换机 SW1 中，输入 trunkport gigabitethernet 0/0/1 to 0/0/3 命令，将物理
duānkǒu GE0/0/1、GE0/0/2、GE0/0/3 jiārù eth-trunk duānkǒu. Yòng xiāngtóng de bùzhòu hé mìnglìng,
端口 GE0/0/1、GE0/0/2、GE0/0/3 加入eth-trunk 端口。用相同的步骤和命令，
pèizhì jiāohuànjī SW2.
配置交换机 SW2。

On switch SW1, enter the command *trunkport gigabitethernet 0/0/1* to *0/0/3* to join the physical ports GE0/0/1, GE0/0/2 and GE0/0/3 to the eth-trunk port. Use the same steps and commands to configure switch SW2.

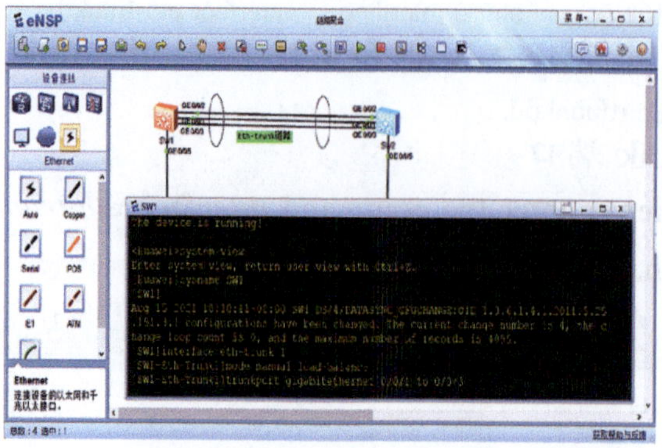

Zài jiāohuànjī SW1 zhōng, yòng display interface eth-trunk 1 mìnglìng, chákàn jiéguǒ.

（5）在交换机 SW1 中，用 display interface eth-trunk 1 命令，查看结果。

On switch SW1, use the command *display interface eth-trunk 1* to view the result.

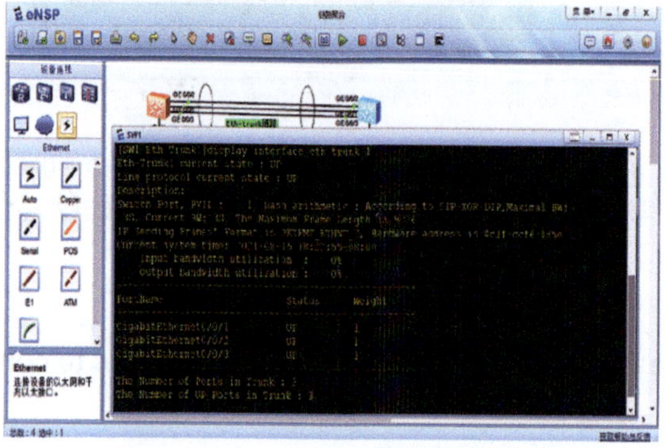

zài jiāohuànjī shang chuàngjiàn biānhào wéi 1 de eth-trunk duānkǒu

① 在交换机上创建编号为 1 的 eth-trunk 端口

Create an eth-trunk port numbered 1 on the switch

pèizhì eth-trunk 1 duānkǒu de gōngzuò móshì

② 配置 eth-trunk 1 端口的工作模式

Configure the working mode of eth-trunk port 1

jiāng wùlǐ duānkǒu GE0/0/1、GE0/0/2、GE0/0/3 jiārù eth-trunk duānkǒu

③ 将物理端口 GE0/0/1、GE0/0/2、GE0/0/3 加入 eth-trunk 端口

Join the physical ports GE0/0/1, GE0/0/2 and GE0/0/3 to the eth-trunk port

chákàn pèizhì jiéguǒ mìnglìng

④ 查看配置结果命令

Command to view the configuration result

A. *mode manual load-balance*

B. *interface eth-trunk 1*

C. *display interface eth-trunk 1*

D. *trunkport gigabitethernet 0/0/1 to 0/0/3*

Pèiduì de jiéguǒ shì:

配对的结果是：

The pairing results:

① ________ ② ________ ③ ________ ④ ________

2. 说一说 Let’s talk

说一说链路聚合配置的步骤。 Talk about the steps of link aggregation configuration.

四、学以致用 xuéyǐzhìyòng Practicing What You Have Learnt

链路聚合如果有一条链路出现故障，只剩下两条链路时，此种情况下，观看查看两台交换机之间的带宽、测试两台电脑的连通性的视频，并回答相关问题。

If one link fails in link aggregation and only two links remain, in this case, watch the video on checking the bandwidth between the two switches and testing the connectivity of the two computers, and answer the related questions.

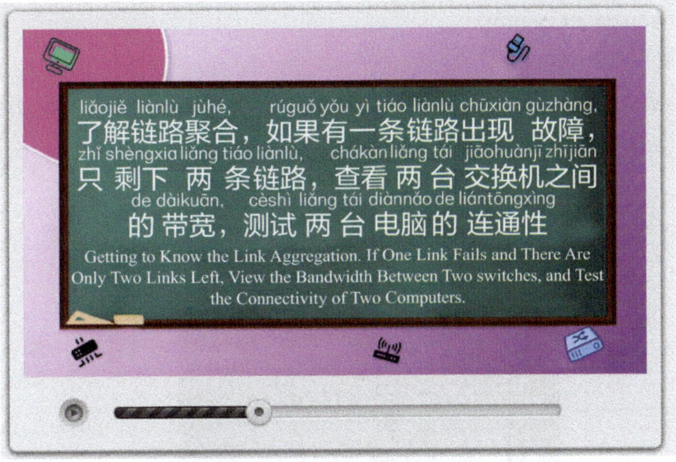

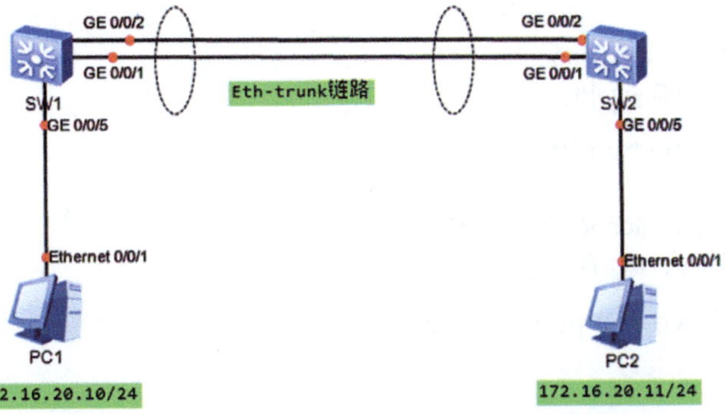

zài jiāohuànjī shang zhíxíng display interface eth-trunk 1 mìnglìng
1. 在交换机上执行 display interface eth-trunk 1 命令
Execute the command *display interface eth-trunk 1* on the switch

Zài jiāohuànjī SW1 shang zhíxíng display interface eth-trunk 1 mìnglìng, lái xiǎnshì zuì dà dàikuān、
（1）在交换机 SW1 上执行 display interface eth-trunk 1 命令，来显示最大带宽、
dāngqián dàikuān jí měi gè jiēkǒu de zhuàngtài.
当前带宽及每个接口的状态。
Execute the command *display interface eth-trunk 1* on switch SW1 to display the maximum bandwidth, current bandwidth, and the status of each interface.

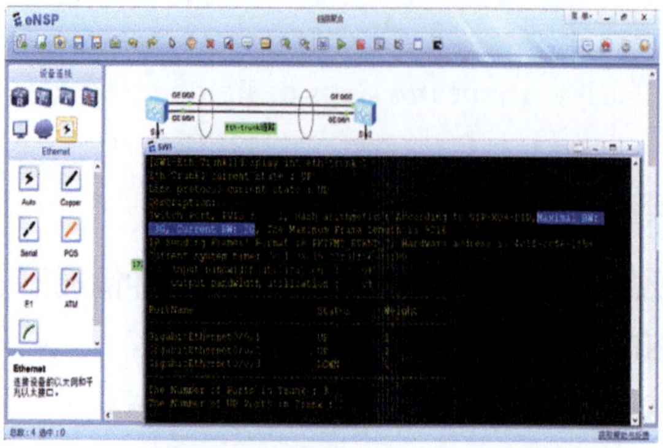

Zài jiāohuànjī SW2 shang zhíxíng display interface eth-trunk 1 mìnglìng, lái xiǎnshì zuì dà dàikuān、
（2）在交换机 SW2 上执行 display interface eth-trunk 1 命令，来显示最大带宽、
dāngqián dàikuān jí měi gè jiēkǒu de zhuàngtài.
当前带宽及每个接口的状态。

Execute the command *display interface eth-trunk 1* on switch SW2 to display the maximum bandwidth, current bandwidth, and the status of each interface.

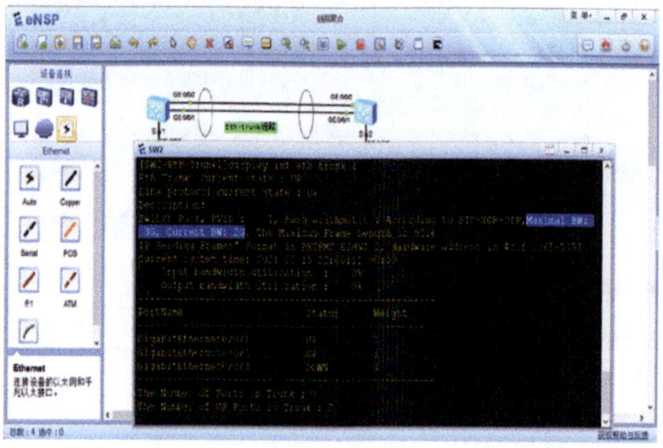

cèshì liǎng tái PC jī de liántōngxìng
2. 测试两台 PC 机的连通性

Test the connectivity of the two PCs

PC1 ping PC2, liǎng tái diànnǎo shì liántōng de.
（1）PC1 ping PC2，两台电脑是连通的。

PC1 ping PC2, so the two computers are connected.

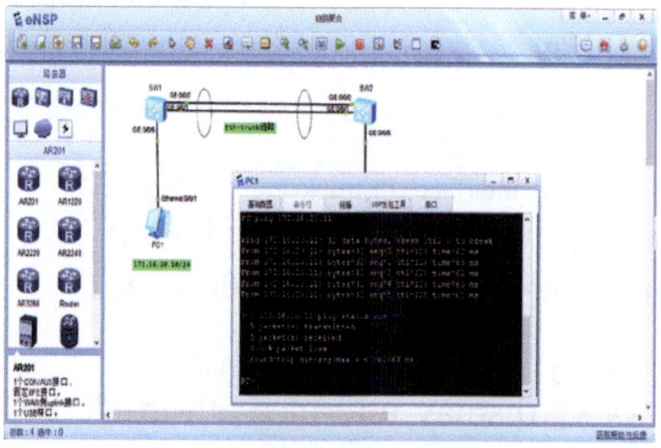

PC2 ping PC1, liǎng tái diànnǎo shì liántōng de.
（2）PC2 ping PC1，两台电脑是连通的。

PC2 ping PC1, so the two computers are connected.

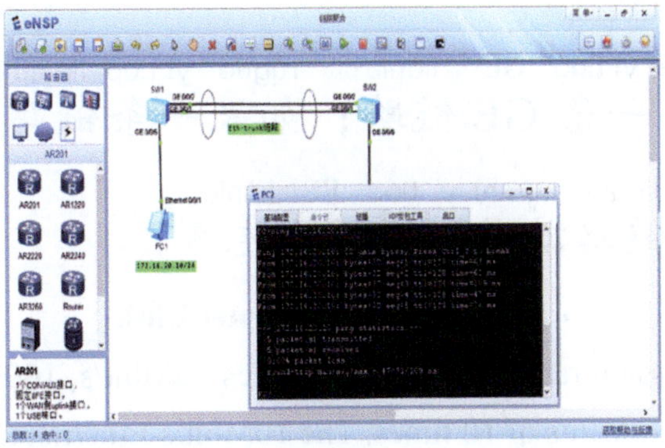

Jiāohuànjī SW1 hé SW2 zhījiān de dāngqián dàikuān shì:
❶ 交换机 SW1 和 SW2 之间的 当前 带宽 是：________________
The current bandwidth between switches SW1 and SW2 is________________

A. 1G　　B. 2G　　C. 3G　　D. 4G

Jiāohuànjī SW1 hé SW2 zhījiān de zuì dà dàikuān shì:
❷ 交换机 SW1 和 SW2 之间的最大 带 宽 是：________________
The maximum bandwidth between switches SW1 and SW2 is________________

A. 1G　　B. 2G　　C. 3G　　D. 4G

五、小知识 xiǎo zhīshi Tips

Yǐtàiwǎng yǔ yǐtàiwǎng liànlù
以太网与以太网链路

Yǐtàiwǎng de xìnxī chuánshūlǜ yǒu: 10Mbit/s、100Mbit/s、1000Mbit/s（1Gbit/s）、
以太网的信息传输率 有：10Mbit/s、100Mbit/s、1000Mbit/s（1Gbit/s）、
10Gbit/s、100Gbit/s, àn 10 bèi guānxi dìzēng. 10Mbit/s yǐtàiwǎng duānkǒu chēngwéi
10Gbit/s、100Gbit/s，按 10 倍关系递增。10Mbit/s 以太网 端口 称为
biāozhǔn yǐtàiwǎng duānkǒu huò 10M kǒu. 100Mbit/s yǐtàiwǎng duānkǒu chēngwéi kuàisù
标准 以太网 端口 或 10M 口。100Mbit/s 以太网 端口 称为 快速
yǐtàiwǎng (Fast Ethernet) duānkǒu huò FE kǒu. 1000Mbit/s yǐtàiwǎng duānkǒu
以太网（Fast Ethernet）端口 或 FE 口。1000Mbit/s 以太网 端口
chēngwéi qiān zhào yǐtàiwǎng (Gigabit Ethernet) duānkǒu huò GE kǒu. 10000Mbit/s
称为 千 兆以太网（Gigabit Ethernet）端口 或 GE 口。10000Mbit/s
yǐtàiwǎng duānkǒu chēngwéi wàn zhào yǐtàiwǎng duānkǒu huò 10GE kǒu. 100000Mbit/s de
以太网 端口 称为 万 兆 以太网 端口 或 10GE 口。100000Mbit/s 的
yǐtàiwǎng duānkǒu cháng chēngwéi 100GE duānkǒu. Yǐtàiwǎng liànlù de shuōfǎ shì yǔ yǐtàiwǎng
以太网 端口 常 称为 100GE 端口。以太网链路的说法是与以太网
duānkǒu de shuōfǎ xiàng duìyìng de. Rúguǒ yì tiáo liànlù liǎng duān de duānkǒu shì GE kǒu,
端口 的说法 相 对应的。如果一条链路 两 端 的端口 是 GE 口，

zé zhè tiáo liànlù jiù chēngwéi yì tiáo GE liànlù; rúguǒ yì tiáo liànlù liǎngduān de duānkǒu shì
则这条链路就称为一条 GE 链路；如果一条链路两端的端口是

FE kǒu, zé chēng zhè tiáo liànlù jiù shì yì tiáo FE liànlù.
FE 口，则称这条链路就是一条 FE 链路。

Ethernet and Ethernet Link

The information transmission rate of Ethernet includes 10Mbit/s, 100Mbit/s, 1000Mbit/S (1Gbit/s), 10Gbit/s and 100Gbit/s, in increments of 10 times. The 10Mbit/s Ethernet port is called standard Ethernet port, or 10M port, 100Mbit/s Ethernet port is called Fast Ethernet port or FE port, 1000Mbit/s Ethernet port is called Gigabit Ethernet port or GE port, 10000Mbit/s Ethernet port is called 10 Gigabit Ethernet port or 10GE port, and 100000Mbit/s Ethernet port is often called 100GE port. The way of saying Ethernet link corresponds to that of Ethernet port. If the ports at both ends of a link are GE ports, the link is called a GE link; and if the ports at both ends of a link are FE ports, the link is called an FE link.

补充专业词语 bǔchōng zhuānyè cíyǔ Supplementary Specialized Vocabulary

06-07

1.	配对	pèi//duì	v.	pair, match
2.	FE 口	FE kǒu	phr.	Fast Ethernet port (FE port)
3.	GE 口	GE kǒu	phr.	Gigabit Ethernet port (GE port)

第二部分 Part 2

汉字 Chinese Characters

一、汉字知识 Hànzì zhīshi Knowledge about Chinese Characters

汉字的偏旁（6） **Radicals of Chinese characters (6)**

偏旁 Radicals	例字 Examples	部件组合 Combinations	结构图示 Illustrations
⺮	笔	⺮+毛	⊟
	篮	⺮+监	⊟
	箱	⺮+相	⊟
	等	⺮+寺	⊟
	管	⺮+官	⊟
	简	⺮+间	⊟
	第	⺮+弟	⊟

（续表）

偏旁 Radicals	例字 Examples	部件组合 Combinations	结构图示 Illustrations
灬	然	肰＋灬	⿱
	点	占＋灬	⿱
	热	执＋灬	⿱
	黑	里＋灬	⿱
	照	昭＋灬	⿱
衤	衬	衤＋寸	⿰
	衫	衤＋彡	⿰
	裤	衤＋库	⿰
雨	需	雨＋而	⿱
	雪	雨＋彐	⿱
	零	雨＋令	⿱
土	城	土＋成	⿰
	地	土＋也	⿰
	场	土＋𠃓	⿰
	坏	土＋不	⿰
	去	土＋厶	⿱

二、汉字认读与书写　Hànzì rèndú yǔ shūxiě　The Recognition and Writing of Chinese Characters

认读下列词语，并试着读写构成词语的汉字。

Recognize the following words, and try to read and write the Chinese characters forming these words.

需要　　第一步　　地址　　点击

需	要	第	一
步	地	址	点
击			

第三部分 Part 3

日常用语 Daily Expressions

1. 我还不能马上说定。Wǒ hái bù néng mǎshàng shuōdìng. I cannot say for certain off-hand.
2. 谢谢您的合作。Xièxie nín de hézuò. Thank you for your cooperation.
3. 如果对某些细节有意见的话，请提出来。Rúguǒ duì mǒu xiē xìjié yǒu yìjiàn dehuà, qǐng tí chulai. If you have any questions on certain details, feel free to ask.

第四部分 Part 4

单元实训 Unit Practical Training

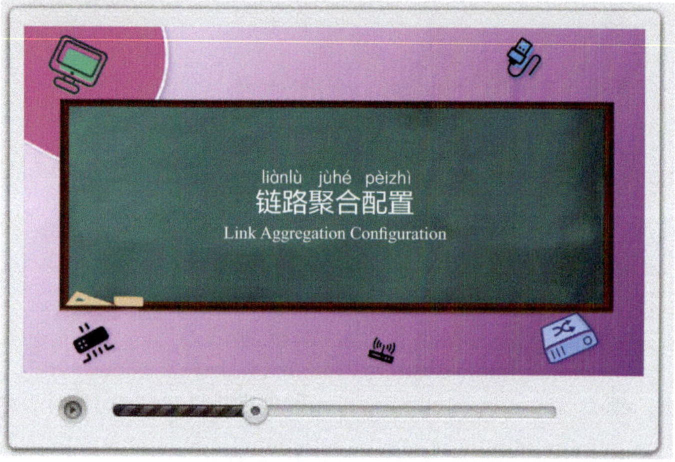

链路聚合配置 liànlù jùhé pèizhì **Link Aggregation Configuration**

实训目的 Training purpose

掌握 interface eth-trunk, mode manual, load-balance, trunkport gigabitethernet, display interface ethtrunk 命令的使用。培养团队合作精神、竞争意识。

To master the use of the commands *interface eth-trunk, mode manual, load-balance, trunkport gigabitethernet, display interface eth-trunk*, and cultivate teamwork spirit and competitive consciousness.

实训组织 Training organization

每组 3 ～ 5 人，选出一个组长。

Each group consists of 3-5 people, and a group leader is selected.

实训内容 Training content

两台交换机用 3 条链路连接，配置链路聚合，测试两台计算机的连通性。

Connect two switches with three links, configure link aggregation, and test the connectivity of two computers.

实训步骤 Training steps

1. 宣布比赛规则及要求：轮流上机操作与实践，每组每人可以多次操作，安排专人记录每位同学操作所花费的时间，其他组同学监督。

Announce the competition rules and requirements: The students take turns to operate and practice on the computer. Each group member can operate for many times, a student is specially assigned to record the time each student takes to operate, and students of other groups supervise.

② 开始比赛。

Start the competition.

小组成员分工合作完成如下操作：绘制网络拓扑图；启动设备，并配置计算机的 IP 地址；配置 SW1 的链路聚合；配置 SW2 的链路聚合；显示 SW1、SW2 的配置结果，并测试两台计算机的连通性。

The group members work together to complete the following operations: draw the network topology diagram, start the equipment and configure the IP address of the computer, configure the link aggregation of SW1, configure the link aggregation of SW2, display the configuration results of SW1 and SW2, and test the connectivity of the two computers.

③ 计算每组同学总共花费的时间及得分。

Calculate the total time and score of each group.

④ 实训结束，教师总结评价。

The training ends. The teacher makes a summary and an evaluation.

第五部分 Part 5

单元小结 *Unit Summary*

cíyǔ
词语
Vocabulary

普通词语 General Vocabulary

1.	当作	dàngzuò	v.	treat/regard...as...
2.	对	duì	m.	pair
3.	包含	bāohán	v.	contain
4.	成员	chéngyuán	n.	member
5.	总和	zǒnghé	n.	sum
6.	有效	yǒuxiào	v.	be effective
7.	增加	zēngjiā	v.	increase
8.	当	dāng	prep.	when
9.	出现	chūxiàn	v.	appear
10.	剩下	shèngxia	phr.	remaining
11.	大部分	dàbùfen	n.	most, the majority
12.	造成	zàochéng	v.	cause
13.	影响	yǐngxiǎng	n.	influence, effect
14.	总	zǒng	adj.	total

cíyǔ
词语
Vocabulary

15.	需求	xūqiú	n.	demand
16.	但	dàn	conj.	but
17.	所以	suǒyǐ	conj.	so
18.	现象	xiànxiàng	n.	phenomenon
19.	整合	zhěnghé	v.	integrate
20.	成	chéng	v.	become, turn into
21.	可	kě	aux.	can
22.	达	dá	v.	reach, achieve

专业词语 Specialized Vocabulary

1.	链路聚合	liànlù jùhé	phr.	link aggregation
2.	带宽	dàikuān	n.	bandwidth
3.	故障	gùzhàng	n.	breakdown, fault
4.	毫秒	háomiǎo	m.	millisecond
5.	拥塞	yōngsè	v.	congest
6.	逻辑链路	luójí liànlù	phr.	logical link

补充专业词语 Supplementary Specialized Vocabulary

1.	配对	pèi//duì	v.	pair, match
2.	FE 口	FE kǒu	phr.	Fast Ethernet port (FE port)
3.	GE 口	GE kǒu	phr.	Gigabit Ethernet port (GE port)

jùzi
句子
Sentences

1. 链路聚合是把两台设备之间的多条物理链路聚合在一起，当作一条逻辑链路来使用。这两台设备可以是一对路由器、一对交换机，或者是一台路由器和一台交换机。
2. 一条聚合链路可以包含多条成员链路，通过聚合几条链路，一个聚合口的带宽可以扩展为所有成员口带宽的总和，这样就有效地增加了逻辑链路的带宽。
3. 当一条链路出现故障时，流量会自动在剩下的链路间重新分配，并且这种故障切换所用的时间是毫秒级的，对大部分应用都不会造成影响。
4. 为解决流量拥塞的问题，可以在 SW1 和 SW2 之间用 3 条 GE 链路，使用链路聚合技术，将这3条GE链路整合成一条最大带宽可达3G的逻辑链路。
5. 用 display 命令可以查看配置结果。

7

Wǎngluò ānquán

网络安全

Network Security

fǎngwèn kòngzhì lièbiǎo de pèizhì guòchéng

访问 控制 列表 的 配置 过程

Configuration Process of Access Control List (ACL)

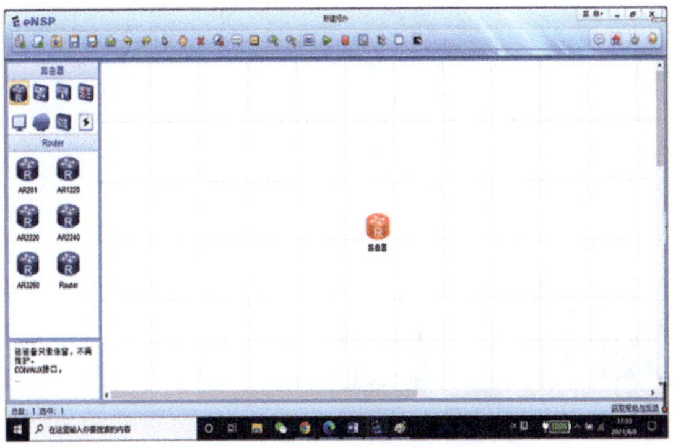

jìnrù lùyóuqì de xìtǒng shìtú

进入路由器的 系统 视图

Enter the System View of the Router

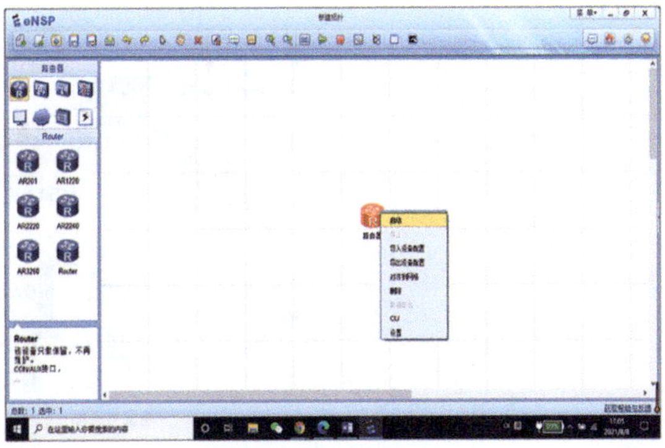

chuàngjiàn ACL

创建 ACL

Create an ACL

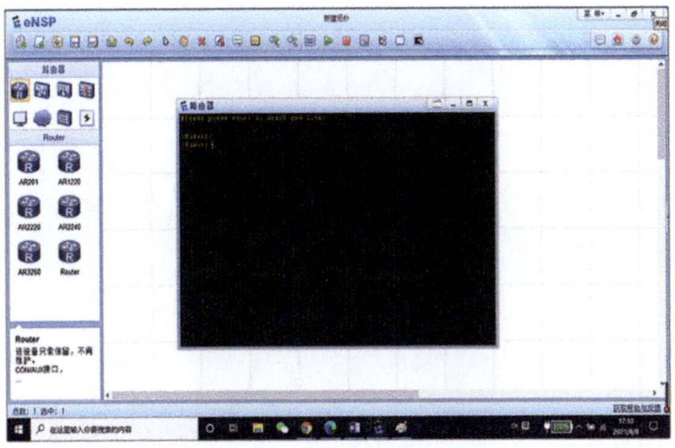

wèi ACL chuàngjiàn guīzé

为 ACL 创建 规则

Create Rules for the ACL

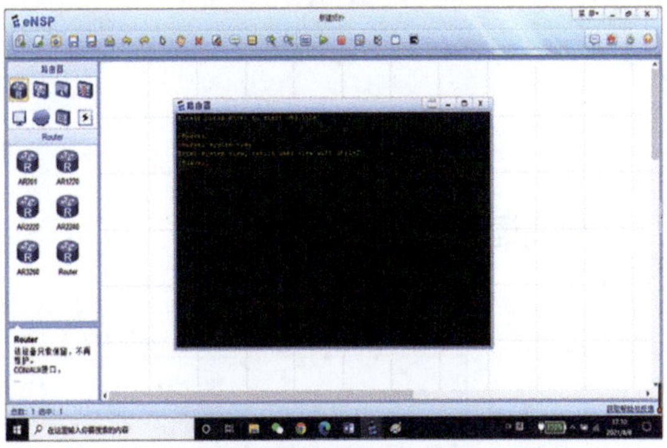

bǎ ACL yìngyòng dào lùyóuqì de chūjiēkǒu

把 ACL 应用 到 路由器的 出接口

Apply the ACL to the Router's Outbound Interface

题解 Introduction

1. 学习内容：ACL 配置的基本步骤、基本分类、基本作用。
   Learning content: The basic steps, classifications and functions of ACL configuration
2. 知识目标：掌握 ACL 配置相关的关键词语，了解汉字的偏旁“走”“忄”“攵”“饣”“禾”，学写相关汉字。
   Knowledge objectives: To master the keywords for ACL configuration, understand the Chinese radicals “走”, “忄”, “攵”, “饣”, “禾”, and learn to write the related Chinese characters
3. 技能目标：学会简单的 ACL 配置，实现网络安全。
   Skill objective: To master simple ACL configuration to realize network security

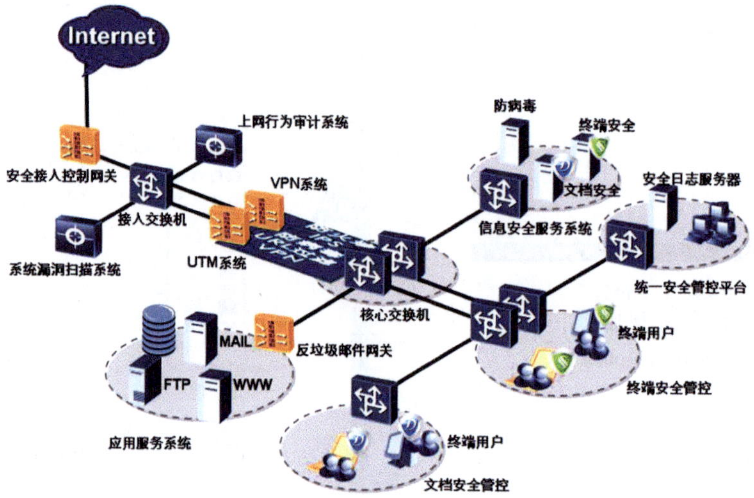

第一部分 Part 1

课文 Texts

一、热身 rèshēn Warm-up

1. 给词语选择对应的图片。 Choose the corresponding pictures for the words.

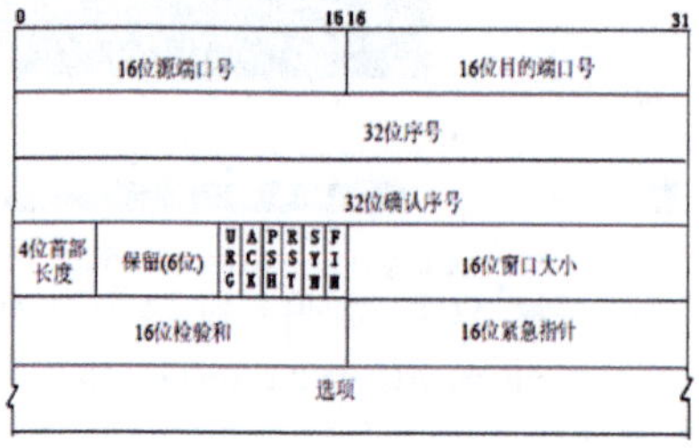

A.

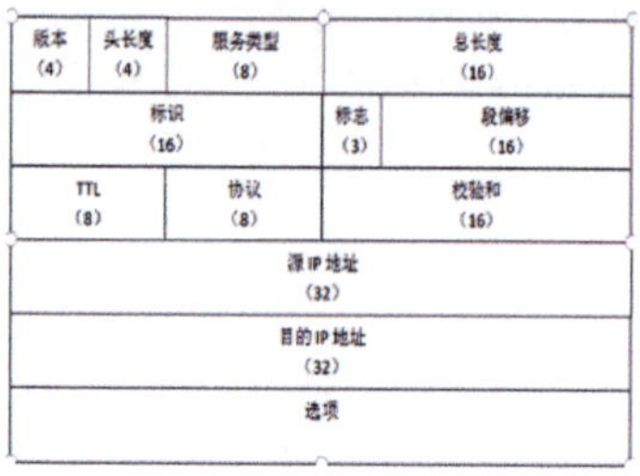

B.

C.

D.

源端口号（16）	目的端口号（16）
总长度 (16)	校验和（16）

E.

MAC 目的地址（48）	MAC 源地址（48）	类型（8）

F.

yǐtàizhēn tóu jiégòu
① 以太帧头结构________________
Ethernet frame header structure

IP bàowén tóu jiégòu
② IP 报文头结构________________
IP message header structure

UDP tóubù jiégòu
③ UDP 头部结构________________
UDP header structure

TCP tóubù jiégòu
④ TCP 头部结构________________
TCP header structure

jiāohuànjī
⑤ 交换机________________
switch

fánghuǒqiáng
⑥ 防火墙________________
firewall

2. 观看介绍访问控制列表在网络安全中的作用的视频，将访问控制列表的配置过程进行排序。

Watch the video introducing the role of Access Control List (ACL) in network security, and sequence the ACL configuration process.

Zàimìnglìngháng pèizhì jièmiàn xià, shūrù system-view, jí jìnrù pèizhì móshì, jìnxíng ACL pèizhì.
A. 在命令行配置界面下，输入 system-view，即进入配置模式，进行 ACL 配置。
In the command line configuration interface, enter the command *system-view* to enter the configuration mode for ACL configuration.

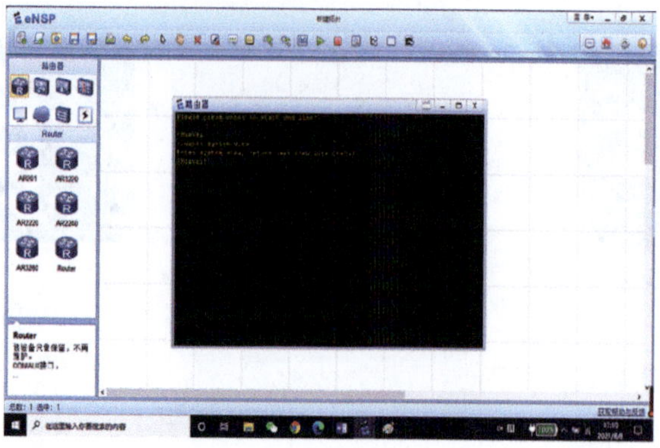

Lùyóuqì qǐdòng hòu, shuāngjī lùyóuqì túbiāo, jìnrù lùyóuqì de mìnglìngháng pèizhì jièmiàn.
B. 路由器启动后，双击路由器图标，进入路由器的命令行配置界面。

After the router is started, double-click the router icon to enter the command line configuration interface of the router.

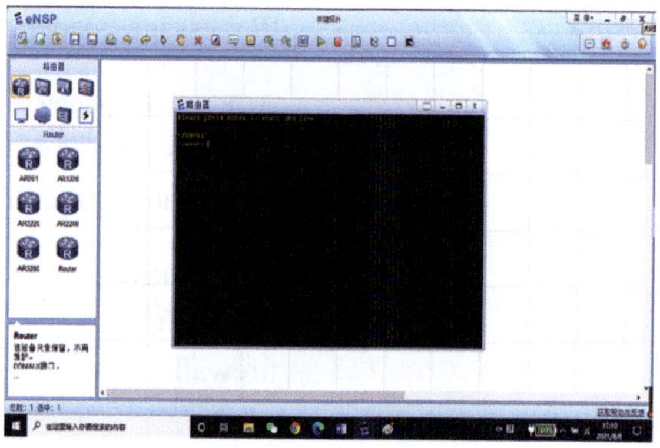

Fàngzhì lùyóuqì shèbèi.
C. 放置路由器设备。

Place the router equipment.

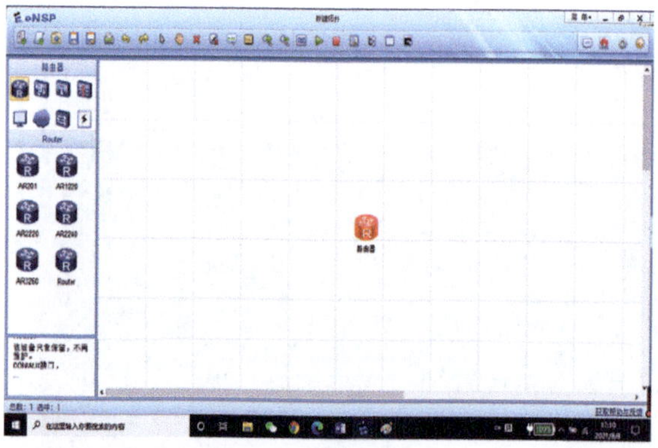

Zài “lùyóuqì” shang dānjī yòujiàn, bìng diǎnjī “qǐdòng”, qǐdòng lùyóuqì.
D. 在“路由器”上单击右键，并点击“启动”，启动路由器。

Right-click on the “Router” and click “Start” to start the router.

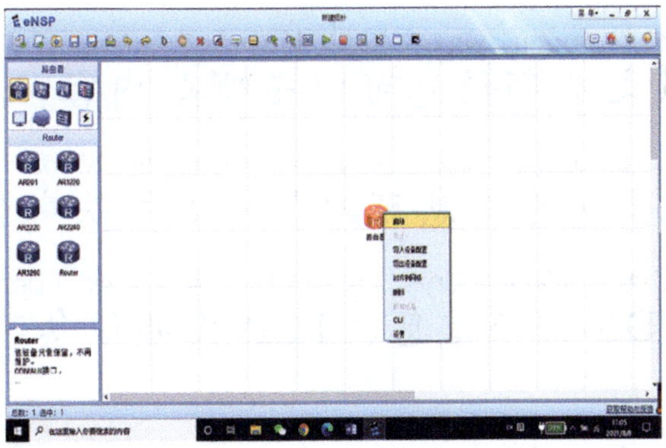

二、课文 kèwén Texts

A 07-01

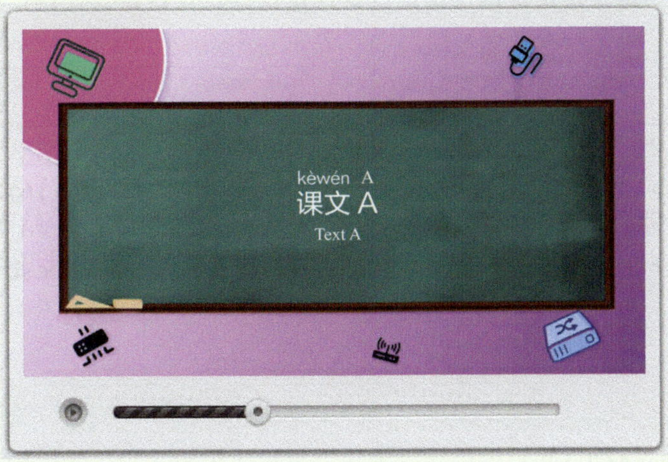

shīfu: Nǐ zhīdào shénme shì ACL ma?
师傅：你知道什么是ACL吗？

túdì: ACL shì Access Control List de suōxiě, jí fǎngwèn kòngzhì lièbiǎo,
徒弟：ACL是Access Control List的缩写，即访问控制列表，

shì yìngyòng zài wǎngluò shèbèi jiēkǒu de zhǐlìng lièbiǎo. Zhèxiē zhǐlìng lièbiǎo yònglái
是应用在网络设备接口的指令列表。这些指令列表用来

gàosu wǎngluò shèbèi gēnjù bàowén de tóubù xìnxī rúhé chǔlǐ bàowén.
告诉网络设备根据报文的头部信息如何处理报文。

shīfu: Zhèlǐ de wǎngluò shèbèi jùtǐ zhǐ shénme?
师傅：这里的网络设备具体指什么？

túdì: Zhèlǐ de wǎngluò shèbèi kěyǐ shì lùyóuqì、jiāohuànjī、fánghuǒqiáng děng.
徒弟：这里的网络设备可以是路由器、交换机、防火墙等。

shīfu: ACL zhōng de bàowén tóubù xìnxī kěyǐ shì nǎxiē nèiróng?
师傅：ACL 中的报文头部信息可以是哪些内容？

túdì: ACL zhōng de bàowén tóubù xìnxī kěyǐ shì yǐtàizhēn tóubù xìnxī、IP bàowén tóubù xìnxī、UDP tóubù xìnxī、TCP tóubù xìnxī děng.
徒弟：ACL 中的报文头部信息可以是以太帧头部信息、IP 报文头部信息、UDP 头部信息、TCP 头部信息等。

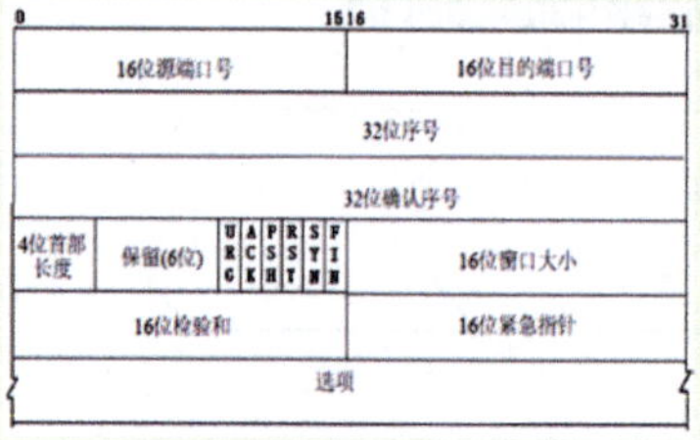

TCP tóubù jiégòu
TCP 头部结构
TCP header structure

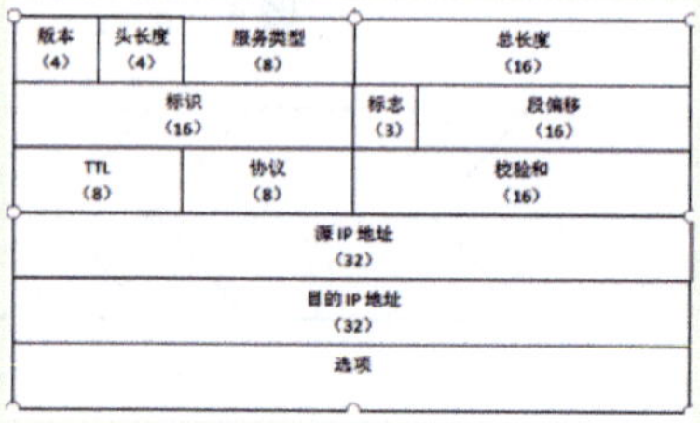

yǐtàizhēn tóu jiégòu
以太帧头结构
Ethernet frame header structure

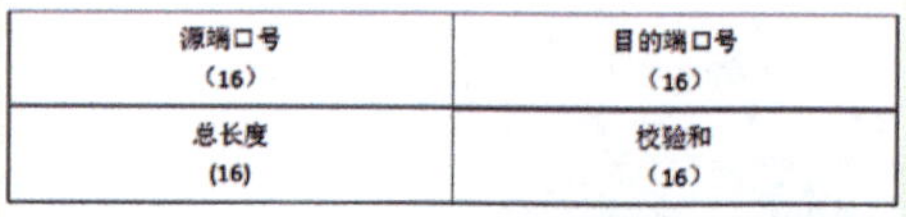

UDP tóubù jiégòu
UDP 头部结构
UDP header structure

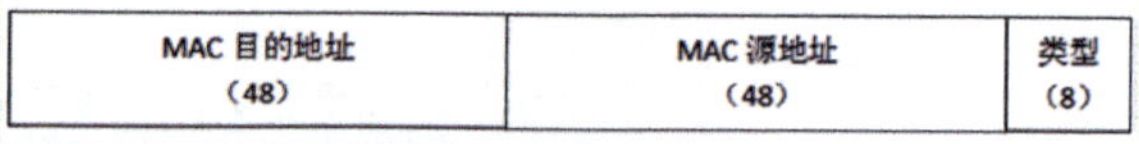

IP bàowén tóu jiégòu
IP 报文头结构
IP message header structure

译文 yìwén Text in English

Master: Hello! Do you know what ACL is?

Apprentice: It is the abbreviation for Access Control List, namely the list of instructions applied to network device interface. The instruction list is used to tell the network device what to do with a message based on the header information of the message.

Master: What does network device specifically refer to here?

Apprentice: The network device here can be a router, a switch, a firewall, etc.

Master: What can the message header information in the ACL be?

Apprentice: It can be Ethernet frame header information, IP message header information, UDP header information, TCP header information, etc.

普通词语 pǔtōng cíyǔ General Vocabulary

07-02

1.	缩写	suōxiě	n.	abbreviation
2.	即	jí		mean
3.	告诉	gàosu	v.	tell

4.	头部	tóubù	n.	header
5.	这里	zhèlǐ	pron.	here

专业词语 zhuānyè cíyǔ Specialized Vocabulary

07-03

1.	访问控制列表	fǎngwèn kòngzhì lièbiǎo	phr.	Access Control List
2.	指令列表	zhǐlìng lièbiǎo	phr.	instruction list
3.	以太帧头部信息	yǐtàizhēn tóubù xìnxī	phr.	Ethernet frame header information
4.	报文头部信息	bàowén tóubù xìnxī	phr.	message header information

B 07-04

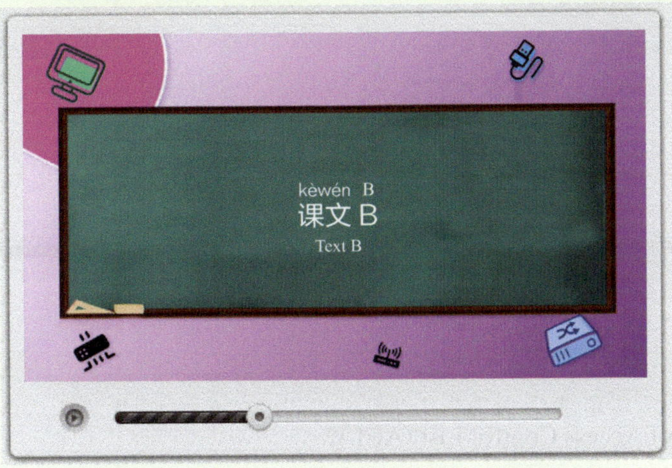

shīfu: Qǐngwèn fǎngwèn kòngzhì lièbiǎo yǒu shénme zuòyòng?
师傅：请问 访问 控制 列表 有 什么 作用？

túdì: Fǎngwèn kòngzhì lièbiǎo yǒu xǔduō yòngtú, bǐrú yùfáng wǎngluò gōngjī, xiànzhì wǎngluò liúliàng, tígāo wǎngluò xìngnéng, shíxiàn cèlüè lùyóu děng.
徒弟：访问 控制 列表 有 许多 用途，比如 预防 网络 攻击，限制 网络 流量，提高 网络 性能，实现 策略 路由 等。

shīfu: Qǐngwèn fǎngwèn kòngzhì lièbiǎo yǒu nǎxiē lèixíng?
师傅：请问 访问 控制 列表 有 哪些 类型？

túdì: Cóng guīzé de jiǎodù kěyǐ jiāng fǎngwèn kòngzhì lièbiǎo fēnwéi jīběn ACL、gāojí ACL、èr céng ACL.
徒弟：从 规则 的 角度 可以 将 访问 控制 列表 分为 基本 ACL、高级 ACL、二层 ACL。

shīfu: Qǐngwèn ACL de shǐyòng fēnwéi nǎ liǎng bù?
师傅：请问 ACL 的 使用 分为 哪 两 步？

túdì: Dì-yī bù shì chuàngjiàn ACL, gēnjù xūyào shèzhì xiāngyìng de guīzé; dì-èr bù shì jiāng ACL yìngyòng dào wǎngluò shèbèi zhǐdìng jiēkǒu de zhǐdìng fāngxiàng (in/out) shang.

徒弟：第一步是创建ACL，根据需要设置相应的规则；第二步是将ACL应用到网络设备指定接口的指定方向(in/out)上。

规则编号：2000~2999	动作：permit 或 deny
源地址	源地址掩码
分片信息(可选)	生效时间(可选)

jīběn ACL
基本ACL
Basic ACL

规则编号：3000~3999	动作：permit 或 deny
源地址	源地址掩码
目的地址	目的地址掩码
TCP/UDP 源端口号	TCP/UDP 目的端口号
分片信息(可选)	生效时间(可选)

gāojí ACL
高级ACL
Advanced ACL

规则编号：4000~4999	动作：permit 或 deny
源 MAC 地址	源 MAC 地址掩码
目的 MAC 地址(可选)	目的 MAC 地址掩码(可选)
分片信息(可选)	生效时间(可选)

èrcéng ACL
二层ACL
Layer 2 ACL

译文 yìwén Text in English

Master: What are the functions of Access Control List (ACL)?

Apprentice: It has many uses, such as preventing network attacks, limiting network traffic, improving network performance, implementing policy-based routing and so on.

Master: What are the types of ACL?

Apprentice: From the perspective of rules, ACL can be divided into basic ACL, advanced ACL, and layer 2 ACL.

Master: What are the two steps to use ACL?

Apprentice: The first step is to create ACL and set the corresponding rules as required. The second step is to apply ACL to the specified direction (in/out) of the specified interface of a network device.

普通词语 pǔtōng cíyǔ General Vocabulary

07-05

1.	预防	yùfáng	v.	prevent
2.	限制	xiànzhì	v.	limit
3.	提高	tí//gāo	v.	improve
4.	规则	guīzé	n.	rule
5.	需要	xūyào	n.	require
6.	相应	xiāngyìng	v.	correspond
7.	方向	fāngxiàng	n.	direction

专业词语 zhuānyè cíyǔ Specialized Vocabulary

07-06

1.	网络攻击	wǎngluò gōngjī	phr.	network attack
2.	网络流量	wǎngluò liúliàng	phr.	network flow, network traffic
3.	网络性能	wǎngluò xìngnéng	phr.	network performance
4.	策略路由	cèlüè lùyóu	phr.	policy-based routing
5.	基本 ACL	jīběn ACL	phr.	basic ACL
6.	高级 ACL	gāojí ACL	phr.	advanced ACL
7.	设置规则	shèzhì guīzé	phr.	set a rule
8.	网络设备	wǎngluò shèbèi	phr.	network device
9.	指定接口	zhǐdìng jiēkǒu	phr.	specified interface
10.	指定方向	zhǐdìng fāngxiàng	phr.	specified direction

三、视听说 shì-tīng-shuō Viewing, Listening, and Speaking

1. 观看介绍访问控制列表的作用的视频，将各种控制列表与其使用规则配对。

Watch the video introducing the functions of ACL, and match the ACLs with their rules of use.

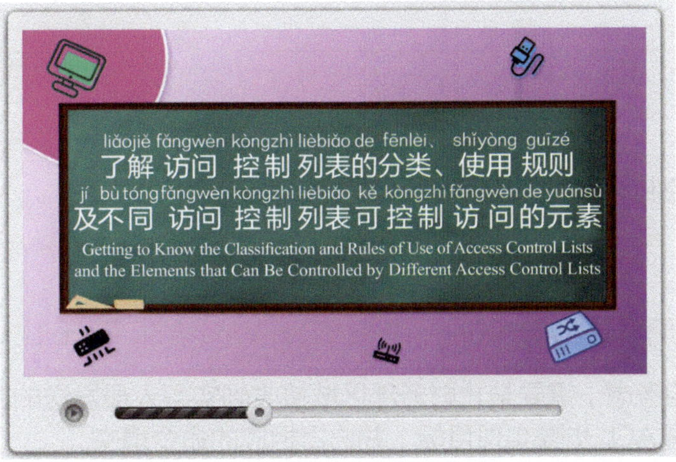

① biāozhǔn ACL
标准 ACL
standard ACL

规则编号：2000~2999	动作：permit 或 deny
源地址	源地址掩码
分片信息(可选)	生效时间(可选)

A. jì kě shǐyòng IPv4 bàowén de yuán IP dìzhǐ, yě kě shǐyòng mùdì IP dìzhǐ、TCP yuán / mùdì duānkǒu、UDP yuán / mùdì duānkǒuhào、shēngxiào shíjiānduàn děng lái dìngyì guīzé

既可使用 IPv4 报文的源 IP 地址，也可使用目的 IP 地址、TCP 源 / 目的端口、UDP 源 / 目的端口号、生效时间段等来定义规则

It can use the source IP address of IPv4 message, and can also use the destination IP address, TCP source/destination port, UDP source/destination port number, effective time period, etc. to define rules.

gāojí ACL
② 高级 ACL
advanced ACL

规则编号：3000~3999	动作：permit 或 deny
源地址	源地址掩码
目的地址	目的地址掩码
TCP/UDP 源端口号	TCP/UDP 目的端口号
分片信息(可选)	生效时间(可选)

èr céng ACL
③ 二层 ACL
layer 2 ACL

规则编号：4000~4999	动作：permit 或 deny
源 MAC 地址	源 MAC 地址掩码
目的 MAC 地址(可选)	目的 MAC 地址掩码(可选)
分片信息(可选)	生效时间(可选)

shǐyòng bàowén de yǐtàizhēn tóubù xìnxī lái dìngyì guīzé, bǐrú gēnjù yuán MAC (Media Access Control) dìzhǐ、mùdì MAC dìzhǐ děng
B. 使用报文的以太帧头部信息来定义规则，比如根据源 MAC（Media Access Control）地址、目的 MAC 地址等
It uses the Ethernet frame header information of the message to define rules, such as the source MAC (Media Access Control) address, destination MAC address, etc.

jǐn shǐyòng bàowén de yuán IP dìzhǐ、fēnpiàn xìnxī hé shēngxiào shíjiānduàn xìnxī lái dìngyì guīzé
C. 仅使用报文的源 IP 地址、分片信息和生效时间段信息来定义规则
It only uses the source IP address, fragment information and effective time period information of the message to define rules.

① ______________ ② ______________ ③ ______________

2. 说一说 Let's talk

说一说不同访问控制列表可控制访问的元素。

Talk about the elements that can be controlled by different Access Control Lists.

四、学以致用 xuéyǐzhìyòng Practicing What You Have Learnt

某公司出于对网络安全方面的考虑，需要禁止财务部区域接收到实习人员发送的 IP 报文。观看视频，看网络安全师如何为财务部写 ACL 步骤实现目标，并选择相应的命令填空。

A company needs to prohibit the finance department from receiving IP messages sent by interns due to considerations of network security. Watch the video on how a cybersecurity expert writes ACL steps for the finance department to achieve the goals and select the corresponding commands to fill in the blanks.

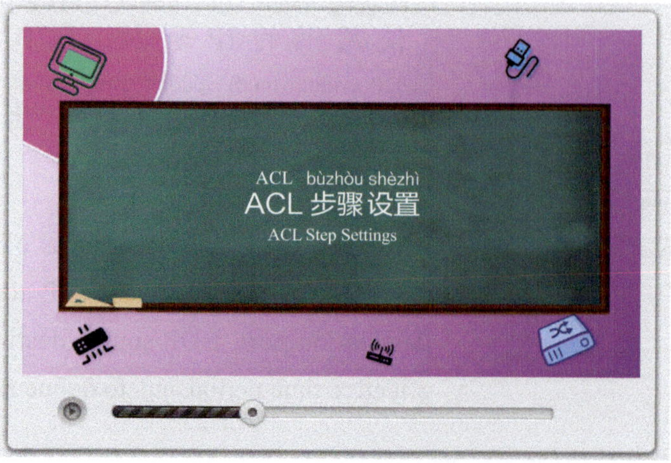

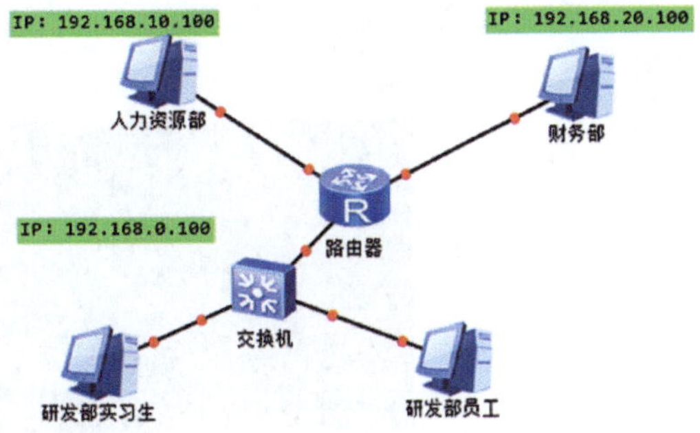

zài lùyóuqì shang jìnxíng ACL pèizhì: zhíxíng mìnglìng acl 2005, chuàngjiàn jīběn guīzé
（1）在路由器上进行 ACL 配置：执行命令 acl 2005，创建基本规则
Configure the ACL on the router: Execute the command *acl 2005* to create basic rules

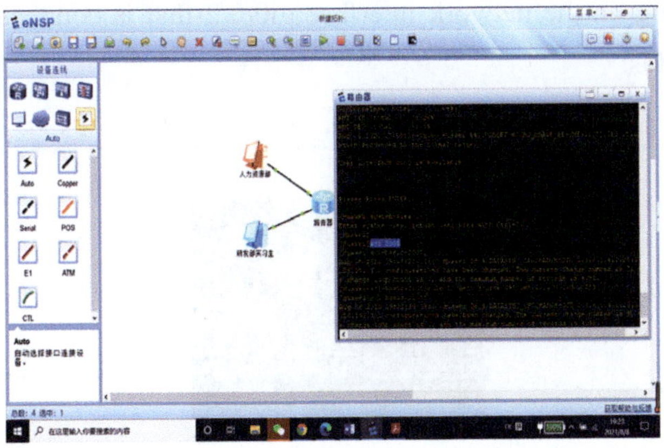

chuàngjiàn ACL guīzé
（2）创建 ACL 规则
Create ACL rules

①

zài jiēkǒu gi0/0/2 shang qǐyòng bàowén guòlǜ
（3）在接口 gi0/0/2 上启用报文过滤
Enable message filtering on interface gi0/0/2

②

Jiéguǒ: cǐshí, yánfābù shíxíshēng de jìsuànjī 192.168.0.100 wúfǎ fǎngwèn cáiwùbù de jìsuànjī 192.168.20.100.
结果：此时，研发部实习生的计算机 192.168.0.100 无法访问财务部的计算机 192.168.20.100.
Result: At this time, the computer 192.168.0.100 of the intern in R&D department cannot access the computer 192.168.20.100 of the finance department.

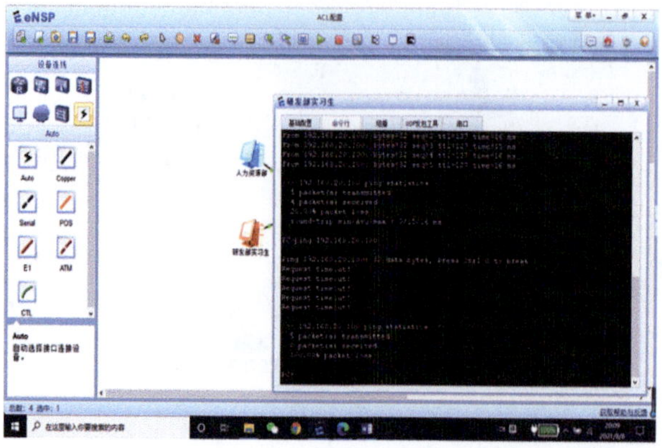

zài yǔ cáiwùbù zhǔjī liánjiē de wǎngluò jiēkǒu gi0/0/2 shang qǐyòng bàowén guòlǜ, mìnglìng wéi:

A. 在与财务部主机连接的网络接口 gi0/0/2 上启用报文过滤，命令为：

Enable message filtering on the network interface gi0/0/2 that is connected to the finance department host, and the command is:

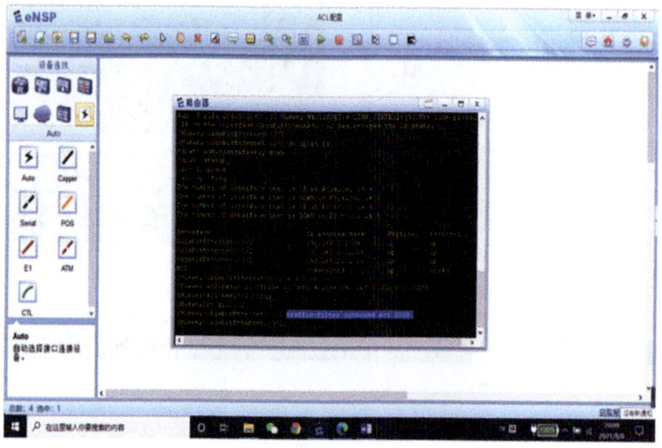

zhíxíng mìnglìng rule 10 deny source 192.168.0.100 0.0.0.255

B. 执行命令 rule 10 deny source 192.168.0.100 0.0.0.255

Execute the command: *rule 10 deny source 192.168.0.100 0.0.0.255*

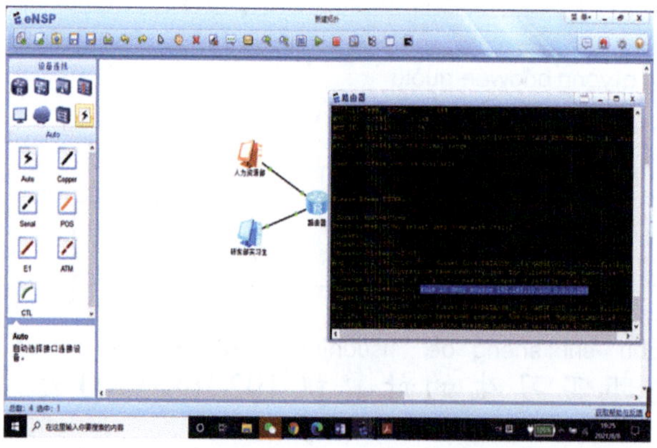

① ______________ ② ______________

五、小知识 xiǎo zhīshi Tips

ACL fēnlèi zhīshi
ACL 分类知识

Yònghù zài chuàngjiàn ACL shí kěyǐ wèi qí zhǐdìng biānhào, tóngshí, wèile biànyú jìyì
用户在创建ACL时可以为其指定编号，同时，为了便于记忆

hé shíbié, yònghù hái kěyǐ chuàngjiàn mìngmíngxíng ACL, jí zài chuàngjiàn ACL shí wèi qí
和识别，用户还可以创建命名型ACL，即在创建ACL时为其

shèzhì míngchēng. Mìngmíngxíng ACL yě kěyǐ shì “míngchēng-shùzì” de xíngshì, jí zài
设置名称。命名型ACL也可以是“名称—数字”的形式，即在

dìngyì mìngmíngxíng ACL shí, tóngshí zhǐdìng ACL biānhào. Rúguǒ bù zhǐdìng biānhào, xìtǒng
定义命名型ACL时，同时指定ACL编号。如果不指定编号，系统

zé huì zìdòng wèi qí fēnpèi yí gè shùzìxíng ACL de biānhào. Bǐrú: acl name test,
则会自动为其分配一个数字型ACL的编号。比如：acl name test，

jí chuàngjiàn yì tiáo míng wéi test de ACL; acl name test 2020 biǎoshì chuàngjiàn yì tiáo
即创建一条名为test的ACL；acl name test 2020表示创建一条

míng wéi test de ACL, qí biānhào wéi 2020.
名为test的ACL，其编号为2020。

Knowledge on Classification of ACLs

When creating an ACL, the user can specify a number for it. At the same time, the user can create a named ACL for easy memory and identification, i.e. the user sets a name for the ACL when creating an ACL. A named ACL can also be in the form of “name-number”, i.e. when defining a named ACL, an ACL number is also specified. If no number is specified, the system will automatically assign a numbered ACL number for it. For example, *acl name test* is to create an ACL named test, while *acl name test 2020* indicates to create an ACL named test and its number is 2020.

补充专业词语 bǔchōng zhuānyè cíyǔ Supplementary Specialized Vocabulary

07-07

1.	源端口	yuánduānkǒu	n.	source port
2.	目的端口	mùdì duānkǒu	phr.	destination port
3.	生效时间段	shēngxiào shíjiānduàn	phr.	effective time period
4.	执行命令	zhíxíng mìnglìng	phr.	execute a command
5.	启用	qǐyòng	v.	start using
6.	报文过滤	bàowén guòlǜ	phr.	message filtering

第二部分 Part 2

汉字 Chinese Characters

一、汉字知识 Hànzì zhīshi Knowledge about Chinese Characters

汉字的偏旁（7） **Radicals of Chinese characters (7)**

偏旁 Radicals	例字 Examples	部件组合 Combinations	结构图示 Illustrations
走	超	走＋召	
	趣	走＋取	
	起	走＋已	
	趟	走＋尚	
忄	忙	忄＋亡	
	快	忄＋夬	
	慢	忄＋曼	
	惯	忄＋贯	
	情	忄＋青	
攵	教	孝＋攵	
	收	丩＋攵	
	数	娄＋攵	
	放	方＋攵	
饣	馆	饣＋官	
	饭	饣＋反	
	饺	饣＋交	
	饼	饣＋并	
	饿	饣＋我	
禾	和	禾＋口	
	种	禾＋中	
	租	禾＋且	
	季	禾＋子	

二、汉字认读与书写 Hànzì rèndú yǔ shūxiě The Recognition and Writing of Chinese Characters

认读下列词语，并试着读写构成词语的汉字。

Recognize the following words, and try to read and write the Chinese characters forming these words.

情况　　网络攻击　　名称　　移动

情				况				网				络			
攻				击				名				称			
移				动											

第三部分 Part 3

日常用语 *Daily Expressions*

1. 我们真诚地希望你们在这里过得愉快。Wǒmen zhēnchéng de xīwàng nǐmen zài zhèlǐ guò de yúkuài. We sincerely hope you'll have a pleasant stay here.
2. 质量比数量更重要。Zhìliàng bǐ shùliàng gèng zhòngyào. Quality is more important than quantity.

第四部分 Part 4

单元实训 *Unit Practical Training*

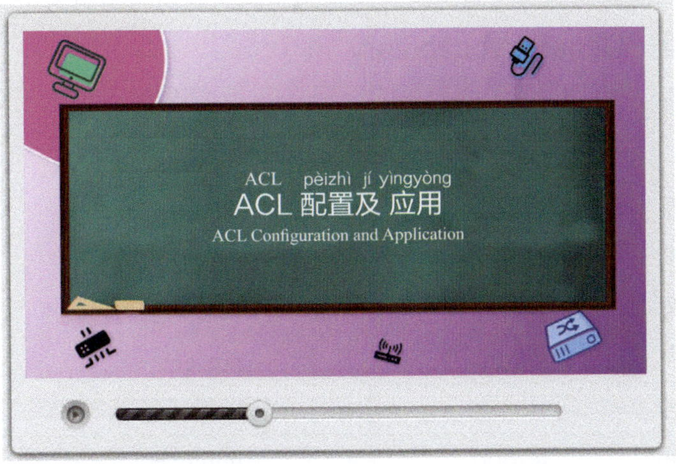

ACL 配置及应用 ACL pèizhì jí yìngyòng ACL Configuration and Application

实训目的 Training purpose

了解访问控制列表的配置方法和应用。

To learn about the configuration method and application of ACL.

实训组织 Training organization

每组 3 人，选出一个组长。

Each group consists of three people, and a group leader is selected.

实训内容 Training content

ACL 的配置和应用。

ACL configuration and application

实训步骤 Training steps

1. 将参加 ACL 配置和应用的人员分成若干小组，每组 3 人。
   Divide the people who participate in ACL configuration and application into groups of three.
2. 第一个人配置标准 ACL，并应用于限制网络流量。
   The first person configures a standard ACL and applies it to limit network traffic.
3. 第二个人配置扩展 ACL，并应用于报文过滤，预防网络攻击。
   The second person configures an extended ACL and applies it to message filtering to prevent network attacks.
4. 第三个人配置基于时间的 ACL，实现基于时间的访问控制。
   The third person configures a time-based ACL to implement time-based access control.
5. 实训结束，教师总结评价。
   The training ends. The teacher makes a summary and an evaluation.

第五部分 Part 5

单元小结 *Unit Summary*

cíyǔ
词语
Vocabulary

普通词语 General Vocabulary

1.	缩写	suōxiě	n.	abbreviation
2.	即	jí		mean
3.	告诉	gàosu	v.	tell
4.	头部	tóubù	n.	header
5.	这里	zhèlǐ	pron.	here
6.	预防	yùfáng	v.	prevent
7.	限制	xiànzhì	v.	limit
8.	提高	tí//gāo	v.	improve
9.	规则	guīzé	n.	rule
10.	需要	xūyào	n.	require
11.	相应	xiāngyìng	v.	correspond
12.	方向	fāngxiàng	n.	direction

cíyǔ
词语
Vocabulary

专业词语 Specialized Vocabulary

1.	访问控制列表	fǎngwèn kòngzhì lièbiǎo	phr.	Access Control List
2.	指令列表	zhǐlìng lièbiǎo	phr.	instruction list
3.	以太帧头部信息	yǐtàizhēn tóubù xìnxī	phr.	Ethernet frame header information
4.	报文头部信息	bàowén tóubù xìnxī	phr.	message header information
5.	网络攻击	wǎngluò gōngjī	phr.	network attack
6.	网络流量	wǎngluò liúliàng	phr.	network flow, network traffic
7.	网络性能	wǎngluò xìngnéng	phr.	network performance
8.	策略路由	cèlüè lùyóu	phr.	policy-based routing
9.	基本 ACL	jīběn ACL	phr.	basic ACL
10.	高级 ACL	gāojí ACL	phr.	advanced ACL
11.	设置规则	shèzhì guīzé	phr.	set a rule
12.	网络设备	wǎngluò shèbèi	phr.	network device
13.	指定接口	zhǐdìng jiēkǒu	phr.	specified interface
14.	指定方向	zhǐdìng fāngxiàng	phr.	specified direction

补充专业词语 Supplementary Specialized Vocabulary

1.	源端口	yuánduānkǒu	n.	source port
2.	目的端口	mùdì duānkǒu	phr.	destination port
3.	生效时间段	shēngxiào shíjiānduàn	phr.	effective time period
4.	执行命令	zhíxíng mìnglìng	phr.	execute a command
5.	启用	qǐyòng	v.	start using
6.	报文过滤	bàowén guòlǜ	phr.	message filtering

jùzi
句子
Sentences

1. 在“路由器”上单击右键，并点击“启动”，启动路由器。
2. 路由器启动后，双击路由器图标，进入路由器的命令行配置界面。
3. 访问控制列表有许多用途，比如预防网络攻击，限制网络流量，提高网络性能，实现策略路由等。
4. ACL 的使用：第一步是创建 ACL，根据需要设置相应的规则；第二步是将 ACL 应用到网络设备指定接口的指定方向 (in/out) 上。

8

Wǎngluò dìzhǐ zhuǎnhuàn
网络地址转换
Network Address Translation

dòngtài wǎngluò dìzhǐ zhuǎnhuàn de pèizhì bùzhòu
动态 网络 地址 转换 的配置 步骤
Configuration Steps of Dynamic Network Address Translation

```
<R2>
<R2>system
Enter system view, return user view with Ctrl+Z.
[R2]nat address-group 1 1.2.3.10 1.2.3.20
```

chuàngjiàn yí gè dìzhǐchí
创建 一个 地址池

Create an Address Pool

```
[R2]acl 2000
[R2-acl-basic-2000]rule permit source any
[R2-acl-basic-2000]quit
```

chuàngjiàn yí gè fǎngwèn kòngzhì lièbiǎo, zài fǎngwèn kòngzhì lièbiǎo
创建 一个 访问 控制 列表，在 访问 控制 列表
zhōng pèizhì xūyào jìnxíng dìzhǐ zhuǎnhuàn de yuándìzhǐ wǎngduàn
中 配置 需要 进行 地址 转换 的 源地址 网段

Create an Access Control List, and Configure the Source Address Network Segment that Needs Address Translation in the Access Control List

```
[R2]int GigabitEthernet 0/0/1
[R2-GigabitEthernet 0/0/1]nat outbound 2000 address-group 1
[R2-GigabitEthernet 0/0/1]quit
```

zài wàiwǎng jiēkǒu xià, jiāng pèizhì de dìzhǐchí hé fǎngwèn
在 外网 接口 下，将 配置 的地址池和 访问
kòngzhì lièbiǎo bǎngdìng
控制 列表 绑定

Bind the Configured Address Pool and Access Control List Together under the External Network Interface

```
[R2]display nat session all
 NAT Session Table Information:

  Portocol        : ICMP(1)
  SrcAddr   Vpn   : 192.168.1.1
  DestAddr  Vpn   : 1.2.3.254
  Type Code IcmpIP  : 0   8    43984
  NAT-Info
   New SrcAddr    : 1.2.3.16
   New DestAddr   : ----
   New IcmpId     : 10240

 Total : 1
```

nèibù zhǔjī yǔ gōnggòng wǎngluò tōngxìn shí, rúguǒ yuándìzhǐ
内部主机 与 公共 网络 通信 时，如果 源地址
mìngzhòng fǎngwèn kòngzhì lièbiǎo zhōng de dìzhǐ fànwéi, zé
命中 访问 控制 列表 中 的地址 范围，则
wǎngguān shèbèi huì cóng dìzhǐchí zhōng xuǎnzé yí gè kě yòng
网关 设备 会 从 地址池 中 选择一个 可 用
de dìzhǐ duì bàowén zhōng de yuándìzhǐ jìnxíng zhuǎnhuàn
的地址 对 报文 中 的 源地址 进行 转换

When an Internal Host Communicates with the Public Network, if the Source Address Hits the Address Range in the Access Control List, the Gateway Device will Select an Available Address from the Address Pool to Convert the Source Address in the Message

题解 Introduction

1. 学习内容：网络地址转换的基本知识与操作步骤、静态网络地址转换与动态网络地址转换的实现。
   Learning content: The basic knowledge and operation steps of network address translation, realization of static and dynamic network address translation
2. 知识目标：掌握网络地址转换相关的关键词语，了解汉字的偏旁“门”“疒”“冂”“车”“贝”，学写相关汉字。
   Knowledge objectives: To master the keywords for network address translation, understand the Chinese radicals “门”, “疒”, “冂”, “车”, “贝”, and learn to write the related Chinese characters
3. 技能目标：学会网络地址转换的操作步骤，实现私有地址间的通信。
   Skill objective: To master the operation steps of network address translation and realize communication between private addresses

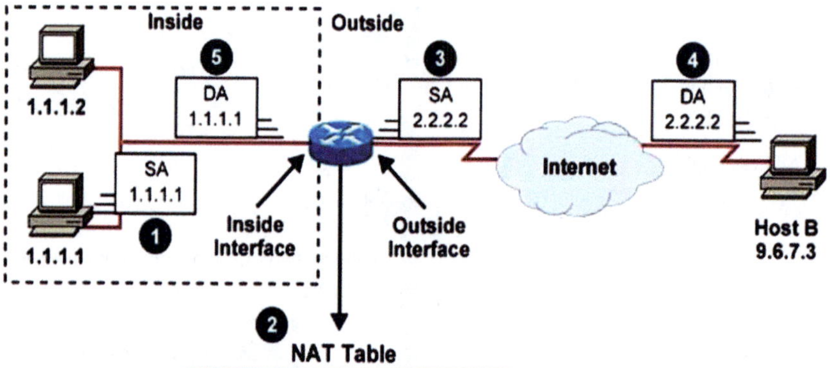

Inside Local IP Address	Inside Global IP Address
1.1.1.2 1.1.1.1	2.2.2.3 2.2.2.2

第一部分 Part 1

课文 Texts

一、热身 rèshēn Warm-up

1. 给下列描述选择对应的图片。Choose the corresponding pictures for the following descriptions.

nat address translation

A.

```
nat address port translation
```

B.

```
[Huawei]nat static
```

C.

```
[Huawei-GigabitEthernet0/0/0]nat outbound
```

D.

```
[Huawei]nat address-group
```

E.

```
[Huawei]display nat session
```

F.

wǎngluò dìzhǐ zhuǎnhuàn bǎngdìng
① 网络 地址 转换 绑定 ______
network address translation binding

jìngtài wǎngluò dìzhǐ zhuǎnhuàn
② 静态 网络 地址 转换 ______
static network address translation

wǎngluò dìzhǐ zhuǎnhuàn
③ 网络 地址 转换 ______
network address translation

wǎngluò dìzhǐ zhuǎnhuàn dìzhǐchí
④ 网络 地址 转换 地址池______
network address translation address pool

xiǎnshì wǎngluò dìzhǐ zhuǎnhuàn huìhuà
⑤ 显示 网络 地址 转换 会话______
displaying network address translation sessions

wǎngluò dìzhǐ duānkǒu zhuǎnhuàn
⑥ 网络 地址 端口 转换 ______
network address port translation

2. 观看介绍网络地址转换的应用场景的视频，将所给词语填入相应的位置。

Watch the video introducing the application scenarios of network address translation, and put the given words in the corresponding positions.

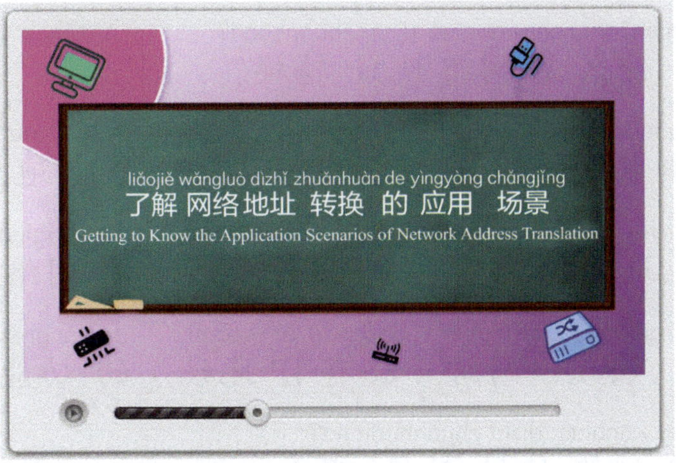

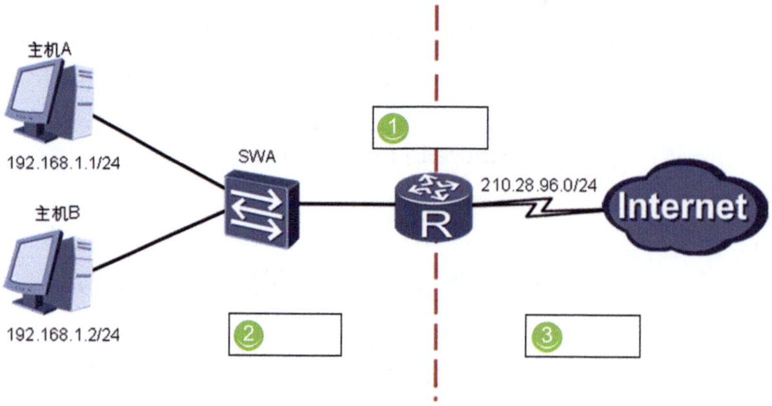

gōnggòng wǎngluò
A. 公共 网络
public network

wǎngguān shèbèi
B. 网关 设备
gateway device

sīyǒu wǎngluò
C. 私有 网络
private network

二、课文 kèwén Texts

A 08-01

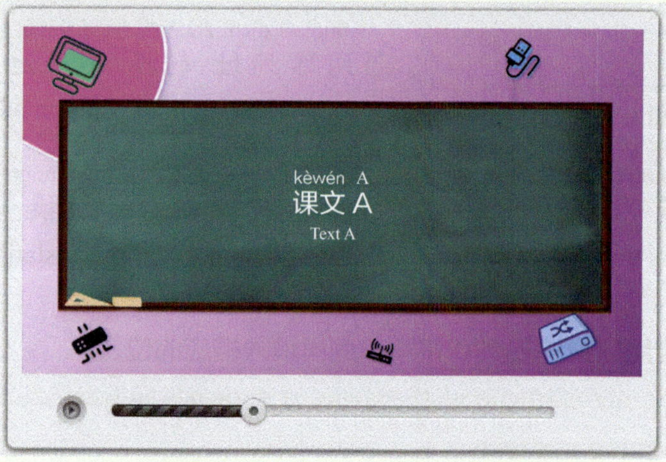

tútdì: Shīfu, qǐngwèn shénme shì wǎngluò dìzhǐ zhuǎnhuàn?
徒弟：师傅，请问 什么 是 网络 地址 转换？

shīfu: Wǎngluò dìzhǐ zhuǎnhuàn shì jiāng IP shùjùbào bàotóu zhōng de IP dìzhǐ zhuǎnhuàn wéi lìng yí gè IP dìzhǐ de guòchéng, zhǔyào yòngyú shíxiàn sīyǒu wǎngluò (sīyǒu IP dìzhǐ) fǎngwèn gōnggòng wǎngluò (gōngyǒu IP dìzhǐ) de gōngnéng.
师傅：网络 地址 转换 是 将 IP 数据报 报头 中 的 IP 地址 转换 为 另 一 个 IP 地址 的 过程，主要 用于 实现 私有 网络（私有 IP 地址）访问 公共 网络（公有 IP 地址）的 功能。

túdì: Wèi shénme xūyào wǎngluò dìzhǐ zhuǎnhuàn ne?
徒弟：为 什么 需要 网络 地址 转换 呢？

shīfu: Yīnwèi sīyǒu dìzhǐ bù néng zài gōngwǎng zhōng lùyóu, jí sīwǎng zhǔjī bù néng yǔ
师傅：因为私有地址不能在公网中路由，即私网主机不能与

gōngwǎng tōngxìn, yě bù néng tōngguò gōngwǎng yǔ lìngwài yí gè sīwǎng tōngxìn.
公网通信，也不能通过公网与另外一个私网通信。

Wǎngluò dìzhǐ zhuǎnhuàn kěyǐ jiějué sīyǒu dìzhǐ jiān de tōngxìn wèntí.
网络地址转换可以解决私有地址间的通信问题。

túdì: Wǎngluò dìzhǐ zhuǎnhuàn yìbān zài shénme shèbèi shang pèizhì ne?
徒弟：网络地址转换一般在什么设备上配置呢？

shīfu: Yìbān zài liánjiē sīwǎng hé gōngwǎng de wǎngguān shèbèi shang pèizhì.
师傅：一般在连接私网和公网的网关设备上配置。

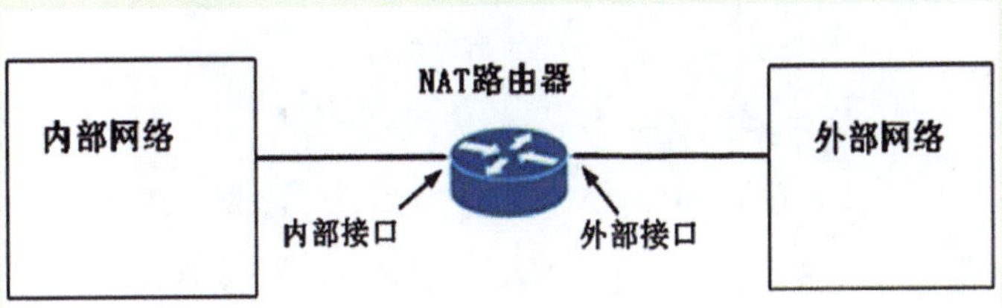

译文 yìwén Text in English

Apprentice: Master, what is network address translation?

Master: It is the process of converting the IP address in the IP datagram header into another IP address. It is mainly used to realize the function of private network (private IP address) accessing public network (public IP address).

Apprentice: Why is network address translation needed?

Master: Because a private address cannot be routed in the public network, that is, the host of the private network cannot communicate with the public network, nor can it communicate with another private network through the public network. Network address translation can solve the communication problem between private addresses.

Apprentice: What device is network address translation generally configured on?

Master: It is generally configured on the gateway device connecting private network and public network.

普通词语 pǔtōng cíyǔ General Vocabulary

08-02

访问	fǎngwèn	v.	access

专业词语 zhuānyè cíyǔ Specialized Vocabulary

08-03

1.	网络地址转换	wǎngluò dìzhǐ zhuǎnhuàn	phr.	network address translation (NAT)
2.	数据报	shùjùbào	n.	datagram
3.	报头	bàotóu	n.	header

4.	私有网络（私网）	sīyǒu wǎngluò (sīwǎng)	phr.	private network
5.	私有 IP 地址	sīyǒu IP dìzhǐ	phr.	private IP address
6.	公共网络（公网）	gōnggòng wǎngluò (gōngwǎng)	phr.	public network
7.	公有 IP 地址	gōngyǒu IP dìzhǐ	phr.	public IP address

B 08-04

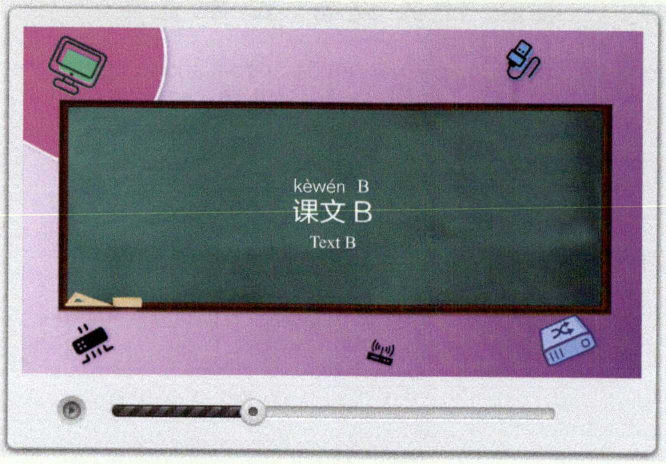

túdì: Shīfu, wǎngluò dìzhǐ zhuǎnhuàn rúhé shíxiàn?
徒弟：师傅，网络地址转换如何实现？

shīfu: Wǎngluò dìzhǐ zhuǎnhuàn yǒu duō zhǒng shíxiàn fāngshì, shìyòng yú bù tóng de chǎngjǐng. Cháng yòng de yǒu jìngtài wǎngluò dìzhǐ zhuǎnhuàn hé dòngtài wǎngluò dìzhǐ zhuǎnhuàn liǎng zhǒng fāngshì.
师傅：网络地址转换有多种实现方式，适用于不同的场景。常用的有静态网络地址转换和动态网络地址转换两种方式。

túdì: Shénme qíngkuàng xià shǐyòng jìngtài wǎngluò dìzhǐ zhuǎnhuàn?
徒弟：什么情况下使用静态网络地址转换？

shīfu: Rúguǒ xiǎng ràng wàibù wǎngluò shǐyòng yí gè zhǐdìng de gōngwǎng dìzhǐ fǎngwèn nèibù fúwùqì, kěyǐ shǐyòng jìngtài wǎngluò dìzhǐ zhuǎnhuàn.
师傅：如果想让外部网络使用一个指定的公网地址访问内部服务器，可以使用静态网络地址转换。

túdì: Dòngtài wǎngluò dìzhǐ zhuǎnhuàn rúhé shíxiàn?
徒弟：动态网络地址转换如何实现？

shīfu: Dòngtài wǎngluò dìzhǐ zhuǎnhuàn tōngguò shǐyòng dìzhǐchí lái shíxiàn, měi gè zhǔjī
师傅：动态网络地址转换通过使用地址池来实现，每个主机

dōu huì cóng dìzhǐchí zhōng fēndào yí gè línshí gōngwǎng dìzhǐ. Wǎngluò dìzhǐ duānkǒu
都会从地址池中分到一个临时公网地址。网络地址端口

zhuǎnhuàn yǔnxǔ duō gè nèibù dìzhǐ yìngshè dào tóng yí gè gōngyǒu dìzhǐ de bù tóng
转换允许多个内部地址映射到同一个公有地址的不同

duānkǒu, zhèyàng kěyǐ tígāo gōngwǎng dìzhǐ de lìyònglǜ.
端口，这样可以提高公网地址的利用率。

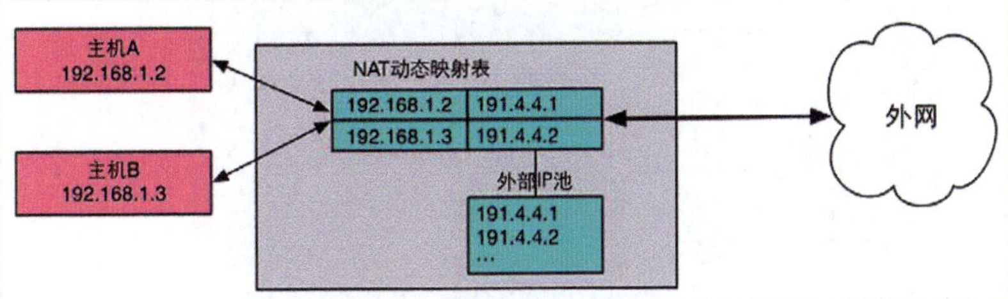

译文 yìwén Text in English

Apprentice: Master, how to implement network address translation?

Master: There are multiple ways to implement it, which are suitable for different scenarios. There are two common methods, namely static network address translation and dynamic network address translation.

Apprentice: Under what circumstances do we use static network address translation?

Master: If you want the external network to use a specified public network address to access the internal server, you can use static network address translation.

Apprentice: How can we implement dynamic network address translation?

Master: The dynamic network address translation is implemented through an address pool, and each host will be assigned a temporary public network address from the address pool. The network address port translation allows multiple internal addresses to be mapped to different ports of the same public address, which can improve the utilization ratio of the public network address.

普通词语 pǔtōng cíyǔ General Vocabulary

08-05

1.	适用于	shìyòng yú	phr.	be suitable for
2.	场景	chǎngjǐng	n.	scenario
3.	内部	nèibù	n.	interior
4.	临时	línshí	adj.	temporary

专业词语 zhuānyè cíyǔ Specialized Vocabulary

08-06

1.	映射	yìngshè	v.	map
2.	利用率	lìyònglǜ	n.	utilization ratio

三、视听说 shì-tīng-shuō Viewing, Listening, and Speaking

1. 观看介绍静态网络地址转换配置的视频，将指令与其对应的中文含义连线。

Watch the video introducing the configuration of static network address translation, and match the commands with their corresponding Chinese meanings.

①

[Huawei]interface GigabitEthernet0/0/1

[Huawei-GigabitEthernet0/0/1] ip address 192.168.1.254 24

②

[Huawei-GigabitEthernet0/0/1] interface Serial1/0/0

[Huawei -Serial1/0/0]ip address 210.28.96.2 24

③

[Huawei-Serial1/0/0]nat static global 210.28.96.1 inside 192.168.1.1

jìnrù Serial1/0/0 jiēkǒu shìtú bìng pèizhì IP dìzhǐ

A. 进入 Serial1/0/0 接口视图并配置 IP 地址

enter the Serial1/0/0 interface view and configure the IP address

jìnrù GigabitEthernet0/0/1 jiēkǒu shìtú bìng pèizhì IP dìzhǐ

B. 进入GigabitEthernet0/0/1 接口视图并配置 IP 地址

enter the GigabitEthernet0/0/1 interface view and configure the IP address

pèizhì sīyǒu IP dìzhǐ yǔ gōngyǒu IP dìzhǐ de yìngshè guānxì

C. 配置私有 IP 地址与公有 IP 地址的映射关系

configure the mapping between the private IP address and the public IP address

2. 说一说 **Let's talk**

说一说静态网络地址转换配置的步骤。

Talk about the configuration steps of static network address translation.

四、学以致用 xuéyǐzhìyòng Practicing What You Have Learnt

观看介绍动态网络地址转换配置的视频，并给配置步骤排序。

Watch the video introducing the configuration of dynamic network address translation, and put the configuration steps in order.

jìnrù fǎngwèn kòngzhì lièbiǎo pèizhì shìtú
A. [Huawei] acl 2000 进入 访问 控制 列表配置视图
Enter the ACL configuration view

chuàngjiàn dìzhǐchí
B. [Huawei] nat address-group 1 210.28.96.1 210.28.96.200 创建 地址池
Create an address pool

jìnrù jiēkǒu shìtú
C. [Huawei]interface serial 0/0/0 进入接口视图
Enter the interface view

xiǎnshì wǎngluò dìzhǐ zhuǎnhuàn pèizhì xìnxī
D. [Huawei]display nat outbound 显示 网络 地址 转换 配置信息
Display NAT configuration information

E. [Huawei -Serial1/0/0]nat outbound 2000 address-group 1 no-pat

jiāng fǎngwèn kòngzhì lièbiǎo yǔ dìzhǐchí bǎngdìng zài jiēkǒu xià
将 访问 控制 列表与地址池 绑定 在接口下
Bind the ACL and the address pool under the interface

F. [Huawei-acl-basic-2000]rule 5 permit source 192.168.1.0 0.0.0.255

pèizhì xūyào wǎngluò dìzhǐ zhuǎnhuàn de yuándìzhǐ wǎngduàn
配置需要网 络地址 转换 的源地址 网段
Configure the source address network segment that needs NAT

① ___ → ② ___ → ③ ___ → ④ ___ → ⑤ ___ → ⑥ ___

五、小知识 xiǎo zhīshi Tips

Lìyòng NAT bǎohù nèibù wǎngluò
利用 NAT 保护内部网络

NAT bùjǐn néng jiějué IP dìzhǐ bùzú de wèntí, érqiě hái nénggòu yǒuxiào de bìmiǎn
NAT 不仅能解决 IP 地址不足的问题，而且还能够有效地避免
láizì wǎngluò wàibù de gōngjī, yǐncáng bìng bǎohù wǎngluò nèibù de jìsuànjī. Yīnwèi jīng NAT
来自网络外部的攻击，隐藏并保护网络内部的计算机。因为经 NAT
zhuǎnhuàn hòu, nèibù zhǔjī de IP dìzhǐ yǐjīng zhuǎnhuàn, wàibù wǎngluò kàn bú dào nèibù zhǔ-
转换后，内部主机的 IP 地址已经转换，外部网络看不到内部主
jī de zhēnshí dìzhǐ. NAT shèbèi kàn qilai jiù xiàng yì tái fúwùqì, duìyú gōngjīzhě lái jiǎng,
机的真实地址。NAT 设备看起来就像一台服务器，对于攻击者来讲，
yào xiǎng tàncè nèibù wǎngluò jùyǒu yídìng de nándù, yīnwèi tā shǒuxiān xūyào gōngpò NAT
要想探测内部网络具有一定的难度，因为他首先需要攻破 NAT
shèbèi, zài gēnjù NAT shèbèi liánjiē dào nèibù wǎngluò jìnxíng pòhuài.
设备，再根据 NAT 设备连接到内部网络进行破坏。

Using NAT to Protect the Internal Network

NAT can not only solve the problem of insufficient IP addresses, but can also effectively prevent attacks from outside the network, hide and protect computers inside the network. Since the IP address of the internal host has been translated after NAT translation, the real address of the internal host cannot be seen by external networks. The NAT device looks like a server. For an attacker, it is difficult to detect the internal network, because he needs to break through the NAT device first, and then connect to the internal network through the NAT device to destroy the network.

补充专业词语 bǔchōng zhuānyè cíyǔ Supplementary Specialized Vocabulary

08-07

1.	源地址	yuándìzhǐ	n.	source address
2.	网段	wǎngduàn	n.	network segment
3.	绑定	bǎngdìng	v.	bind

第二部分 Part 2

汉字 Chinese Characters

一、汉字知识 Hànzì zhīshi Knowledge about Chinese Characters

汉字的偏旁（8） **Radicals of Chinese characters (8)**

偏旁 Radicals	例字 Examples	部件组合 Combinations	结构图示 Illustrations
门	问	门＋口	⿵
	闻	门＋耳	⿵
	间	门＋日	⿵
	闹	门＋市	⿵
疒	病	疒＋丙	⿸
	瘦	疒＋叟	⿸
冂	网	冂＋㐅㐅	⿵
	同	冂＋𠮛	⿵
	冈	冂＋㐅	⿵
车	辆	车＋两	⿰
	轻	车＋圣	⿰
	较	车＋交	⿰
	辅	车＋甫	⿰
贝	费	弗＋贝	⿱
	赛	𡨄＋贝	⿱
	贵	𠀐＋贝	⿱

二、汉字认读与书写 Hànzì rèndú yǔ shūxiě The Recognition and Writing of Chinese Characters

认读下列词语，并试着读写构成词语的汉字。

Recognize the following words, and try to read and write the Chinese characters forming these words.

访问　　痕迹　　网段　　转换　　比赛

访				问				痕				迹			
网				段				转				换			
比				赛											

第三部分 Part 3

日常用语 Daily Expressions

1. 我想也许将来我们可以合作。Wǒ xiǎng yěxǔ jiānglái wǒmen kěyǐ hézuò. I think we may be able to work together in the future.
2. 我们想把生意扩大到中国市场。Wǒmen xiǎng bǎ shēngyi kuòdà dào Zhōngguó shìchǎng. We are thinking of expanding our business into the Chinese market.

第四部分 Part 4

单元实训 Unit Practical Training

配置静态网络地址转换 pèizhì jìngtài wǎngluò dìzhǐ zhuǎnhuàn Configuring Static NAT

实训目的 Training purpose

了解静态网络地址转换的配置方法和步骤。

To learn about the configuration methods and steps of static NAT.

实训组织 Training organization

每组 3 人，选出一个组长。

Each group consists of three people, and a group leader is selected.

实训内容 Training content

配置静态网络地址转换

The configuration of static NAT

实训步骤 Training steps

1. 将参加实训的人员分成若干小组，每组 3 人。轮流上机操作与实践。
   Divide the trainees into groups of three and ask them to take turns operating and practicing on the computer.
2. 运行 eNSP 软件，新建拓扑如下图所示。
   Run the eNSP software and create a new topology as shown in the figure below.

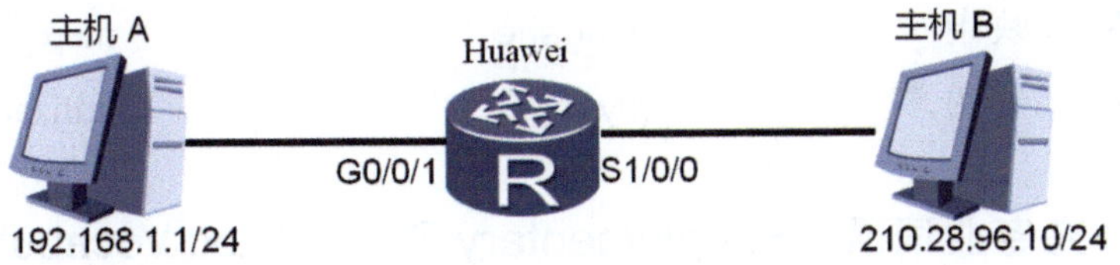

③ 路由器 Huawei 配置好接口地址。
Configure the interface address of Huawei router.

④ 在 Huawei 上配置静态网络地址转换。
Configure static network address translation on Huawei.

⑤ 查看配置。
View configuration.

⑥ 实训结束，教师总结评价。
The training ends. The teacher makes a summary and an evaluation.

第五部分 Part 5

单元小结 Unit Summary

cíyǔ
词语
Vocabulary

普通词语 General Vocabulary

1.	访问	fǎngwèn	v.	access
2.	适用于	shìyòng yú	phr.	be suitable for
3.	场景	chǎngjǐng	n.	scenario
4.	内部	nèibù	n.	interior
5.	临时	línshí	adj.	temporary

专业词语 Specialized Vocabulary

1.	网络地址转换	wǎngluò dìzhǐ zhuǎnhuàn	phr.	network address translation (NAT)
2.	数据报	shùjùbào	n.	datagram
3.	报头	bàotóu	n.	header
4.	私有网络（私网）	sīyǒu wǎngluò (sīwǎng)	phr.	private network
5.	私有 IP 地址	sīyǒu IP dìzhǐ	phr.	private IP address
6.	公共网络（公网）	gōnggòng wǎngluò (gōngwǎng)	phr.	public network
7.	公有 IP 地址	gōngyǒu IP dìzhǐ	phr.	public IP address

cíyǔ
词语
Vocabulary

8.	映射	yìngshè	v.	map
9.	利用率	lìyònglǜ	n.	utilization ratio

补充专业词语 Supplementary Specialized Vocabulary

1.	源地址	yuándìzhǐ	n.	source address
2.	网段	wǎngduàn	n.	network segment
3.	绑定	bǎngdìng	v.	bind

jùzi
句子
Sentences

1. 网络地址转换是将IP数据报报头中的IP地址转换为另一个IP地址的过程，主要用于实现私有网络访问公共网络的功能。
2. 网络地址转换常用的有静态网络地址转换和动态网络地址转换两种方式。
3. 如果想让外部网络使用一个指定的公网地址访问内部服务器，可以使用静态网络地址转换。
4. 动态网络地址转换通过使用地址池来实现。

9

Diǎn dào diǎn xiéyì PPP

点到点协议 PPP

Point-to-Point Protocol PPP

PPP pèizhì de cāozuò guòchéng

PPP 配置 的 操作 过程

Operation Process of PPP Configuration

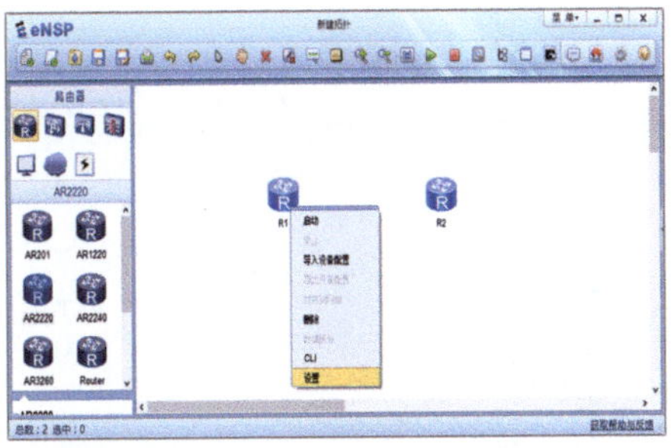

qǐdòng eNSP, fàngzhì lùyóuqì R1、R2

启动 eNSP, 放置 路由器 R1、R2

Start eNSP, Place Routers R1 and R2

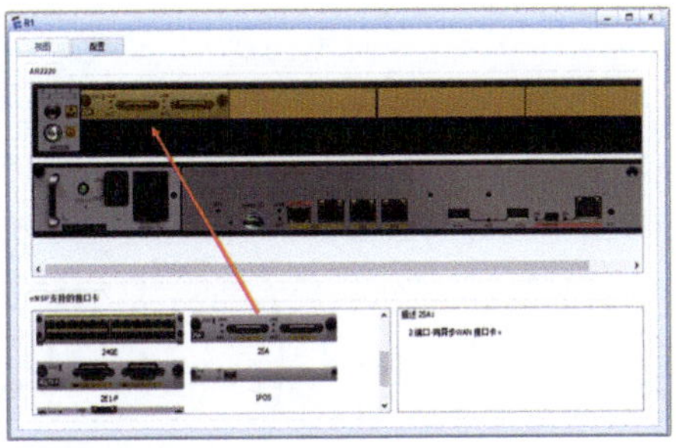

jiāng 2SA tuōdòng dào lùyóuqì R1、R2

将 2SA 拖动 到 路由器 R1、R2

Drag 2SA to Routers R1 and R2

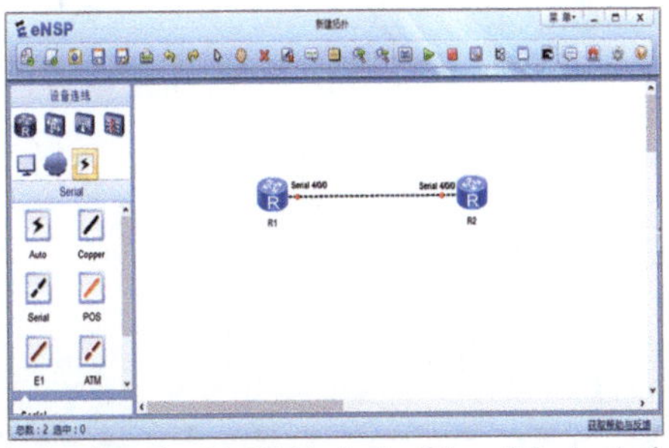

yòng chuànxíngxiàn liánjiē lùyóuqì R1、R2 de chuànxíng jiēkǒu

用 串行线 连接路由器 R1、R2 的 串行 接口

Connect the Serial Interfaces of Routers R1 and R2 with a Serial Cable

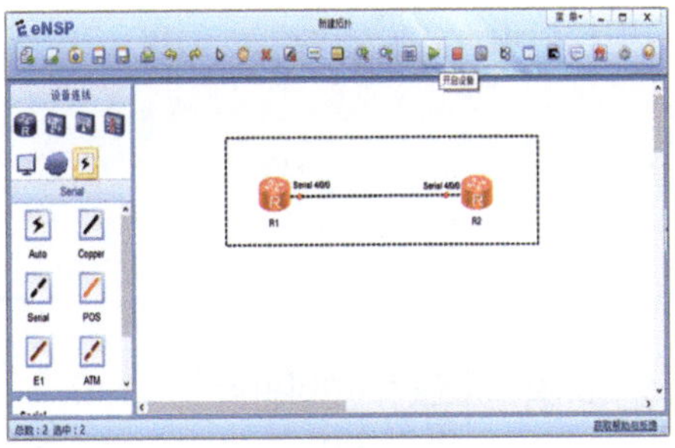

qǐdòng R1、R2

启动 R1、R2

Start R1 and R2

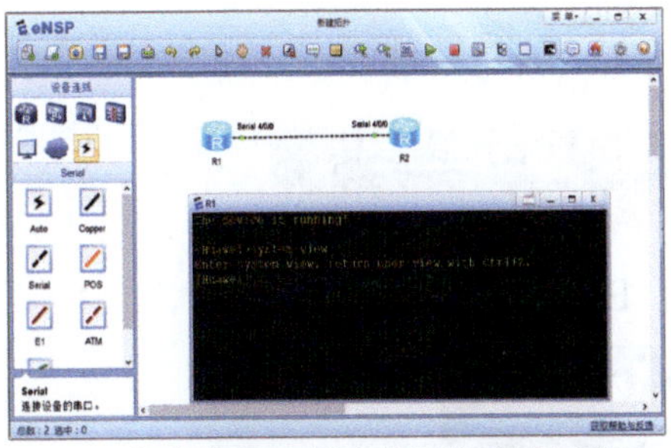

jìnrù xìtǒng shìtú kāishǐ pèizhì PPP

进入系统 视图 开始 配置 PPP

Enter the System View to Start PPP Configuration

题解 Introduction

1. 学习内容：PPP 的内涵和功能、串行接口的连接。
   Learning content: The connotation and functions of PPP, and the connection of serial interfaces
2. 知识目标：掌握 PPP 相关的关键词语，了解汉字的偏旁“耳”“欠”“冫”“彳”，学写相关汉字。
   Knowledge objectives: To master the keywords for PPP, understand the Chinese radicals “耳”, “欠”, “冫”, “彳”, and learn to write the related Chinese characters
3. 技能目标：学会两个网络之间串行口的连接，实现数据传输。
   Skill objective: To master the connection of serial ports between two networks and realize data transmission

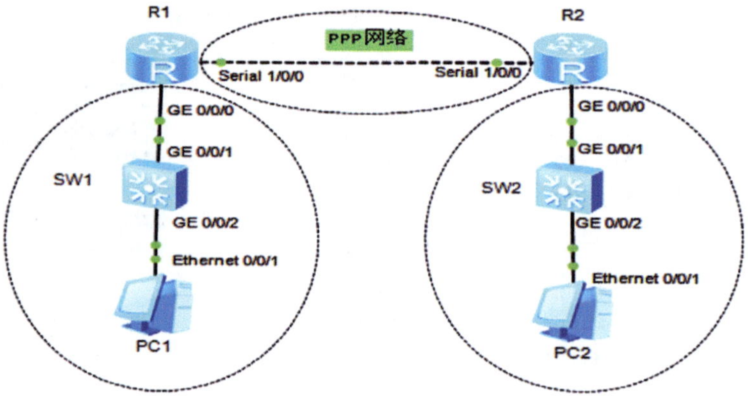

第一部分 Part 1

课文 Texts

一、热身 rèshēn Warm-up

1. 给词语选择对应的图片。 **Choose the corresponding pictures for the words.**

A.

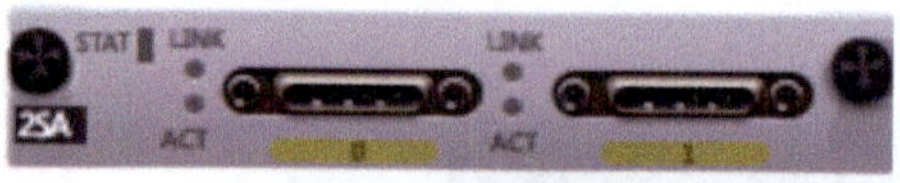

B.

C.

D.

E.

F.

PC jī shang de chuànxíng tōngxìn duānkǒu
① PC 机 上 的 串行 通信 端口
serial communication port on PC

RS-232C jiēkǒu
② RS-232C 接口
RS-232C interface

PCI zhuǎn chuànkǒukǎ COM kǒu、 RS232 9 zhēn shèbèi
③ PCI 转 串口卡 COM 口、RS232 9 针 设备
PCI to serial card COM port, RS232 9-pin device

eNSP liánjiē shèbèi de chuànkǒuxiàn
④ eNSP 连接设备的 串口线
eNSP serial port cable connecting equipment

AR2220 lùyóuqì
⑤ AR2220 路由器
AR2220 router

2SA: 2 duānkǒu WAN jiēkǒukǎ
⑥ 2SA：2 端口 WAN 接口卡
2SA: 2-port WAN interface card

2. 观看介绍 PPP 配置的操作视频，给操作过程排序。

Watch the video introducing the operation of PPP configuration and sequence the operation process.

Xuǎnzhòng liǎng tái lùyóuqì, diǎnjī "kāiqǐ shèbèi", qǐdòng suǒyǒu shèbèi.
A. 选中 两 台路由器，点击 "开启设备"，启动 所有 设备。
Select two routers and click "Turn on the Device" to start all the devices.

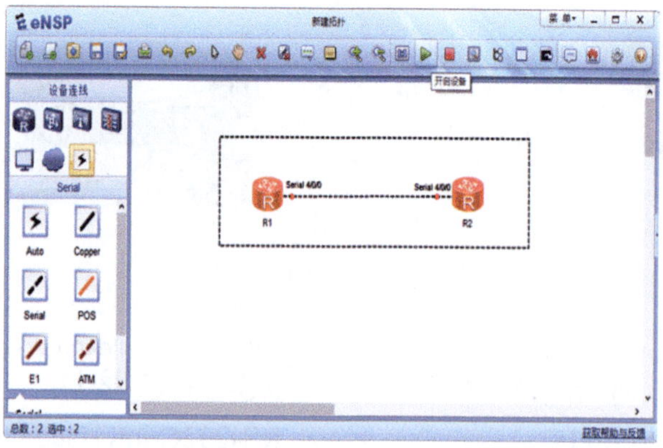

Yòng chuànxíngxiàn liánjiē liǎng tái lùyóuqì de Serial 4/0/0 jiēkǒu.
B. 用 串行线 连接 两 台路由器的 Serial 4/0/0 接口。
Connect the serial 4/0/0 interfaces of the two routers with a serial line.

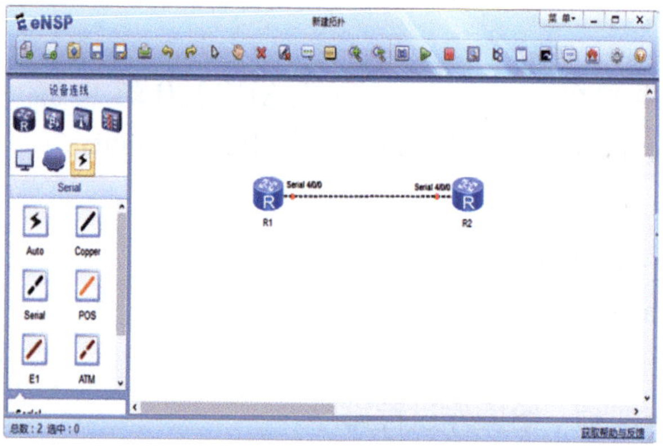

Jiāng 2SA tuōdòng dào lùyóuqì, yòng xiāngtóng de fāngfǎ shèzhì lùyóuqì R2.
C. 将 2SA 拖动 到路由器，用 相同 的方法 设置路由器 R2。
Drag 2SA to the router and set up router R2 in the same way.

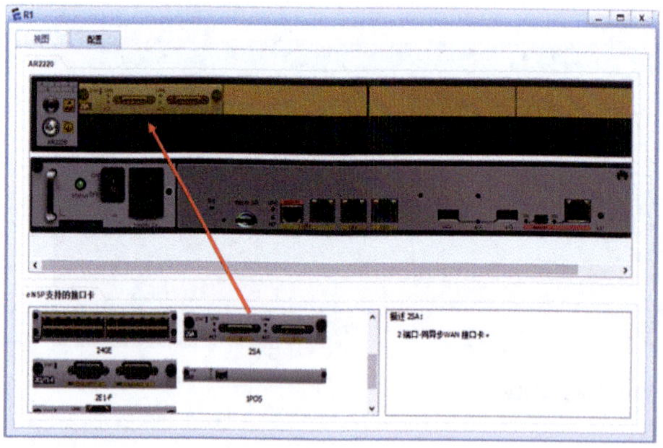

Suǒyǒu shèbèi qǐdòng hòu, shuāngjī lùyóuqì R1 túbiāo, jìnrù lùyóuqì de mìnglìngháng jièmiàn. Zài mìnglìngháng jièmiàn, shūrù system-view, jìnrù xìtǒng shìtú, jiù kěyǐ kāishǐ PPP de pèizhì le.
D. 所有设备 启动 后，双击 路由器 R1 图标，进入路由器的 命令行 界面。在命令行 界面，输入 system-view，进入系统视图，就可以开始 PPP 的配置了。

After starting all the devices, double-click the router R1 icon to enter the command line interface of the router. In the command line interface, enter *system-view* to enter the system view and start PPP configuration.

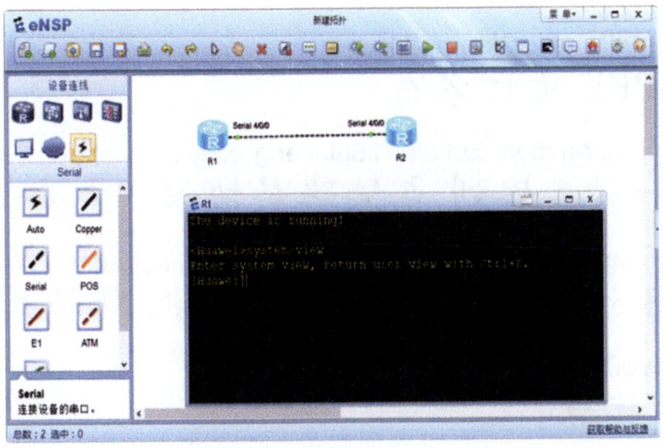

Qǐdòng eNSP, fàngzhì liǎng tái lùyóuqì, yòujī lùyóuqì R1 de "shèzhì".
E. 启动 eNSP，放置两台路由器，右击路由器 R1 的"设置"。
Start eNSP, place 2 routers, and right-click "Settings" of router R1.

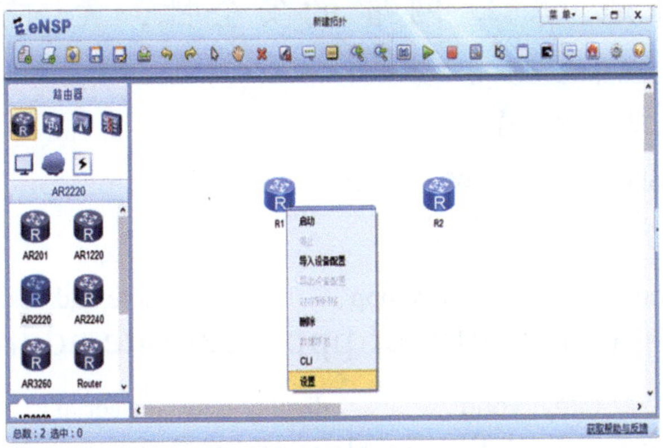

二、课文 kèwén Texts

A 09-01

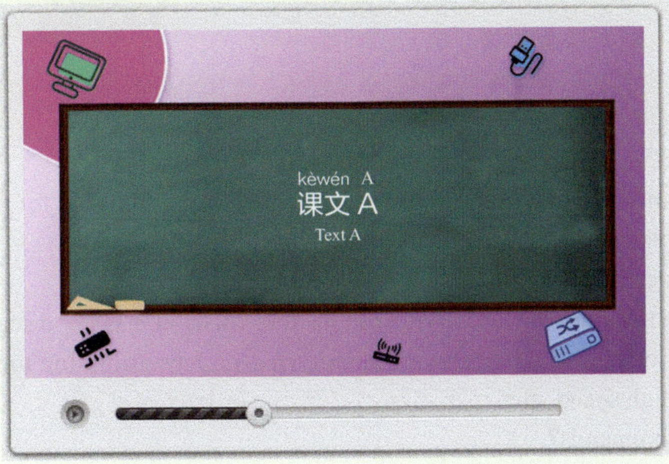

túdì: shīfu, qǐngwèn PPP shì shénme?
徒弟：师傅，请问 PPP 是什么？

shīfu: PPP xiéyì shì yì zhǒng diǎn dào diǎn liànlùcéng xiéyì, zhǔyào yòngyú zài quánshuānggōng de tóng-yìbù liànlù shang jìnxíng diǎn dào diǎn de shùjù chuánshū.
师傅：PPP 协议是一种点到点链路层协议，主要用于在全双工的同异步链路上进行点到点的数据传输。

túdì: Tā jùyǒu shénme yōudiǎn?
徒弟：它具有什么优点？

shīfu: Zhīchí tóngbù chuánshū、yìbù chuánshū, yǒu hěn hǎo de kuòzhǎnxìng, tígōng rènzhèng xiéyì lái gèng hǎo de bǎozhèng wǎngluò de ānquánxìng, wú chóngchuán jīzhì, wǎngluò kāixiāo xiǎo、sùdù kuài děng.
师傅：支持同步传输、异步传输，有很好的扩展性，提供认证协议来更好地保证网络的安全性，无重传机制，网络开销小、速度快等。

túdì: Tā de zhǔyào mìnglìng yǒu nǎ xiē?
徒弟：它的主要命令有哪些？

shīfu: Zhǔyào mìnglìng yǒu link-protocol ppp、remote address、ip address ppp-negotiate, kěyǐ yòng display interface serial chákàn jiéguǒ.
师傅：主要命令有 link-protocol ppp、remote address、ip address ppp-negotiate，可以用 display interface serial 查看结果。

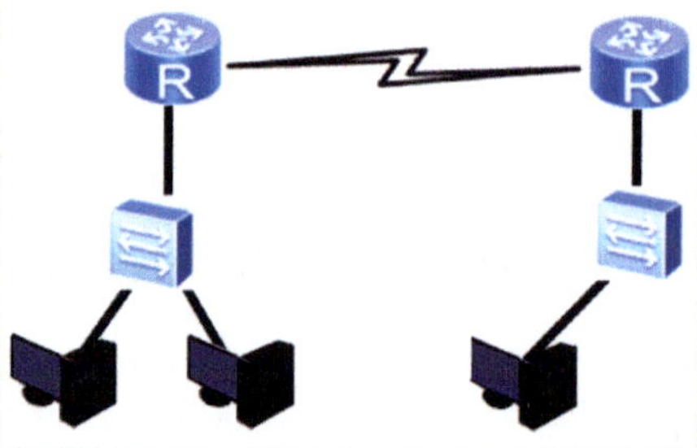

译文 yìwén Text in English

Apprentice: Master, what is PPP?

Master: The PPP protocol is a point-to-point link layer protocol, which is mainly used for point-to-point data transmission on full duplex synchronous and asynchronous links.

Apprentice: What advantages does it have?

Master: It supports synchronous transmission and asynchronous transmission, has good scalability, provides authentication protocol to better ensure network security, has no retransmission mechanism, low network overhead and high speed, etc.

Apprentice: What are its main commands?

Master: The main commands are *link-protocol ppp*, *remote address*, *ip address ppp-negotiate*. You can use *display interface serial* to view the results.

普通词语 pǔtōng cíyǔ General Vocabulary

09-02

1.	更好	gèng hǎo	phr.	better
2.	保证	bǎozhèng	v.	ensure
3.	无	wú	v.	be without
4.	小	xiǎo	adj.	small, low
5.	速度	sùdù	n.	speed
6.	快	kuài	adj.	fast
7.	结果	jiéguǒ	n.	result

专业词语 zhuānyè cíyǔ Specialized Vocabulary

09-03

1.	点到点	diǎn dào diǎn	phr.	point-to-point
2.	全双工	quánshuānggōng	n.	full duplex
3.	同异步链路	tóng-yìbù liànlù	phr.	synchronous and asynchronous link
4.	传输	chuánshū	v.	transmit
5.	同步	tóngbù	v.	(be) synchronous
6.	异步	yìbù	v.	(be) asynchronous
7.	扩展性	kuòzhǎnxìng	n.	scalability, expansibility
8.	认证协议	rènzhèng xiéyì	phr.	authentication protocol
9.	安全性	ānquánxìng	n.	security
10.	重传机制	chóngchuán jīzhì	phr.	retransmission mechanism
11.	网络开销	wǎngluò kāixiāo	phr.	network overhead

B

09-04

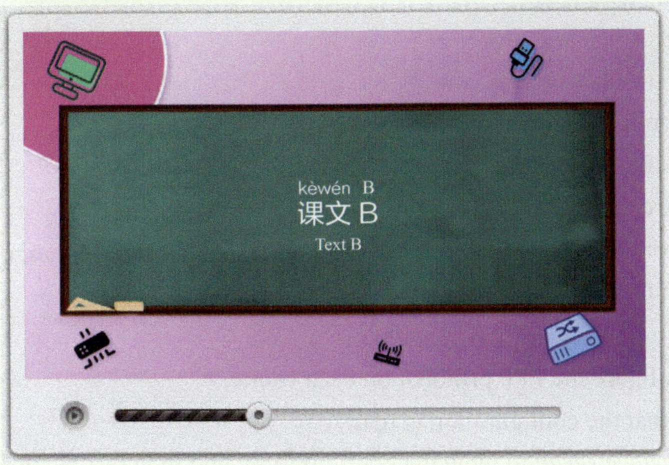

túdì: PPP zài shénme duānkǒu pèizhì ne?
徒弟：PPP在什么端口配置呢？

shīfu: Zài lùyóuqì de chuànxíng jiēkǒu shang pèizhì.
师傅：在路由器的串行接口上配置。

túdì: PPP xiéyì zěnme pèizhì ne?
徒弟：PPP协议怎么配置呢？

shīfu: Zài eNSP zhōng, huìzhì wǎngluò tuòpūtú, shǐyòng liǎng tái lùyóuqì, měi tái lùyóuqì tiānjiā chuànxíng jiēkǒu, ránhòu yòng chuànxíngxiàn liánjiē liǎng tái lùyóuqì.
师傅：在eNSP中，绘制网络拓扑图，使用两台路由器，每台路由器添加串行接口，然后用串行线连接两台路由器。

túdì: Ránhòu ne?
徒弟：然后呢？

shīfu: Qǐdòng lùyóuqì, zài měi tái lùyóuqì shang jìnxíng PPP xiéyì pèizhì.
师傅：启动路由器，在每台路由器上进行PPP协议配置。

túdì: Nà wǒmen zěnme cái néng zhīdào pèizhì hǎo le ne?
徒弟：那我们怎么才能知道配置好了呢？

shīfu: Wǒmen kěyǐ yòng Display interface serial chákàn pèizhì, ránhòu cèshì lùyóuqì zhījiān de liántōngxìng.
师傅：我们可以用Display interface serial查看配置，然后测试路由器之间的连通性。

译文 yìwén Text in English

Apprentice: What port is PPP configured on?

Master: It is configured on the serial interface of the router.

Apprentice: How do we configure the PPP protocol?

Master: In eNSP, draw the network topology diagram, use two routers, add a serial interface to each router, and then connect the two routers with a serial line.

Apprentice: And then?

Master: Start the routers and configure the PPP protocol on each router.

Apprentice: How can we know that the configuration is ready?

Master: We can use *Display interface serial* to view the configuration, and then test the connectivity between the routers.

专业词语 zhuānyè cíyǔ Specialized Vocabulary

09-06

1.	串行接口	chuànxíng jiēkǒu	phr.	serial interface
2.	串行线	chuànxíngxiàn	n.	serial line

三、视听说 shì-tīng-shuō Viewing, Listening, and Speaking

1. 观看介绍 PPP 协议配置的视频，将配置命令进行配对，并写出配对结果。

Watch the video introducing PPP protocol configuration, match the configuration commands with their meanings, and write the matching results.

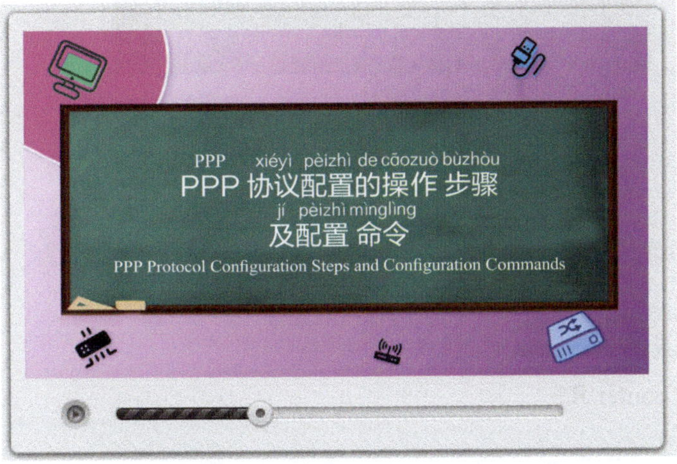

lùyóuqì de pèizhì
(1) 路由器的配置
the configuration of routers

lùyóuqì R1 de pèizhì
① 路由器 R1 的配置
the configuration of router R1

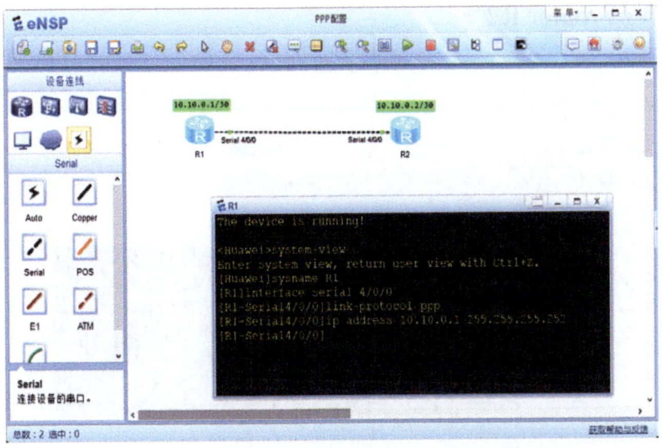

lùyóuqì R2 de pèizhì
② 路由器 R2 的配置
the configuration of router R2

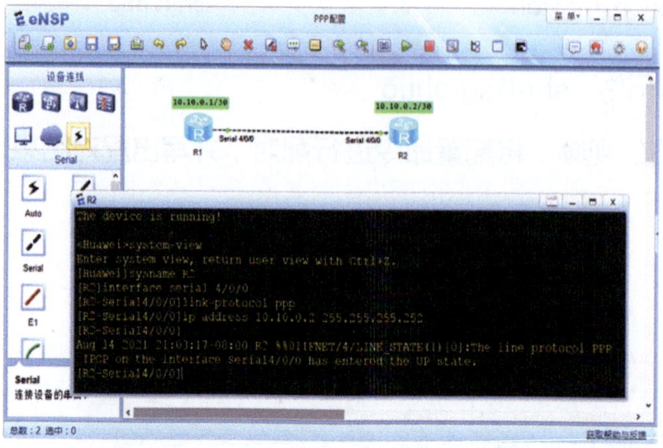

chákàn pèizhì jiéguǒ
（2）查看配置结果
view the configuration results

lùyóuqì R1 de pèizhì jiéguǒ
① 路由器 R1 的配置结果
the configuration result of router R1

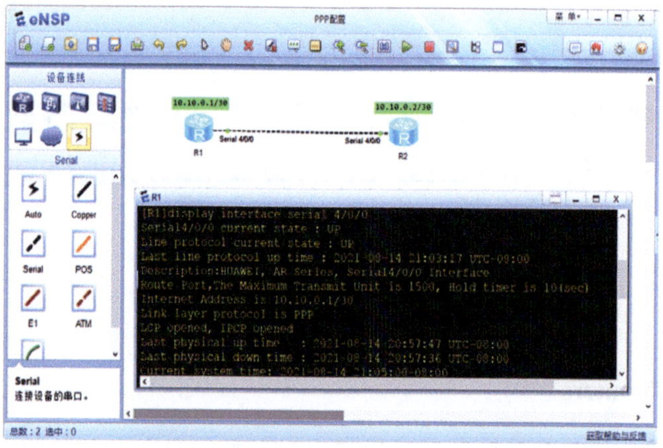

lùyóuqì R2 de pèizhì jiéguǒ
② 路由器 R2 的配置结果
the configuration result of router R2

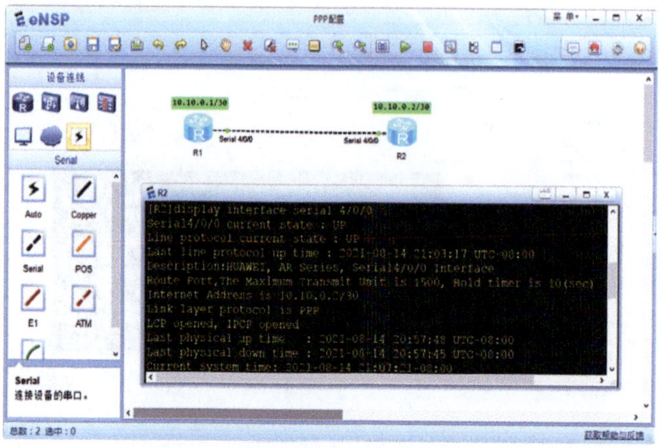

jìnrù chuànxíng jiēkǒu mìnglìng
① 进入 串行 接口 命令
Command for entering the serial interface

A. link-protocol ppp

pèizhì jiēkǒu de IP dìzhǐ mìnglìng
② 配置接口的 IP 地址 命令
Command for configuring the IP address of the interface

B. ping 10.10.0.2

lùyóuqì pèizhì PPP xiéyì
③ 路由器配置 PPP 协议
Configuring the PPP protocol for the router

C. interface serial 4/0/0

chákàn pèizhì jiéguǒ mìnglìng
④ 查看配置结果 命令
Command for viewing the configuration results

D. ip address 10.10.0.1 255.255.255.252

cèshì jiéguǒ mìnglìng
⑤ 测试结果 命令
Command for the test result

E. display interface serial 4/0/0

Pèiduì jiéguǒ:
配对结果：
Pairing results:

① ________ ② ________ ③ ________ ④ ________ ⑤ ________

2. 说一说 Let's talk

说一说 PPP 协议的配置步骤。 **Talk about the configuration steps of the PPP protocol.**

四、学以致用 xuéyǐzhìyòng Practicing What You Have Learnt

观看介绍 R1、R2 串行接口配置过程的视频，选择需要的正确命令。

Watch the video introducing the configuration process of R1 and R2 serial interfaces and select the correct commands required.

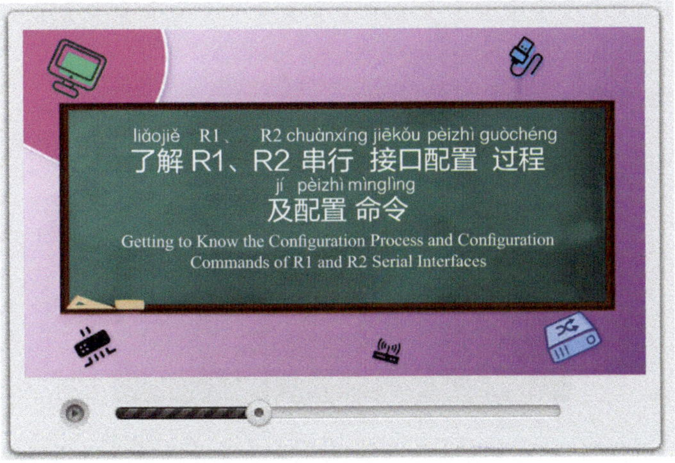

Rú tú suǒ shì, liǎng tái lùyóuqì R1、 R2 yòng chuànxíngxiàn liánjiē, lùyóuqì R2 de chuànkǒu IP dìzhǐ yóu lùyóuqì R1 tígōng.
如图所示，两台路由器R1、R2用串行线连接，路由器R2的串口IP地址由路由器R1提供。

As shown in the figure, two routers R1 and R2 are connected by a serial line, and the serial port IP address of router R2 is provided by router R1.

Lùyóuqì R1、 R2 yòng chuànxíngxiàn liánjiē chuànxíng jiēkǒu, lùyóuqì R1 de IP dìzhǐ wéi 10.10.0.1/30, lùyóuqì R2 de IP dìzhǐ yóu R1 tígōng, R2 de IP dìzhǐ wéi 10.10.0.2.
路由器R1、R2用串行线连接串行接口，路由器R1的IP地址为10.10.0.1/30，路由器R2的IP地址由R1提供，R2的IP地址为10.10.0.2。

Connect the serial interfaces of routers R1 and R2 with a serial line. The IP address of router R1 is 10.10.0.1/30, the IP address of router R2 is provided by R1, and the IP address of R2 is 10.10.0.2.

lùyóuqì R1 de pèizhì
（1）路由器R1的配置

Configuration of router R1

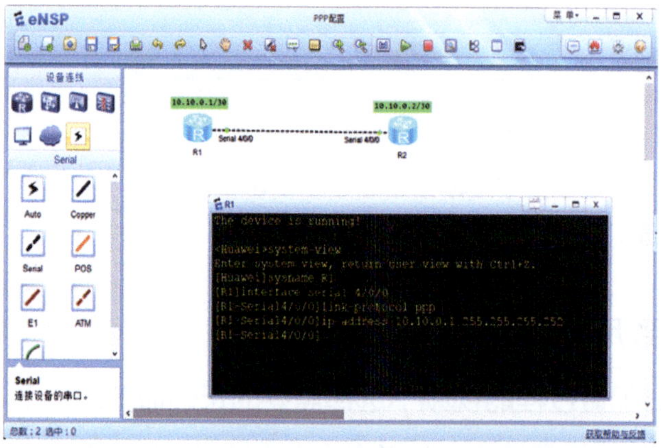

lùyóuqì R2 de pèizhì
（2）路由器R2的配置

Configuration of router R2

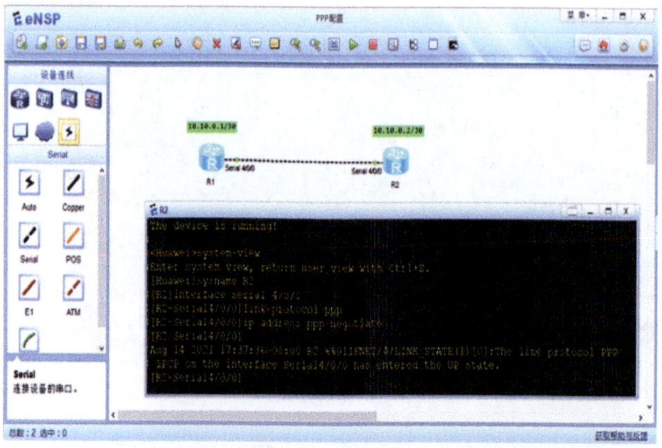

Zài lùyóuqì R1 shang zhǐdìng fēnpèi gěi lùyóuqì R2 de Serial 4/0/0 jiēkǒu de IP dìzhǐ wéi 10.10.0.2,
① 在路由器 R1 上 指定分配给路由器 R2的 Serial 4/0/0 接口的 IP 地址为 10.10.0.2，
mìnglìng shì
命令是____________ The command to specify the IP address assigned to the Serial 4/0/0 interface of router R2 on router R1 as 10.10.0.2 is__________

Lùyóuqì R2 de IP dìzhǐ, xīwàng yóu Lùyóuqì R1 de duìduān jiēkǒu fēnpèi de mìnglìng shì
② 路由器R2的IP地址，希望由路由器R1的对端接口分配的命令是__________

The command that the IP address of router R2 to be assigned by the peer side interface of R1 is__________

A. display interface serial

B. link-protocol ppp

C. remote address

D. ip address ppp-negotiate

五、小知识 xiǎo zhīshi Tips

Chuànxíng shùjù chuánsòng de tèdiǎn
串行数据传送的特点

Chuànxíng shùjù chuánsòng de tèdiǎn shì: Shùjù chuánsòng àn wèi shùnxù jìnxíng, zuì shǎo zhǐ xūyào yì gēn chuánshūxiàn jí kě wánchéng, jiéshěng chuánshūxiàn; chuánshū jùlí cháng, kě dádào shù qiān qiānmǐ; chuànxíng tōngxìn de kàng gānrǎo nénglì shífēn qiángdà, qí xìnhào jiān de hùxiāng gānrǎo wánquán kěyǐ hūlüè. PC jī shang de chuànxíng jiēkǒu de míngchēng yǒu duō zhǒng shuōfǎ: 232 kǒu、chuànkǒu、tōngxìnkǒu、COM kǒu、yìbùkǒu děng.

串行数据传送的特点是：数据传送按位顺序进行，最少只需要一根传输线即可完成，节省传输线；传输距离长，可达到数千千米；串行通信的抗干扰能力十分强大，其信号间的互相干扰完全可以忽略。PC机上的串行接口的名称有多种说法：232口、串口、通信口、COM口、异步口等。

Characteristics of Serial Data Transmission

The characteristics of serial data transmission are as follows: data transmission is carried out in bit order, which can be completed with a minimum of one transmission line, thus saving transmission lines. It boasts of long transmission distance, up to thousands of kilometers. The anti-interference ability of serial communication is very strong, and the mutual interference between its signals can be completely ignored. There are many names of the serial interface on PCs: 232 port, serial port, communication port, COM port, asynchronous port, etc.

补充专业词语 bǔchōng zhuānyè cíyǔ Supplementary Specialized Vocabulary

01-07

1.	串行数据	chuànxíng shùjù	phr.	serial data
2.	异步口	yìbùkǒu	n.	asynchronous port

第二部分 Part 2

汉字 Chinese Characters

一、汉字知识 Hànzì zhīshi Knowledge about Chinese Characters

汉字的偏旁（9） **Radicals of Chinese characters (9)**

偏旁 Radicals	例字 Examples	部件组合 Combinations	结构图示 Illustrations
耳	聊	耳＋卯	
	职	耳＋只	
	取	耳＋又	
	联	耳＋关	
欠	歌	哥＋欠	
	歉	兼＋欠	
	欢	又＋欠	
冫	冷	冫＋令	
	准	冫＋隹	
	次	冫＋欠	
彳	行	彳＋亍	
	得	彳＋㝵	
	律	彳＋聿	
	很	彳＋艮	

二、汉字认读与书写 Hànzì rèndú yǔ shūxiě The Recognition and Writing of Chinese Characters

认读下列词语，并试着读写构成词语的汉字。

Recognize the following words, and try to read and write the Chinese characters forming these words.

冷接子　　命令行　　聚合　　逻辑

冷				接				子				命			
令				行				聚				合			
逻				辑											

第三部分 Part 3

日常用语 *Daily Expressions*

1. 我们很乐意帮忙。Wǒmen hěn lèyì bāngmáng. We are happy to be of help.
2. 我保证通力合作。Wǒ bǎozhèng tōnglì hézuò. I can assure you of our full cooperation.
3. 所有这些产品都是我们的畅销货。Suǒyǒu zhèxiē chǎnpǐn dōu shì wǒmen de chàngxiāohuò. All these articles are our bestsellers.

第四部分 Part 4

单元实训 *Unit Practical Training*

配置 PPP pèizhì PPP Configuring PPP

实训目的 Training purpose

掌握 PPP 协议配置步骤，并能独立完成配置，让路由器之间能互相通信，培养团队合作精神和竞争意识。

To master the PPP protocol configuration steps, and be able to complete the configuration independently to enable routers to communicate with each other, and cultivate teamwork spirit and competitive consciousness.

实训组织 Training organization

每组 3 ～ 5 人，选出一个组长。

Each group consists of 3-5 people, and a group leader is selected.

实训内容 Training content

配置两台路由器的 PPP。

Configuring the PPP of two routers.

实训步骤 Training steps

1. 宣布比赛规则及要求：每组每人可以多次操作，安排专人记录每位同学操作所花费的时间，其他组同学监督。

   Announce the competition rules and requirements: Each group member can operate for many times. A student is specially assigned to record the time each student takes to operate, and students of other groups supervise.

2. 开始比赛。

   Start the competition.

   第一个人绘制网络拓扑图。

   The first person draws the network topology diagram.

   第二个人启动设备，配置 R1 的 PPP。

   The second person starts the device and configures the PPP of R1.

   第三个人配置 R2 的 PPP，显示 R1、R2 配置结果，并测试两台路由器的连通性。

   The third person configures the PPP of R2, displays the configuration results of R1 and R2, and tests the connectivity of the two routers.

3. 计算每组同学总共花费的时间及得分，老师总结评价。

   Calculate the total time and score of each group, and the teacher makes a summary and an evaluation.

第五部分 Part 5

单元小结 Unit Summary

cíyǔ
词语
Vocabulary

普通词语 General Vocabulary

1.	更好	gèng hǎo	phr.	better
2.	保证	bǎozhèng	v.	ensure
3.	无	wú	v.	be without
4.	小	xiǎo	adj.	small, low
5.	速度	sùdù	n.	speed
6.	快	kuài	adj.	fast
7.	结果	jiéguǒ	n.	result

专业词语 Specialized Vocabulary

1.	点到点	diǎn dào diǎn	phr.	point-to-point
2.	全双工	quánshuānggōng	n.	full duplex
3.	同异步链路	tóng-yìbù liànlù	phr.	synchronous and asynchronous link
4.	传输	chuánshū	v.	transmit
5.	同步	tóngbù	v.	(be) synchronous
6.	异步	yìbù	v.	(be) asynchronous
7.	扩展性	kuòzhǎnxìng	n.	scalability, expansibility
8.	认证协议	rènzhèng xiéyì	phr.	authentication protocol
9.	安全性	ānquánxìng	n.	security
10.	重传机制	chóngchuán jīzhì	phr.	retransmission mechanism
11.	网络开销	wǎngluò kāixiāo	phr.	network overhead
12.	串行接口	chuànxíng jiēkǒu	phr.	serial interface
13.	串行线	chuànxíngxiàn	n.	serial line

补充专业词语 Supplementary Specialized Vocabulary

1.	串行数据	chuànxíng shùjù	phr.	serial data
2.	异步口	yìbùkǒu	n.	asynchronous port

jùzi
句子
Sentences

1. PPP 协议是一种点到点链路层协议，主要用于在全双工的同异步链路上进行点到点的数据传输。
2. PPP 支持同步传输、异步传输，有很好的扩展性，提供认证协议来更好地保证网络的安全性，无重传机制，网络开销小、速度快。
3. PPP 在路由器的串行接口上配置。在 eNSP 中，绘制网络拓扑图，使用两台路由器，每台路由器添加串行接口，然后用串行线连接两台路由器。
4. 启动路由器，在每台路由器上进行 PPP 协议配置。可以用 Display interface serial 查看配置，然后测试路由器之间的连通性。

10

Wǎngluò guǎnlǐ

网络管理

Network Management

wǎngluò guǎnlǐ xìtǒng ruǎnjiàn gōngjù de gōngnéng

网络 管理 系统 软件 工具的 功能

Functions of Software Tools of Network Management System

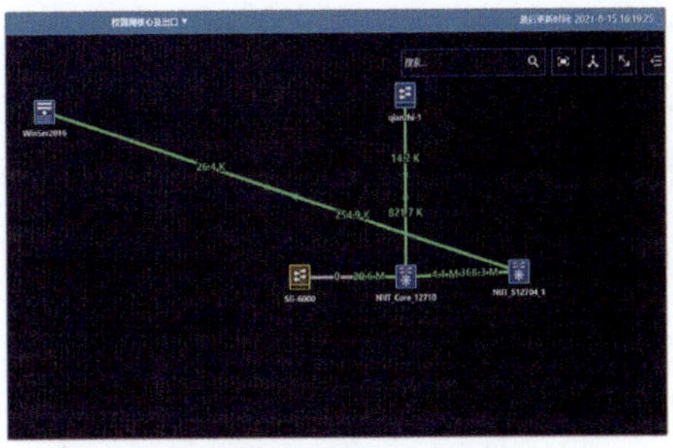

wǎngluò tuòpūtú de xiǎnshì

网络 拓扑图的 显示

Display of Network Topology Diagram

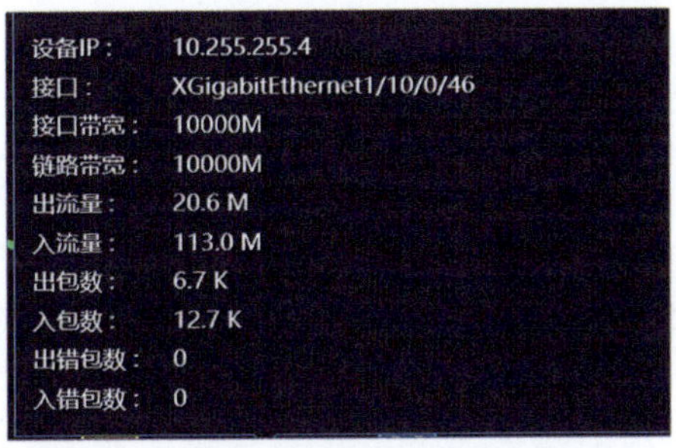

wǎngluò shèbèi duānkǒu zhuàngtài de jiānshì yǔ fēnxī

网络 设备 端口 状态 的监视与分析

Monitoring and Analysis of Network Equipment Port Status

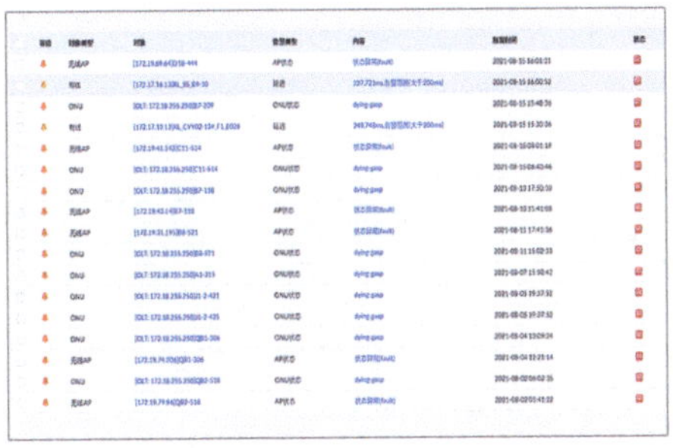

wǎngluò xìngnéng shùjù de jiānshì yǔ fēnxī

网络 性能 数据的监视与分析

Monitoring and Analysis of Network Performance Data

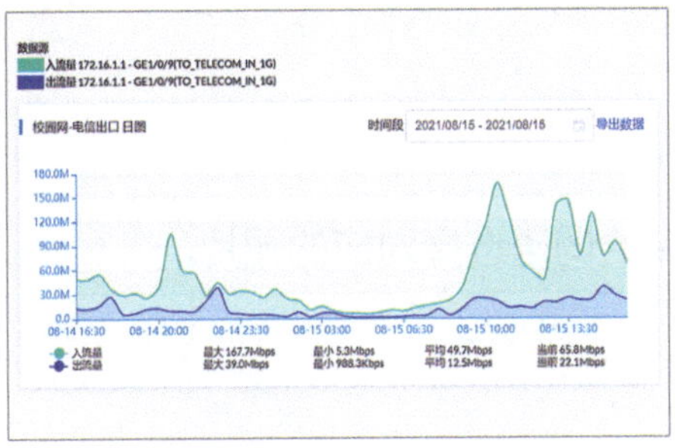

gùzhàng de bàojǐng yǔ zhěnduàn

故障 的 报警 与 诊断

Fault Alarm and Diagnosis

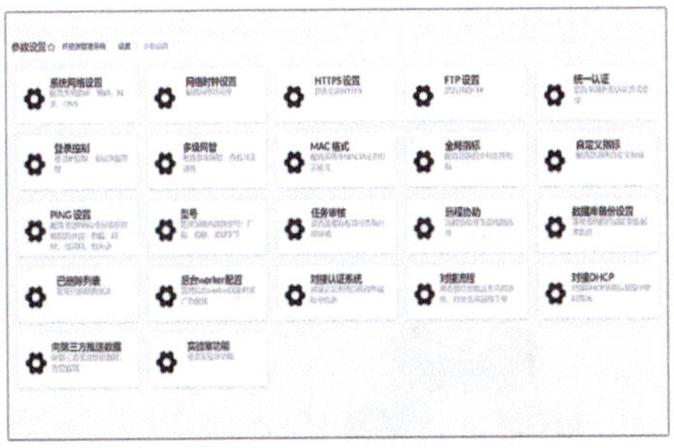

yuǎnchéng pèizhì

远程 配置

Remote Configuration

题解 Introduction

1. 学习内容：网络管理的基本知识与操作步骤，网络拓扑、设备状态和告警信息的查看。
   Learning content: The basic knowledge and operation steps of network management, the viewing of network topology, device status and alarm information
2. 知识目标：掌握网络管理相关的关键词语，了解汉字的偏旁“穴”“田”“力”“牛”，学写相关汉字。
   Knowledge objectives: To master the keywords for network management, understand the Chinese radicals “穴”,“田”,“力”,“牛”, and learn to write the related Chinese characters
3. 技能目标：学会网络管理的操作步骤，提高网络管理效率。
   Skill objective: To master the operation steps of network management and improve network management efficiency

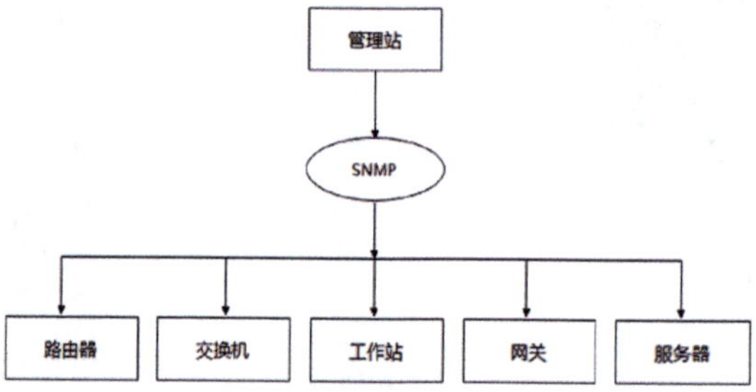

第一部分 Part 1

课文 Texts

一、热身 rèshēn Warm-up

1. 给词语选择对应的图片。 **Choose the corresponding pictures for the words.**

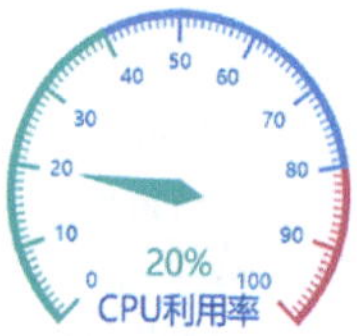

A.

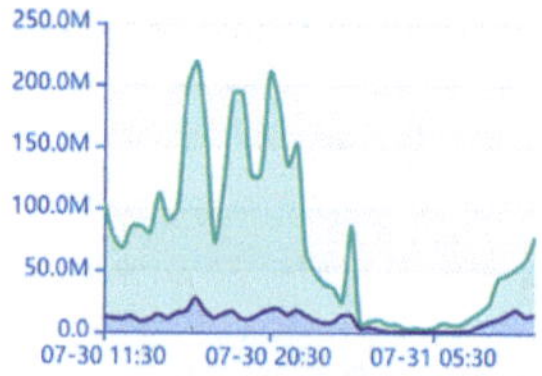

B.

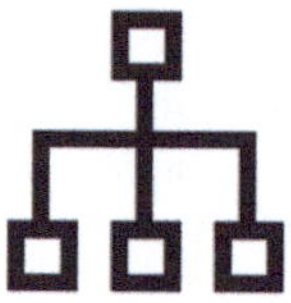

C.

D.

E.

F.

shèbèi guǎnlǐ
① 设备管理________________
device management

tuòpū guǎnlǐ
② 拓扑管理________________
topology management

gàojǐng guǎnlǐ
③ 告警管理________________
warning management

wǎngluò shèzhì
④ 网络设置________________
network setting

liúliàng
⑤ 流量________________
traffic

CPU lìyònglǜ
⑥ CPU利用率________________
CPU utilization ratio

2. 观看介绍网络管理系统的统计信息总览的视频，为下列描述选择对应的图片。

Watch the video introducing the statistical information overview of the network management system, and choose the corresponding pictures for the following descriptions.

A.

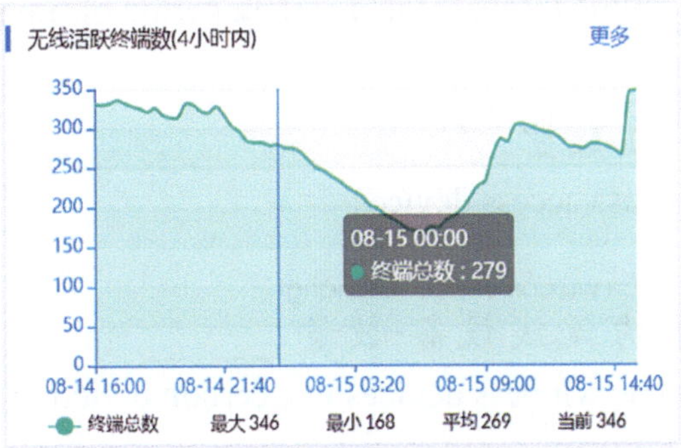

B.

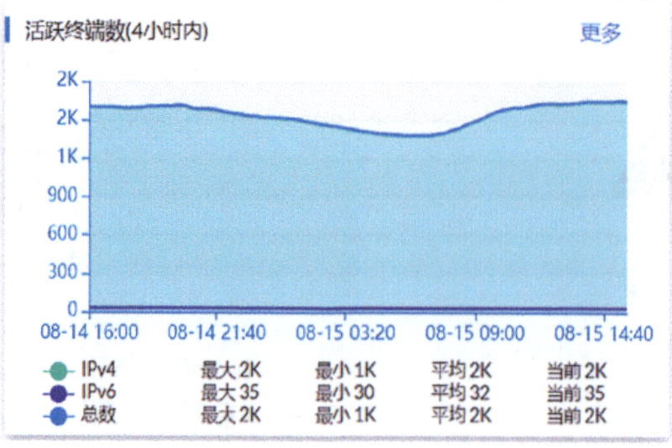

C.

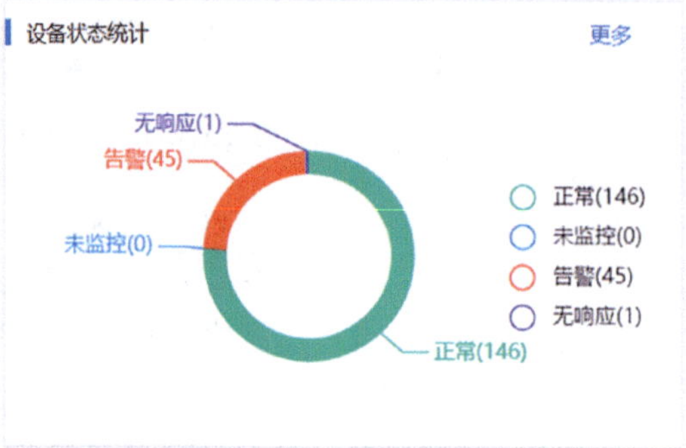

D.

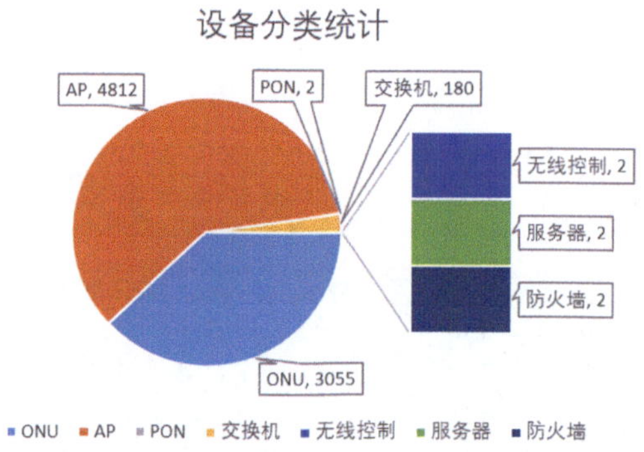

dāngqián zhèngcháng de shèbèi shùliàng

① 当前　正常　的设备 数量 ______

The current number of normal devices

mǒu shíduàn nèi zàixiàn de zuì dà zhōngduān shùliàng

② 某 时段 内在线的最大 终端　数量 ______

The maximum number of online terminals in a certain period of time

dāngqián wúxiàn jiērù shèbèi de shùliàng

③ 当前 无线接入设备的 数量 ______

The current number of wireless access devices

mǒu shíduàn nèi zàixiàn de píngjūn wúxiàn shèbèi shùliàng

④ 某 时段 内在线的平均无线设备 数量 ______

The average number of online wireless devices in a certain period of time

二、课文 kèwén Texts

A 10-01

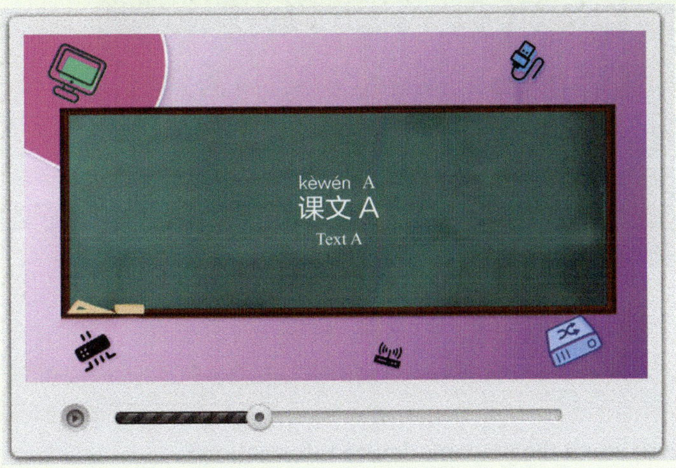

túdì: Shīfu, qǐngwèn rúhé liǎojiě wǎngluò shèbèi xìnxī?
徒弟：师傅，请问如何了解网络设备信息？

shīfu: Tōngguò wǎngluò guǎnlǐ ruǎnjiàn kěyǐ jiāncè wǎngluò zhōng suǒyǒu de shèbèi xìnxī.
师傅：通过网络管理软件可以监测网络中所有的设备信息。

túdì: Zěnme cāozuò ne?
徒弟：怎么操作呢？

shīfu: Shǒuxiān, dǎkāi wǎngluò guǎnlǐ ruǎnjiàn; ránhòu, zài diànnǎo píngmù shang kěyǐ shíshí xiǎnshì wǎngluò de tuòpūtú. Zài tuòpūtú zhōng kěyǐ kàndào wǎngluò shèbèi de túbiāo, rú lùyóuqì、jiāohuànjī de túbiāo děng.
师傅：首先，打开网络管理软件；然后，在电脑屏幕上可以实时显示网络的拓扑图。在拓扑图中可以看到网络设备的图标，如路由器、交换机的图标等。

túdì: Xià yí bù ne?
徒弟：下一步呢？

shīfu: Zuìhòu, yòng shǔbiāo dānjī mǒu gè shèbèi túbiāo, yǐ xià tú zhōng de shèbèi XL_ZZL_1F_S5720 wéi lì, túbiāo biān shang huì zìdòng xiǎnshì gāi shèbèi de míngchēng、IP dìzhǐ、ānfàng wèizhì、gōngzuò zhuàngtài、CPU lìyònglǜ hé nèicún lìyònglǜ. Zhèyàng, wǒmen jiù liǎojiě dào le wǎngluò shèbèi xìnxī.
师傅：最后，用鼠标单击某个设备图标，以下图中的设备XL_ZZL_1F_S5720为例，图标边上会自动显示该设备的名称、IP地址、安放位置、工作状态、CPU利用率和内存利用率。这样，我们就了解到了网络设备信息。

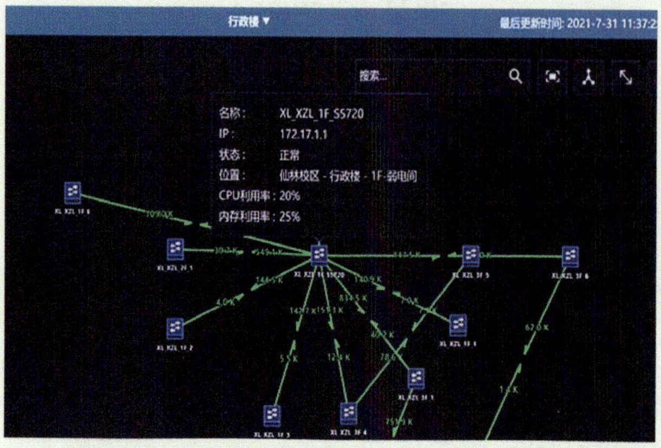

译文 yìwén Text in English

Apprentice: Master, how do I learn about the network device information?

Master: You can use the network management software to monitor the information of all the devices on the network.

Apprentice: How do I operate it?

Master: First, open the network management software, and then the network topology diagram can be displayed on the computer screen in real time. In the topology diagram, you can see the icons of network devices, such as the router, switch and so on.

Apprentice: What's the next step?

Master: Finally, click a device icon with the mouse. Take the device XL_ZZL_1F_S5720 in the following diagram as an example. The name, IP address, placement location, working status, CPU utilization ratio and memory utilization ratio of the device are automatically displayed next to the icon. In this way, we'll know the network device information.

普通词语 pǔtōng cíyǔ General Vocabulary

10-02

1.	监测	jiāncè	v.	monitor
2.	屏幕	píngmù	n.	screen
3.	实时	shíshí	adv.	in real time
4.	看到	kàndào	phr.	see
5.	边上	biān shang	phr.	(on the) side

专业词语 zhuānyè cíyǔ Specialized Vocabulary

10-03

1.	单击	dānjī	v.	click
2.	安放位置	ānfàng wèizhì	phr.	placement location
3.	CPU 利用率	CPU lìyònglǜ	phr.	CPU utilization ratio
4.	内存利用率	nèicún lìyònglǜ	phr.	memory utilization ratio
5.	工作状态	gōngzuò zhuàngtài	phr.	working status

B 10-04

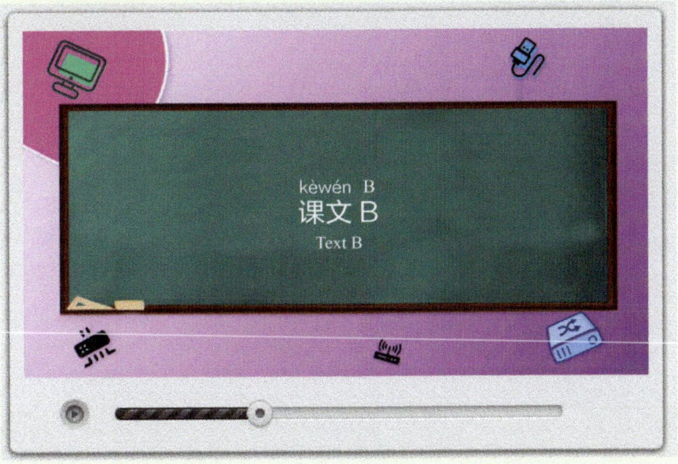

túdì: Zěnme pànduàn wǎngluò shèbèi shìfǒu fāshēng gùzhàng le?
徒弟：怎么判断网络设备是否发生故障了？

shīfu: Kěyǐ gēnjù shèbèi de túbiāo yánsè lái pànduàn. Zài wǎngluò guǎnlǐ ruǎnjiàn zhōng, dāng shèbèi fāshēng gùzhàng shí, qí túbiāo de yánsè huì fāshēng biànhuà.
师傅：可以根据设备的图标颜色来判断。在网络管理软件中，当设备发生故障时，其图标的颜色会发生变化。

túdì: Rúhé zhǎodào zhèxiē shèbèi de gōngzuò zhuàngtài xìnxī ne? Nín kěyǐ cāozuò shìfàn yíxià ma?
徒弟：如何找到这些设备的工作状态信息呢？您可以操作示范一下吗？

shīfu: Hǎo de. Yǐ míngchēng wéi TT_CORE_S12700E-8 de shèbèi wéi lì, dānjī gāi shèbèi túbiāo, zài "shèbèi xìnxī" miànbǎn zhōng, wǒmen kěyǐ kāndào diūbāolǜ wéi "0%", yánchí wéi "1.25 ms", zhuàngtài wéi "zhèngcháng".
师傅：好的。以名称为 TT_CORE_S12700E-8 的设备为例，单击该设备图标，在"设备信息"面板中，我们可以看到丢包率为"0%"，延迟为"1.25 ms"，状态为"正常"。

túdì: Zài nǎlǐ chákàn xiángxì xìnxī?
徒弟：在哪里查看详细信息？

shīfu: Zài "dāngqián zhuàngtài" miànbǎn, kě chákàn "diūbāolǜ、yánchí、CPU lìyònglǜ、nèicún lìyònglǜ" de xiángxì xìnxī.
师傅：在"当前状态"面板，可查看"丢包率、延迟、CPU 利用率、内存利用率"的详细信息。

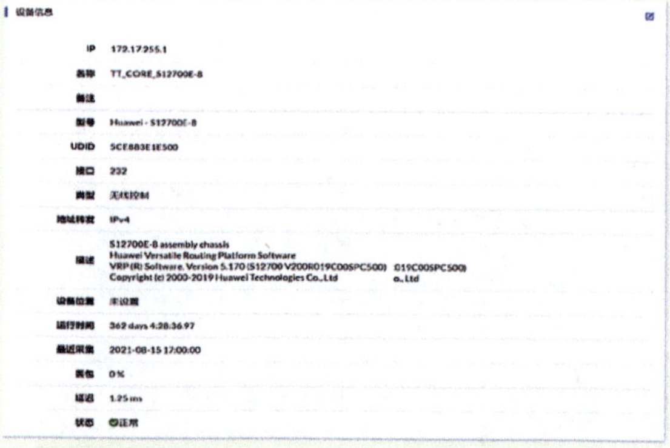

译文 yìwén Text in English

Apprentice: How can we tell whether a network device has been out of order or not?

Master: It can be judged by the color of the device icon. In the network management software, when a device is out of order, the color of its icon will change.

Apprentice: How can we find the information on working status of these devices? Could you demonstrate the operation?

Master: OK. Take the device TT_CORE_S12700E-8 as an example. Click the device icon. In the "Device Information" panel, we can see that the packet loss rate is "0 %", the delay is "1.25 ms", and the status is "Normal".

Apprentice: Where can I view the details?

Master: In the "Current Status" panel, you can view the detailed information of Packet Loss Rate, Delay, CPU Utilization and Memory Utilization.

普通词语 pǔtōng cíyǔ General Vocabulary

10-05

1.	颜色	yánsè	n.	color
2.	判断	pànduàn	v.	judge, tell
3.	其	qí	pron.	its
4.	示范	shìfàn	v.	demonstrate
5.	一下	yíxià	q.	*used after a verb to indicate one action/attempt*
6.	正常	zhèngcháng	adj.	normal
7.	详细	xiángxì	adj.	detailed

专业词语 zhuānyè cíyǔ Specialized Vocabulary

10-06

1.	发生故障	fāshēng gùzhàng	phr.	out of order
2.	面板	miànbǎn	n.	panel
3.	丢包率	diūbāolǜ	n.	packet loss rate
4.	延迟	yánchí	v.	delay

三、视听说　shì-tīng-shuō　Viewing, Listening, and Speaking

1. 观看介绍网络管理系统软件工具的功能的视频，给功能描述选择对应的图片。

Watch the video introducing the functions of software tools of the network management system, and choose the corresponding pictures for the function descriptions.

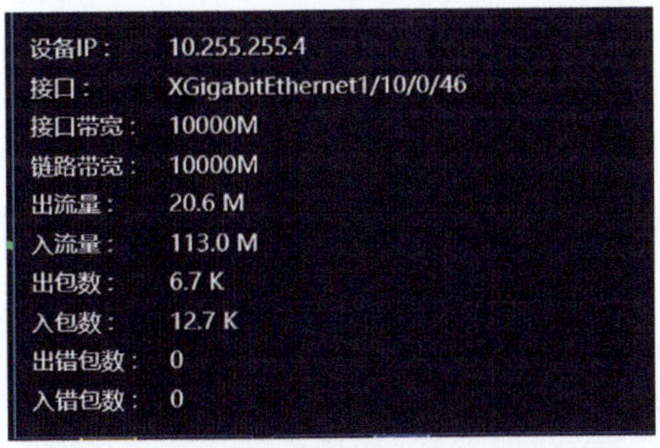

A.

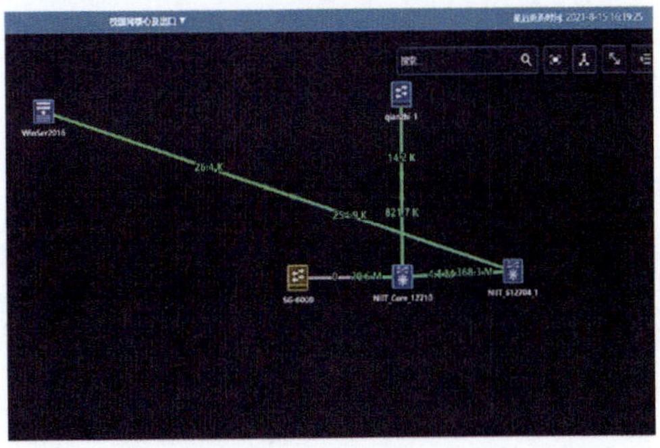

B.

C.

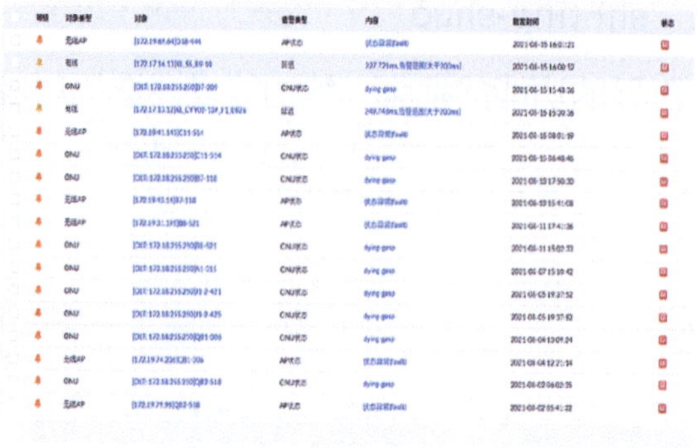

D.

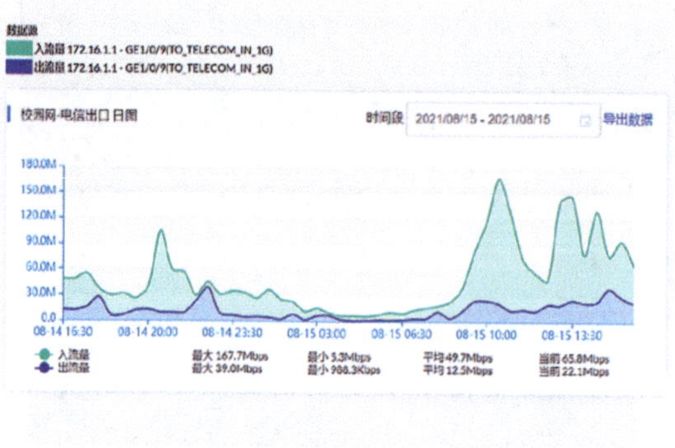

E.

yuǎnchéng pèizhì
① 远程 配置______
remote configuration

gùzhàng de bàojǐng yǔ zhěnduàn
② 故障的报警与诊断______
fault alarm and diagnosis

wǎngluò tuòpūtú de xiǎnshì
③ 网络拓扑图的显示______
display of network topology diagram

wǎngluò xìngnéng shùjù de jiānshì yǔ fēnxī
④ 网络性能数据的监视与分析______
monitoring and analysis of network performance data

wǎngluò shèbèi duānkǒu zhuàngtài de jiānshì yǔ fēnxī
⑤ 网络设备端口状态的监视与分析______
monitoring and analysis of network device port status

2. 说一说 Let's talk

说一说网络管理系统软件工具的功能。

Talk about the functions of software tools of the network management system.

四、学以致用 xuéyǐzhìyòng Practicing What You Have Learnt

观看介绍网络管理系统流量统计的视频，根据网络流量统计报表判断以下时间点是否会发生告警，并在“是”或者“否”后面画“√”。

Watch the video introducing the traffic statistics of the network management system, judge whether a warning will occur at the following time points according to the network traffic statistics report. Put a tick (√) after “是” or “否”.

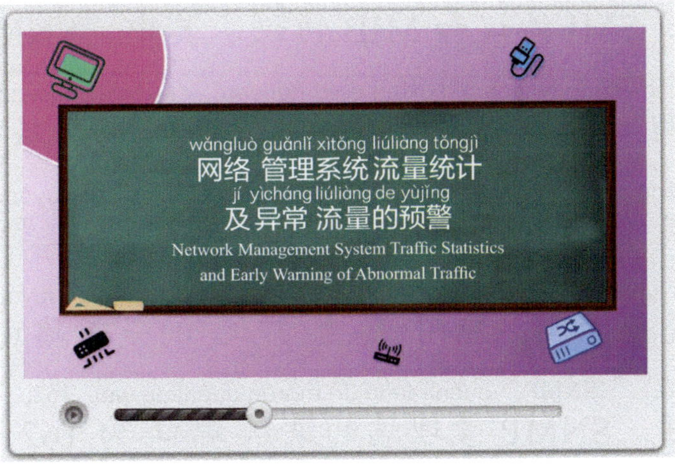

xùhào 序号 Number	shíjiān 时间 Time	rùliúliàng 入流量（bps） Inflow	chūliúliàng 出流量（bps） Outflow	shìfǒu huì fāshēng gàojǐng 是否会 发生 告警 Whether there will be a warning?
1	2021-08-14 16:30:00	47527850	13068138	shì 是___ / fǒu 否___ Yes. No.
2	2021-08-14 17:00:00	38216362	12318645	shì 是___ / fǒu 否___ Yes. No.
3	2021-08-14 17:30:00	54666901	5964978	shì 是___ / fǒu 否___ Yes. No.
4	2021-08-14 18:00:00	36745123	27639712	shì 是___ / fǒu 否___ Yes. No.

五、小知识 xiǎo zhīshi Tips

SNMP 协议

SNMP xiéyì

Zài TCP/IP wǎngluò zhōng, wǎngluò guǎnlǐ xìtǒng zǒnggòng yǒu sān gè xiāngguān xiéyì, fēnbié shì SNMP xiéyì、SMI xiéyì hé MIB xiéyì. Qízhōng, SNMP shì héxīn xiéyì, SNMP wèiyú liǎng zhǒng wǎngluò móxíng de dǐngcéng, jí yìngyòngcéng, shǔyú yìngyòngcéng xiéyì, zài chuánshūcéng yīkào UDP xiéyì jìnxíng chuánshū. Tā zhǔyào yòngyú zài júyùwǎng zhōng duì shèbèi jìnxíng guǎnlǐ, yìngyòng zuì wéi guǎngfàn de shì duì lùyóuqì、jiāohuànjī děng wǎngluò shèbèi de guǎnlǐ. SNMP guǎnlǐduān de mòrèn duānkǒu wéi 162, zhǔyào yònglái jiēshōu gàojǐng xiāoxi.

在TCP/IP网络中，网络管理系统总共有3个相关协议，分别是SNMP协议、SMI协议和MIB协议。其中，SNMP是核心协议，SNMP位于两种网络模型的顶层，即应用层，属于应用层协议，在传输层依靠UDP协议进行传输。它主要用于在局域网中对设备进行管理，应用最为广泛的是对路由器、交换机等网络设备的管理。SNMP管理端的默认端口为162，主要用来接收告警消息。

SNMP Protocol

There are three protocols related to the network management system on TCP/IP networks: the SNMP protocol, SMI protocol and MIB protocol respectively. Among them, SNMP is the core protocol. It is located at the top of the two network models, that is, the application layer. It is an application layer protocol and relies on the UDP protocol for transmission at the transport layer. It is mainly used to manage devices in local area network. It is most widely used to manage network devices, such as routers and switches. The default port of SNMP manager is 162, which is mainly used to receive warning messages.

补充专业词语 bǔchōng zhuānyè cíyǔ Supplementary Specialized Vocabulary

10-07

1.	SNMP 协议	SNMP xiéyì	phr.	SNMP (Simple Network Management Protocol) Protocol
2.	SMI 协议	SMI xiéyì	phr.	SMI (Serial Management Interface) Protocol
3.	MIB 协议	MIB xiéyì	phr.	MIB (Management Information Base) Protocol
4.	网络模型	wǎngluò móxíng	phr.	network model
5.	传输层	chuánshūcéng	n.	transport layer
6.	告警	gàojǐng	v.	warn

第二部分 Part 2

汉字 Chinese Characters

一、汉字知识 Hànzì zhīshi Knowledge about Chinese Characters

汉字的偏旁（10） Radicals of Chinese characters (10)

偏旁 Radicals	例字 Examples	部件组合 Combinations	结构图示 Illustrations
穴	空	穴＋工	
	突	穴＋犬	
	穿	穴＋牙	
田	男	田＋力	
	累	田＋糸	
	思	田＋心	
	备	夂＋田	
	留	卯＋田	
力	加	力＋口	
	动	云＋力	
	努	奴＋力	
牛	物	牛＋勿	
	特	牛＋寺	

二、汉字认读与书写 Hànzì rèndú yǔ shūxiě The Recognition and Writing of Chinese Characters

认读下列词语，并试着读写构成词语的汉字。

Recognize the following words, and try to read and write the Chinese characters forming these words.

空格　　详细　　动态　　协议　　告警

空				格				详				细			
动				态				协				议			
告				警											

第三部分 Part 3

日常用语 Daily Expressions

1. 这是我们的共同愿望。Zhè shì wǒmen de gòngtóng yuànwàng. This is our common wish.
2. 百闻不如一见。Bǎi wén bùrú yí jiàn. Seeing is believing.
3. 英雄所见略同！ Yīngxióng suǒ jiàn lüè tóng! Great minds think alike!

第四部分 Part 4

单元实训 Unit Practical Training

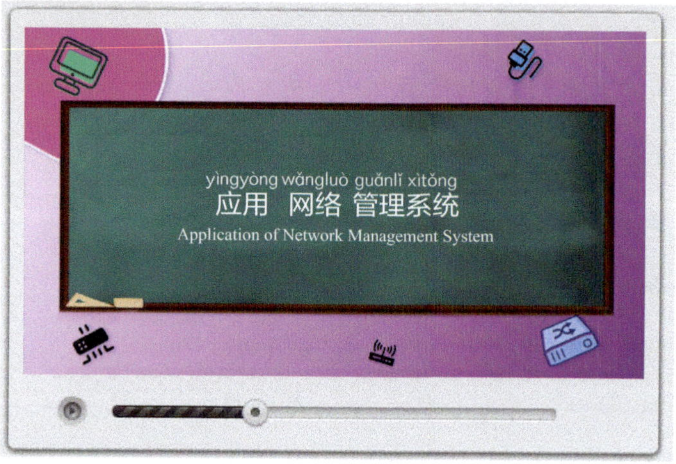

应用网络管理系统 yìngyòng wǎngluò guǎnlǐ xìtǒng

Application of Network Management System

实训目的 Training purpose

了解网络管理的方法，收集、分析和处理来自各个设备的管理信息。

To learn about the methods of network management, collect, analyze and process management information from various devices.

实训组织 Training organization

每组 3 人，选出一个组长。

Each group consists of three people, and a group leader is selected.

实训内容 Training content

应用网络管理系统查看网络拓扑图。

Using the network management system to view the network topology diagram.

实训步骤 Training steps

1. 将参加实训的人员分成若干小组，每组 3 人，轮流上机操作。

   Divide the trainees into groups of three and ask them to take turns operating and practicing on the computer.

② 登录网络管理系统，查看某个被管理的设备的信息。

Logon to the network management system to view the information of a managed device.

③ 在需要被管理的各个设备上进行一些简单的配置操作。

Perform some simple configuration operations on each device that needs to be managed.

④ 收集、分析和处理来自各个设备的管理信息之后，将网络的各种情况以图像、表格、文字等形式呈现和记录下来，然后以作业方式提交。

After collecting, analyzing and processing the management information from each device, present and record various situations of the network in the form of images, tables, texts, etc., and then submit the assignment.

⑤ 实训结束，教师总结评价。

The training ends. The teacher makes a summary and an evaluation.

第五部分 Part 5

单元小结 Unit Summary

cíyǔ
词语
Vocabulary

普通词语 General Vocabulary

1.	监测	jiāncè	v.	monitor
2.	屏幕	píngmù	n.	screen
3.	实时	shíshí	adv.	in real time
4.	看到	kàndào	phr.	see
5.	边上	biān shang	phr.	(on the) side
6.	颜色	yánsè	n.	color
7.	判断	pànduàn	v.	judge, tell
8.	其	qí	pron.	its
9.	示范	shìfàn	v.	demonstrate
10.	一下	yíxià	q.	*used after a verb to indicate one action/attempt*
11.	正常	zhèngcháng	adj.	normal
12.	详细	xiángxì	adj.	detailed

专业词语 Specialized Vocabulary

1.	单击	dānjī	v.	click
2.	安放位置	ānfàng wèizhì	phr.	placement location
3.	CPU 利用率	CPU lìyònglǜ	phr.	CPU utilization ratio
4.	内存利用率	nèicún lìyònglǜ	phr.	memory utilization ratio
5.	工作状态	gōngzuò zhuàngtài	phr.	working status

cíyǔ
词语
Vocabulary

6.	发生故障	fāshēng gùzhàng	phr.	out of order
7.	面板	miànbǎn	n.	panel
8.	丢包率	diūbāolǜ	n.	packet loss rate
9.	延迟	yánchí	v.	delay

补充专业词语 Supplementary Specialized Vocabulary

1.	SNMP 协议	SNMP xiéyì	phr.	SNMP (Simple Network Management Protocol) Protocol
2.	SMI 协议	SMI xiéyì	phr.	SMI (Serial Management Interface) Protocol
3.	MIB 协议	MIB xiéyì	phr.	MIB (Management Information Base) Protocol
4.	网络模型	wǎngluò móxíng	phr.	network model
5.	传输层	chuánshūcéng	n.	transport layer
6.	告警	gàojǐng	v.	warn

jùzi
句子
Sentences

1. 通过网络管理软件可以监测网络中所有的设备信息。
2. 首先，打开网络管理软件；然后，在电脑上实时显示网络拓扑图。在拓扑图中可以看到网络设备的图标，如路由器、交换机的图标等。
3. 最后，用鼠标单击某个设备图标，图标边上会自动显示该设备的名称、IP地址、安放位置、工作状态、CPU利用率和内存利用率等信息。
4. 在网络管理中，可以根据设备的图标颜色来判断设备是否发生了故障。

附录　Appendixes

词语总表　Vocabulary

序号	生词	拼音	词性	词义	普通 G/专业 S	所属单元
1	安放位置	ānfàng wèizhì	phr.	placement location	S	10A
2	安全	ānquán	n.	security	G	4A
3	安全性	ānquánxìng	n.	security	S	9A
4	绑定	bǎngdìng	v.	bind	S	8
5	包含	bāohán	v.	contain	G	6A
6	保护	bǎohù	v.	protect	G	4A
7	保证	bǎozhèng	v.	ensure	G	9A
8	报头	bàotóu	n.	header	S	8A
9	报文	bàowén	n.	message	S	4B
10	报文过滤	bàowén guòlǜ	phr.	message filtering	S	7
11	报文头部信息	bàowén tóubù xìnxī	phr.	message header information	S	7A
12	必须	bìxū	adv.	must	G	4B
13	边上	biān shang	phr.	(on the) side	G	10A
14	变化	biànhuà	n.	change	G	1A
15	并且	bìngqiě	conj.	and	G	2A
16	不断	búduàn	adv.	constantly	G	2A
17	策略路由	cèlüè lùyóu	phr.	policy-based routing	S	7B
18	层	céng	n.	layer	S	4A
19	常	cháng	adv.	frequently	G	2B
20	常见	cháng jiàn	phr.	common	G	2B
21	场景	chǎngjǐng	n.	scenario	G	8B
22	成	chéng	v.	become, turn into	G	6B
23	成员	chéngyuán	n.	member	G	6A
24	重传机制	chóngchuán jīzhì	phr.	retransmission mechanism	S	9A
25	出错	chū cuò	phr.	make a mistake	G	3A
26	出现	chūxiàn	v.	appear	G	6A
27	传输	chuánshū	v.	transmit	S	9A
28	传输层	chuánshūcéng	n.	transport layer	S	10
29	传统	chuántǒng	adj.	traditional	G	5B
30	串行接口	chuànxíng jiēkǒu	phr.	serial interface	S	9B
31	串行数据	chuànxíng shùjù	phr.	serial data	S	9

（续表）

序号	生词	拼音	词性	词义	普通 G/专业 S	所属单元
32	串行线	chuànxíngxiàn	n.	serial line	S	9B
33	此时	cǐshí	n.	this moment	G	5B
34	达	dá	v.	reach, achieve	G	6B
35	打开	dǎ//kāi	v.	turn on, switch on	G	1A
36	大部分	dàbùfen	n.	most, the majority	G	6A
37	大大	dàdà	adv.	greatly	G	3A
38	大型	dàxíng	adj.	large, large-scale	G	2B
39	带宽	dàikuān	n.	bandwidth	S	6A
40	单臂路由	dānbì lùyóu	phr.	single-arm routing, router-on-a-stick routing	S	4
41	单击	dānjī	v.	click	S	10A
42	但	dàn	conj.	but	G	6B
43	当	dāng	prep.	when	G	6A
44	当作	dàngzuò	v.	treat/regard...as...	G	6A
45	点到点	diǎn dào diǎn	phr.	point-to-point	S	9A
46	丢包率	diūbāolǜ	n.	packet loss rate	S	10B
47	动态路由	dòngtài lùyóu	phr.	dynamic routing	S	1A
48	动态路由表	dòngtài lùyóubiǎo	phr.	dynamic routing table	S	2
49	对	duì	m.	pair	G	6A
50	而	ér	conj.	*used to show a contrast*	G	2A
51	发生	fāshēng	v.	happen	G	1A
52	发生故障	fāshēng gùzhàng	phr.	out of order	S	10B
53	发送	fāsòng	v.	send	G	1A
54	方便	fāngbiàn	v.	provide convenience for	G	5A
55	方向	fāngxiàng	n.	direction	G	7B
56	防止	fángzhǐ	v.	prevent	G	4A
57	访问	fǎngwèn	v.	access	G	8A
58	访问控制列表	fǎngwèn kòngzhì lièbiǎo	phr.	Access Control List	S	7A
59	非常	fēicháng	adv.	very	G	3A
60	分别	fēnbié	adv.	respectively	G	2A
61	风暴	fēngbào	n.	storm	S	4A
62	服务器	fúwùqì	n.	server	S	5A
63	该	gāi	pron.	the, this	G	3A
64	改变	gǎibiàn	v.	change	G	2A

（续表）

序号	生词	拼音	词性	词义	普通 G/ 专业 S	所属单元
65	概念	gàiniàn	n.	concept	G	2A
66	高级 ACL	gāojí ACL	phr.	advanced ACL	S	7B
67	告警	gàojǐng	v.	warn	S	10
68	告诉	gàosu	v.	tell	G	7A
69	隔	gé	v.	(be) after/at an interval	G	1A
70	隔离	gélí	v.	isolate	G	4A
71	各个	gègè	pron.	each	G	3A
72	更新	gēngxīn	v.	update	G	1A
73	更好	gèng hǎo	phr.	better	G	9A
74	工作	gōngzuò	n.	work	G	3A
75	工作状态	gōngzuò zhuàngtài	phr.	working status	S	10A
76	公共网络（公网）	gōnggòng wǎngluò (gōngwǎng)	phr.	public network	S	8A
77	公有 IP 地址	gōngyǒu IP dìzhǐ	phr.	public IP address	S	8A
78	共	gòng	adv.	together	G	5A
79	故障	gùzhàng	n.	breakdown, fault	S	6A
80	管理距离	guǎnlǐ jùlí	phr.	administrative distance	S	1
81	广播	guǎngbō	v.	broadcast	G	1A
82	广播风暴	guǎngbō fēngbào	phr.	broadcast storm	S	4A
83	广播功能	guǎngbō gōngnéng	phr.	broadcast function	S	4
84	广播域	guǎngbōyù	phr.	broadcast domain	S	4A
85	规则	guīzé	n.	rule	G	7B
86	还	hái	adv.	still	G	2B
87	毫秒	háomiǎo	m.	millisecond	S	6A
88	耗费	hàofèi	v.	consume	G	3A
89	何	hé	pron.	what	G	2B
90	环境	huánjìng	n.	environment	G	2B
91	会	huì	aux.	can, be able to	G	2A
92	基本 ACL	jīběn ACL	phr.	basic ACL	S	7B
93	即	jí		mean	G	7A
94	即使	jíshǐ	conj.	even if	G	1A
95	计数单位	jìshù dānwèi	phr.	counting unit	S	1B
96	既	jì	conj.	(to be echoed by 且，又，也，etc.) both...and...	G	3A

（续表）

序号	生词	拼音	词性	词义	普通 G/专业 S	所属单元
97	加入	jiārù	v.	join	G	3A
98	监测	jiāncè	v.	monitor	G	10A
99	减少	jiǎnshǎo	v.	reduce	G	3A
100	见	jiàn	v.	meet	G	2B
101	建立	jiànlì	v.	establish	G	2A
102	接收	jiēshōu	v.	receive	G	5B
103	结果	jiéguǒ	n.	result	G	9A
104	解决	jiějué	v.	solve	G	3A
105	经常	jīngcháng	adv.	frequently	G	3A
106	精力	jīnglì	n.	energy	G	3A
107	静态路由表	jìngtài lùyóubiǎo	phr.	static routing table	S	2
108	具有	jùyǒu	v.	have	G	4B
109	距离矢量	jùlí shǐliàng	phr.	distance vector	S	1B
110	距离向量	jùlí xiàngliàng	phr.	distance vector	S	1
111	开启	kāiqǐ	v.	start	G	3B
112	看到	kàndào	phr.	see	G	10A
113	考虑	kǎolǜ	v.	consider	G	3A
114	可	kě	aux.	can	G	6B
115	可是	kěshì	conj.	but	G	3B
116	快	kuài	adj.	fast	G	9A
117	扩展性	kuòzhǎnxìng	n.	scalability, expansibility	S	9A
118	利用率	lìyònglǜ	n.	utilization ratio	S	8B
119	链路	liànlù	n.	link	S	2A
120	链路层	liànlùcéng	n.	link layer	S	4A
121	链路聚合	liànlù jùhé	phr.	link aggregation	S	6A
122	临时	línshí	adj.	temporary	G	8B
123	另外	lìngwài	pron.	other, another	G	4B
124	路由表	lùyóubiǎo	n.	routing table	S	1A
125	路由环路	lùyóu huánlù	phr.	routing loop	S	2
126	路由器	lùyóuqì	n.	router	S	2A
127	路由条目	lùyóu tiáomù	phr.	routing entry	S	2A
128	路由跳数	lùyóu tiàoshù	phr.	routing hop count	S	1B
129	逻辑链路	luójí liànlù	phr.	logical link	S	6B

（续表）

序号	生词	拼音	词性	词义	普通 G/专业 S	所属单元
130	面板	miànbǎn	n.	panel	S	10B
131	秒	miǎo	m.	second	G	1A
132	默认	mòrèn	v.	do by default	G	3B
133	目的端口	mùdì duānkǒu	phr.	destination port	S	7
134	目前	mùqián	n.	the present	G	4B
135	难道	nándào	adv.	*used in a rhetorical question for emphasis*	G	3A
136	内部	nèibù	n.	interior	G	8B
137	内存利用率	nèicún lìyònglǜ	phr.	memory utilization ratio	S	10A
138	判断	pànduàn	v.	judge, tell	G	10B
139	配对	pèi//duì	v.	pair, match	S	6
140	配合	pèihé	v.	(be) in conjunction with	G	4A
141	批量创建	pīliàng chuàngjiàn	phr.	create... in batches	S	4
142	屏幕	píngmù	n.	screen	G	10A
143	其	qí	pron.	its	G	10B
144	企业	qǐyè	n.	enterprise	G	5A
145	启用	qǐyòng	v.	start using	S	7
146	且	qiě	conj.	and	G	3A
147	区域划分	qūyù huàfēn	phr.	area division	S	2
148	全称	quánchēng	n.	full name	G	3A
149	全局	quánjú	n.	being global	S	3B
150	全双工	quánshuānggōng	n.	full duplex	S	9A
151	认证协议	rènzhèng xiéyì	phr.	authentication protocol	S	9A
152	任何	rènhé	pron.	any	G	1A
153	容易	róngyì	adj.	easy	G	3A
154	设置规则	shèzhì guīzé	phr.	set a rule	S	7B
155	涉及	shèjí	v.	involve	G	3A
156	生成	shēngchéng	v.	generate	G	5B
157	生效时间段	shēngxiào shíjiānduàn	phr.	effective time period	S	7
158	剩下	shèngxia	phr.	remaining	G	6A
159	实时	shíshí	adv.	in real time	G	10A
160	使能	shǐnéng	v.	enable	S	3B
161	示范	shìfàn	v.	demonstrate	G	10B
162	适当	shìdàng	adj.	appropriate	G	2A

（续表）

序号	生词	拼音	词性	词义	普通 G/专业 S	所属单元
163	适合	shìhé	v.	be suitable for	G	1B
164	适用于	shìyòng yú	phr.	be suitable for	G	8B
165	属性	shǔxìng	n.	attribute	S	3
166	数据包	shùjùbāo	n.	data packet	S	2A
167	数据报	shùjùbào	n.	datagram	S	8A
168	数量	shùliàng	n.	number	G	3A
169	私有 IP 地址	sīyǒu IP dìzhǐ	phr.	private IP address	S	8A
170	私有网络（私网）	sīyǒu wǎngluò (sīwǎng)	phr.	private network	S	8A
171	速度	sùdù	n.	speed	G	9A
172	缩写	suōxiě	n.	abbreviation	G	7A
173	所以	suǒyǐ	conj.	so	G	6B
174	太	tài	adv.	too	G	3A
175	特别	tèbié	adv.	especially	G	3A
176	提高	tí//gāo	v.	improve	G	7B
177	调整	tiáozhěng	v.	adjust	G	2A
178	同步	tóngbù	v.	(be) synchronous	S	9A
179	同异步链路	tóng-yìbù liànlù	phr.	synchronous and asynchronous link	S	9A
180	头部	tóubù	n.	header	G	7A
181	完	wán	v.	finish	G	1A
182	网段	wǎngduàn	n.	network segment	S	8
183	网络层	wǎngluòcéng	n.	network layer	S	4A
184	网络地址转换	wǎngluò dìzhǐ zhuǎnhuàn	phr.	network address translation (NAT)	S	8A
185	网络攻击	wǎngluò gōngjī	phr.	network attack	S	7B
186	网络开销	wǎngluò kāixiāo	phr.	network overhead	S	9A
187	网络流量	wǎngluò liúliàng	phr.	network flow, network traffic	S	7B
188	网络模型	wǎngluò móxíng	phr.	network model	S	10
189	网络设备	wǎngluò shèbèi	phr.	network device	S	7B
190	网络性能	wǎngluò xìngnéng	phr.	network performance	S	7B
191	问题	wèntí	n.	problem	G	3A
192	无	wú	v.	be without	G	9A
193	无法	wúfǎ	v.	cannot	G	5B

（续表）

序号	生词	拼音	词性	词义	普通 G/专业 S	所属单元
194	物理链路	wùlǐ liànlù	phr.	physical link	S	4
195	现象	xiànxiàng	n.	phenomenon	G	6B
196	限制	xiànzhì	v.	limit	G	7B
197	相对	xiāngduì	adj.	relative	G	2A
198	相关	xiāngguān	v.	relate	G	3B
199	相邻	xiānglín	adj.	adjacent	G	1A
200	相应	xiāngyìng	v.	correspond	G	7B
201	详细	xiángxì	adj.	detailed	G	10B
202	向	xiàng	prep.	to	G	5B
203	消息中转	xiāoxi zhōngzhuǎn	phr.	message transfer	S	5A
204	小	xiǎo	adj.	small, low	G	9A
205	小型	xiǎoxíng	adj.	small, small-scale	G	1B
206	协助	xiézhù	v.	assist	G	5B
207	修改	xiūgǎi	v.	modify	G	5B
208	需求	xūqiú	n.	demand	G	6B
209	需要	xūyào	n.	require	G	7B
210	延迟	yánchí	v.	delay	S	10B
211	颜色	yánsè	n.	color	G	10B
212	一下	yíxià	q.	*used after a verb to indicate one action/attempt*	G	10B
213	以太帧头部信息	yǐtàizhēn tóubù xìnxī	phr.	Ethernet frame header information	S	7A
214	异步	yìbù	v.	(be) asynchronous	S	9A
215	异步口	yìbùkǒu	n.	asynchronous port	S	9
216	影响	yǐngxiǎng	n.	influence, effect	G	6A
217	应答	yìngdá	v.	respond	G	5B
218	应用层	yìngyòngcéng	n.	application layer	S	1
219	映射	yìngshè	v.	map	S	8B
220	拥塞	yōngsè	v.	congest	S	6B
221	有效	yǒuxiào	v.	be effective	G	6A
222	预防	yùfáng	v.	prevent	G	7B
223	源地址	yuándìzhǐ	n.	source address	S	8
224	源端口	yuánduānkǒu	n.	source port	S	7
225	允许	yǔnxǔ	v.	allow	G	3B

（续表）

序号	生词	拼音	词性	词义	普通 G/专业 S	所属单元
226	造成	zàochéng	v.	cause	G	6A
227	则	zé	conj.	then	G	3A
228	增加	zēngjiā	v.	increase	G	6A
229	这里	zhèlǐ	pron.	here	G	7A
230	整个	zhěnggè	adj.	whole	G	1A
231	整合	zhěnghé	v.	integrate	G	6B
232	正常	zhèngcháng	adj.	normal	G	10B
233	之前	zhīqián	n.	before	G	3B
234	执行命令	zhíxíng mìnglìng	phr.	execute a command	S	7
235	指	zhǐ	v.	refer to	G	2A
236	指定方向	zhǐdìng fāngxiàng	phr.	specified direction	S	7B
237	指定接口	zhǐdìng jiēkǒu	phr.	specified interface	S	7B
238	指令列表	zhǐlìng lièbiǎo	phr.	instruction list	S	7A
239	中文	Zhōngwén	n.	Chinese (language)	G	3A
240	终端	zhōngduān	n.	terminal	G	5A
241	周期性	zhōuqīxìng	n.	periodicity	S	1A
242	注册	zhù//cè	v.	register	S	3A
243	注销	zhùxiāo	v.	logout, unregister	S	3A
244	注意	zhùyì	v.	pay attention to	G	3B
245	转发	zhuǎnfā	v.	forward	G	4B
246	资源	zīyuán	n.	resource	G	5A
247	自动	zìdòng	adv.	automatically	G	2A
248	自治系统	zìzhì xìtǒng	phr.	As (Autonomous System)	S	1
249	总	zǒng	adj.	total	G	6B
250	总和	zǒnghé	n.	sum	G	6A
251	最终	zuìzhōng	n.	finally	G	5A
252	作为	zuòwéi	v.	regard as	G	1B
253	作业要求	zuòyè yāoqiú	phr.	operation requirement	S	1
254	ARP			Address Resolution Protocol	S	4
255	BGP			Border Gateway Protocol	S	2B
256	CPU 利用率	CPU lìyònglǜ	phr.	CPU utilization ratio	S	10A
257	DHCP			Dynamic Host Configuration Protocol	S	5A
258	DHCP Relay 组网	DHCP Relay zǔwǎng	phr.	DHCP Relay networking	S	5

（续表）

序号	生词	拼音	词性	词义	普通 G/专业 S	所属单元
259	DHCP 典型组网	DHCP diǎnxíng zǔwǎng	phr.	typical DHCP networking	S	5
260	DHCP 中继代理	DHCP zhōngjì dàilǐ	phr.	DHCP relay agent	S	5
261	DHCP 组网	DHCP zǔwǎng	phr.	DHCP networking	S	5B
262	eNSP 软件	eNSP ruǎnjiàn	phr.	eNSP software	S	1A
263	FE 口	FE kǒu	phr.	Fast Ethernet port (FE port)	S	6
264	GARP			Generic Attribute Registration Protocol	S	3
265	GE 口	GE kǒu	phr.	Gigabit Ethernet port (GE port)	S	6
266	GVRP			GARP VLAN Registration Protocol	S	3A
267	IS-IS			Intermediate System-to-Intermediate System	S	2B
268	MIB 协议	MIB xiéyì	phr.	MIB (Management Information Base) Protocol	S	10
269	OSPF			Open Shortest Path First	S	2A
270	ping 通	ping tōng	phr.	ping each other	S	1
271	RIP 动态路由	RIP dòngtài lùyóu	phr.	RIP dynamic routing	S	1A
272	SMI 协议	SMI xiéyì	phr.	SMI (Serial Management Interface) Protocol	S	10
273	SNMP 协议	SNMP xiéyì	phr.	SNMP (Simple Network Management Protocol) Protocol	S	10
274	VLANIF			Virtual Local Area Network Interface	S	4

视频脚本　Video Scripts

第一单元　RIP 组建网络

一、热身

小机器人：在 eNSP 中绘制网络拓扑图的流程：

第一步，启动 eNSP 软件；

第二步，选中左边的“路由器”设备及型号，拖动路由器到工作区，重复此步骤，再拖动一台路由器到工作区；

第三步，选择左上角的“终端设备”，选中左侧的 PC 拖动到工作区，重复此步骤，再拖动一台 PC 到工作区；

第四步，选中所有设备，按启动键启动设备；

第五步，选择左上角的“设备连线”按钮，选中 copper 线；

第六步，在路由器上右击鼠标选中 G 口，拖动线缆到另一台路由器上，右击鼠标选择 G 口进行设备连线，重复此步骤，完成路由器与 PC 机之间的连线。

三、视听说

小机器人：RIP 路由配置的实际操作过程，主要包括三个方面的内容和要求：

1. 前期准备；2. 基本配置；3. 配置的保存和连通性的测试。

前期准备主要包括：下载并安装 eNSP 软件，绘制网络拓扑图。

基本配置主要包括：配置计算机的 IP 地址、子网掩码和网关；配置 RIP 路由。

配置的保存和连通性的测试主要包括：用 save 命令保存配置，用 Display ip routing-table 查看路由的配置信息；测试每台 PC 之间能互相 ping 通。

四、学以致用

徒弟：RIP 路由配置包括哪些步骤？

师傅：RIP 路由配置有以下六个步骤：

第一步，下载并安装 eNSP 软件；

第二步，打开 eNSP 软件，绘制网络拓扑图；

第三步，启动所需设备；

第四步，打开路由器，进行 RIP 路由配置；

第五步，打开计算机，配置 IP 地址，子网掩码和网关；

第六步，保存配置，并测试计算机连通性。

第二单元　OSPF 组建网络

一、热身

小机器人：让我们来学习如何设置 OSPF 的设备地址：

第一步：选中所有的 eNSP 的设备并启动；

第二步：双击 PC1，设置 IP 地址，子网掩码和网关，点击“应用”按钮。

第三步：双击 PC2，重复第二步操作。

第四步：双击 R1，配置 R1 的 OSPF 动态路由。

第五步：双击 R2，配置 R2 的 OSPF 动态路由。

三、视听说

徒弟：师傅，OSPF 路由配置的流程是什么？

师傅：OSPF 路由配置的流程主要有五个步骤：

第一步，下载并安装 eNSP 软件；打开 eNSP 软件，绘制网络拓扑图。

第二步，启动所需网络设备。

第三步，打开计算机，配置 IP 地址，子网掩码和网关。

第四步，每台路由器都配置 OSPF 动态路由协议。

第五步，保存配置，测试每台 PC 之间能互相 ping 通。

四、学以致用

小机器人：RIP 协议是一种典型的距离矢量协议，它的最大网络直径为 15，也就是说 RIP 协议所能传递路由信息的最大跳数就是 15 跳，超过 15 跳就表示不可达；OSPF 协议是一种典型的链路状态协议，是当前最主流的 IGP 协议，无论是园区网络、大型企业乃至于运营商，都很喜欢用 OSPF。在实际运用中，RIP 适合用于小型的网络环境，OSPF 适合用于大型的网络环境；RIP 不支持区域划分，OSPF 能够支持多区域划分，可管理性更强。

第三单元　动态虚拟局域网

一、热身

徒弟：GVRP 的注册模式有几种？

师傅：主要分为 Normal 模式、Fixed 模式和 Forbidden 模式三种。这三种模式各自的特点和功能是：

1. Normal 模式：允许接口动态注册、注销 VLAN，传播动态 VLAN 及静态 VLAN。
2. Fixed 模式：不能动态注册或注销 VLAN，只能发送静态 VLAN 注册信息。
3. Forbidden 模式：不能动态注册或注销 VLAN，只保留 VLAN1 的信息。

徒弟：那么接口启用 GVRP 协议时默认什么模式？

师傅：默认 Normal 模式。

三、视听说

小机器人：一起来学习 GVRP 的主要配置思路和如何查看配置结果吧。首先，要在所有的交换机上全局使能 GVRP；然后，在 trunk 端口下使能 GVRP；之后就可以查看交换机上所有 VLAN 的汇总信息了，包括静态创建、动态创建以及保留的 VLAN 情况。

四、学以致用

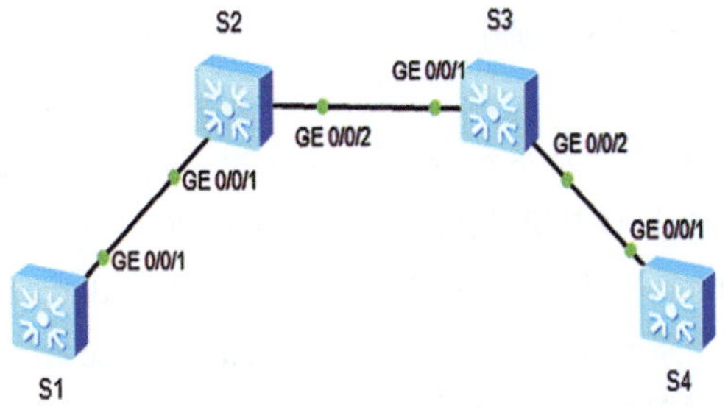

小机器人：一起来学习如何配置交换机吧。首先，对交换机 S1 进行配置，全局使能 GVRP，创建 VLAN，设置 GE0/0/1 端口类型为 trunk，允许所有的 VLAN 通过，并在此端口下使能 GVRP；然后，配置 S2，设置 GE0/0/1 和 GE0/0/2 端口类型为 trunk，允许所有的 VLAN 通过，并在上述端口下使能 GVRP；接下来配置 S3，与 S2 类似；之后配置 S4，设置 GE0/0/1 端口类型为 trunk，允许所有的 VLAN 通过，并在此端口下使能 GVRP。

第四单元　VLAN 间路由

一、热身

徒弟：三层交换机是怎样部署 VLAN 间路由的？

师傅：三层交换机是通过配置 VLANIF 接口来实现 VLAN 路由的。比如主机 A 和主机 B 分别属于 VLAN 2 和 VLAN 3，地址分别是 192.168.2.0/24 和 192.168.3.0/24 网段；那么需要在三层交换机上创建 VLANIF 2 和 VLANIF 3 接口，分配配置 192.168.2.0/24 和 192.168.3.0/24 网段地址；然后在主机上设置网关地址为对应的 VLANIF 接口地址，主机 A 和主机 B 就能实现 VLAN 间通信了。

徒弟：VLANIF 接口是什么接口？

师傅：VLANIF 接口是 VLAN Interface 的简称。它是一种逻辑接口，并不是设备上真实存在的端口。它可以创建，也可以删除。

三、视听说

徒弟：学习单臂路由实现 VLAN 间路由的配置，先要学什么？

师傅：首先要了解配置操作的中文含义。比如，[SWA-GigabitEthernet0/0/1]port link-type trunk 对应的中文含义是“配置接口为 trunk 类型接口”，[SWA-GigabitEthernet0/0/1]port trunk allow-pass vlan 2 3 是设置 trunk 接口允许通过的 VLAN ID，[RTA-GigabitEthernet0/0/1.1]arp broadcast enable 的操作含义是“使能 ARP 广播功能”。

四、学以致用

徒弟：三层交换机配置 VLAN 路由有哪几个步骤？

师傅：总共有五个步骤：

首先，批量创建 VLAN 2 和 VLAN 3；第二步，将接口 GE0/0/1 和接口 GE0/0/2 分别加入 VLAN 2 和 VLAN 3；第三步，创建 VLANIF 接口；第四步，在 VLANIF 接口下配置 IP 地址；最后，验证主机 A 与主机 B 能否正常通信。

第五单元　DHCP 中继代理配置

一、热身

小机器人：DHCP Relay 配置的前提条件包括：（1）完成基于全局地址池的 DHCP Server 配置；（2）DHCP Server 与 DHCP Relay 接口之间路由可达；（3）DHCP Relay 接口与 DHCP Client 在同一网段；（4）DHCP Client 的缺省网关地址应为 DHCP Relay 接口的 IP 地址。

三、视听说

徒弟：配置一个 DHCP Relay 接口包括哪些步骤？

师傅：有以下六个步骤：

第一步，执行命令 system-view，进入系统视图；第二步，执行命令 dhcp enable，开启 DHCP 服务；第三步，执行命令 interface，进入 DHCP Relay 接口视图；第四步，执行命令 ip relay address，在 DHCP Relay 接口上指定 DHCP Server 的 IP 地址；第五步，执行命令 dhcp select relay，将 DHCP Relay 接口上的配置信息应用到当前接口。第六步，执行命令 dhcp relay source-ip agent-ip，将 DHCP 请求报文的源 IP 地址设置为配置了 DHCP 中继的接口 IP 地址。

四、学以致用

小机器人：（1）为实现DHCP Server对跨网段的DHCP Client分配IP地址及其他网络参数，需要配置全局地址池，并为 DHCP Client 指定出口网关、域名后缀、DNS Server 地址等。具体为：

a. 开启 DHCP 服务；

b. 为 DHCP Client 配置动态分配 IP 地址及其他网络参数；

c. 添加 DHCP Server 到 DHCP Relay 接口之间的路由，保证两者之间路由可达。

（2）为实现不同网段的 DHCP Client 和 DHCP Server 能相互通信，需要配置 DHCP Relay 功能。具体为：

a. 开启 DHCP 服务；

b. 在 Relay 接口下配置 DHCP ServerIP 地址。

（3）为实现 DHCP Client 能自动获取 DHCP Server 分配 IP 地址及其他网络参数，需要配置 DHCP Client 的 TCP/IP 属性为“自动获得 IP 地址”和“自动获得 DNS 服务器地址”。

第六单元　链路聚合

一、热身

小机器人：一起学习链路聚合配置的操作吧。首先在 eNSP 放置两台交换机，两台 PC，将两台交换机的 GE 0/0/1、GE0/0/2、GE 0/0/3 接口互连，PC1 与 SW1 连接，PC2 与 SW2 连接。选中所有设备，启动所有设备。然后，双击交换机 SW1 图标，进入交换机的命令行界面。在命令行界面，输入 system-view，进入系统视图，就可以开始链路聚合的配置了。

三、视听说

设置两台电脑的IP地址、子网掩码。在交换机使用interface eth-trunk 1 命令，创建编号为 1 的Eth-trunk端口。使用 mode manual load-balance 命令，配置 eth-trunk 1 端口的工作模式。使用 trunkport gigabitethernet 0/0/1 to 0/0/3 命令，将物理端口加入 eth-trunk 端口。用 display interface eth-trunk 1 命令，查看结果。

四、学以致用

小机器人：现在把链路 GE 0/0/3 删除，还剩下 2 条链路。在交换机上执行 display interfale eth-trunk 1 命令，显示 Maximal BW: 3G, Current BW: 2G。GigabitEthernet0/0/3 接口的状态是 DOWN。GigabitEthernet0/0/1、GigabitEthernet0/0/2 接口的状态是 UP。用 ping 命令测试两台电脑 PC1、PC2 的连通性，PC1 和 PC2 是连通的。说明断开一条链路，当前带宽减少，但网络还是通的。

第七单元　网络安全

一、热身

小机器人：访问控制列表有许多用途，比如预防网络攻击、限制网络流量、提高网络性能、实现策略路由等。要配置一个控制列表，第一，先进入路由器的系统视图；第二，创建 ACL；第三，为 ACL 创建规则；第四，把创建的 ACL 应用到路由器的出接口上。

三、视听说

A：ACL 怎么分类？

B：按照规则所使用的报文字段不同，可以将 ACL 分为基本 ACL、高级 ACL、二层 ACL 等。

A：它们之间的区别是什么？

B：标准 ACL 仅使用报文的源 IP 地址、分片信息和生效时间段信息来定义规则；高级 ACL 既可使用 IPv4 报文的源 IP 地址，也可使用目的 IP 地址、TCP 源 / 目的端口、UDP 源 / 目的端口号、生效时间段等来定义规则；二层 ACL 是使用报文的以太帧头信息来定义规则，如根据源 MAC（Media Access Control）地址、目的 MAC 地址等。

四、学以致用

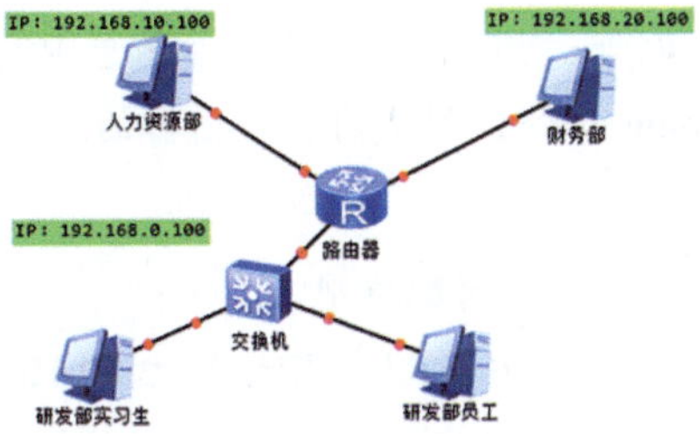

小机器人：如图所示，某公司网络包含了研发部区域、人力资源部区域和财务部区域。在研发部区域中，有一台专供实习人员使用的 PC，该 PC 的 IP 地址为 172.16.10.100/24。处于网络安全方面的考虑，需要禁止财务部区域接收到实习人员发送的 IP 报文。我们可以在路由器 R 上配置基本 ACL，根据源 IP 地址信息识别实习人员发出的 IP 报文，然后在 GE1/0/3 接口的出方向（Outbound 方向）上拒绝放行源 IP 地址为 192.168.0.100 0.0.0.255 的 IP 报文。

第八单元　网络地址转换

一、热身

小机器人：请看视频中这个拓扑图。图中的网关设备将网络分成了两个部分：企业或家庭所使用的网络为私有网络，使用的是私有地址；运营商维护的网络为公共网络，使用的是公有地址。私有地址不能在公网中路由。网络地址转换一般部署在连接内网和外网的网关设备上。这个图中的网关设备是路由器。

三、视听说

徒弟：静态网络地址转换应该如何配置？

师傅：首先，需要将网关设备，也就是路由器的内网接口和外网接口配置好 IP 地址，这个是内外网通信的前提。所以，先进入 GE0/0/1 接口视图，配置好内网接口 IP 地址；然后进入 serial0/0/1 接口，配置好外网接口地址。NAT 只要一条配置就好了。比如，配置内网地址 192.168.1.1 和外网地址 200.28.96.1 的映射，这样，内网主机 192.168.1.1 在与外网通信时，源地址就会被转换成 200.28.96.1 这个外网地址了。如果需要多个内部主机与外网通信，每个主机都需要配置一条映射。

四、学以致用

徒弟：动态网络地址转换如何配置？

师傅：首先，它需要创建一个地址池；第二步是创建一个访问控制列表，在访问控制列表中配置需要进行地址转换的源地址网段；然后，再在外网接口下将配置的地址池和访问控制列表绑定在一起。这样，当有内部主机与公共网络通信时，如果源地址命中访问控制列表中的地址范围，则网关设备会从地址池中选择一个可用的地址对报文中的源地址进行转换。

第九单元　点到点协议 PPP

一、热身

小机器人：一起学习 PPP 的配置吧！启动 eNSP，放置两台路由器，右击路由器 R1 的“设置”；将 2SA 拖动到路由器，用相同的方法设置路由器 R2；用串行线连接两台路由器的 Serial 4/0/0 接口；选中两台路由器，点击“开启设备”，启动所有设备；所有设备启动后，双击路由器 R1 图标，进入路由器的命令行界面；在命令行界面，输入 system-view，进入系统视图，就可以开始 PPP 的配置了。

三、视听说

小机器人：PPP 协议配置操作步骤如图所示，两台路由器 R1、R2 用串行线连接，路由器 R1、R2 的串行接口的链路层协议配置为 PPP，配置路由器 R1 的串口 IP 地址为 10.10.0.1/30，R2 的串口 IP 地址为 10.10.0.2/30，用命令查看 R1、R2 的结果，用 ping 命令测试结果。

第一步，启动所有设备，双击路由器 R1 图标，执行 interface serial 4/0/0 命令，进入 Serial 4/0/0 接口；第二步，执行 link-protocol ppp 命令，将当前接口的链路层协议配置为 PPP；第三步，执行 ip address 10.10.0.1 255.255.255.252 命令，为接口配置 IP 地址；用相同的方法，配置 R2；第四步，执行 display interface serial 4/0/0 命令，查看结果；第五步，执行 ping 命令，测试两台路由器的连通性。

四、学以致用

小机器人：一起来学习对两个路由器串行接口进行配置吧。

路由器R1、R2用串行线连接串行接口，路由器R1的IP地址为 10.10.0.1/30，路由器R2的IP地址由R1提供，

R2 的 IP 地址为 10.10.0.2。

运行 eNSP，画好拓扑图，启动所有设备。

（1）路由器 R1 的配置

进入路由器 R1 的串行口 Serial 4/0/0，将接口的链路层协议配置为 PPP，配置 Serial 4/0/0 接口的 IP 地址为 10.10.0.1，子网掩码 255.255.255.252。在 R1 执行命令 remote address 10.10.0.2，指定分配给路由器 R2 的 Serial 4/0/0 接口的 IP 地址为 10.10.0.2。

（2）路由器 R2 的配置

进入路由器 R2 的串行口 Serial 4/0/0，将接口的链路层协议配置为 PPP。路由器 R2 的接口 Serial 4/0/0 输入 ip address ppp-negotiate 命令，表示由对端接口，R1 的 Serial 4/0/0 分配一个 IP 地址给自己。在路由器 R1、R2 上分别执行命令 display interface serial 4/0/0，查看配置结果。

第十单元　网络管理

一、热身

小机器人：网络管理系统中，系统为不同种类的设备、不同厂家生产的设备、不同型号的设备，定义一个统一的接口和协议，同时，因为网络设备众多，为了能及时得到设备的重要状态，还要求设备能主动地汇报重要的状态信息。管理员可以使用统一的外观界面，面对所有网络和位于不同物理空间的设备信息进行管理，从而大大提高网络管理的效率，简化网络管理员的工作。对于网络管理，管理员可以查看的设备统计信息包括设备的配置、参数、状态等信息，采用的操作是读取和设置。下面，我们介绍相关的网络管理统计信息。主要有如下几个方面：（1）当前正常的设备数量；（2）某时段内在线的最大终端数量；（3）当前无线接入设备的数量；（4）某时段内在线的平均无线设备数量。

三、视听说

徒弟：为什么网管员的电脑如此神奇？

师傅：是因为网管员在自己的电脑上运行了某种统称为“网络管理系统”的软件工具，该工具的功能强大，可以非常高效地管理网络。

徒弟：有哪些功能？

师傅：主要有以下几个功能：网络拓扑图的显示、网络设备端口状态的监视与分析、网络性能数据的监视与分析、故障的报警与诊断、远程配置。

四、学以致用

徒弟：什么是流量统计功能？

师傅：流量统计就是统计某一段时间内各个上网设备（电脑、手机、移动 PAD），或者一个网段的上网设备使用了多少流量，以及这些流量都用在哪些网络协议上了。

徒弟：如何在网络管理软件中，使用某个接口的流量统计信息？

师傅：在网络管理软件中，可以在流量菜单下选择相应的接口，通过综合数据报表查看统计信息。

徒弟：可以根据该信息判断出一些异常的流量。通过查看某个时段内流入、流出的流量大小，以此判别异常流量的预警。只要以下有一个条件满足，就会产生流量告警：当入口流量＞入口网络流量基准线阈值 *（1+ 流量阈值），会发生告警；或当出口流量＞出口网络流量基准线阈值 *（1+ 流量阈值），也会发生告警。

参考答案 Reference Answers

第一单元

一、热身

1. ①E ②C ③B ④A ⑤F ⑥D
2. ①D ②E ③A ④C ⑤B ⑥F

三、视听说

1. ①C F ②A E ③B D

四、学以致用

①A ②E ③C ④D ⑤F ⑥B

第二单元

一、热身

1. ①F ②E ③B ④D ⑤A ⑥C
2. ①D ②C ③A ④E ⑤B

三、视听说

1. ①E ②D ③C ④A ⑤B

四、学以致用

①B、C、E

②A、D、F

第三单元

一、热身

1. ①A ②B ③C ④D ⑤E ⑥F
2. ①B ②C ③A

三、视听说

1. ①没有动态 VLAN。

   ②有动态 VLAN，为 VLAN10~VLAN20（共 11 个）。

四、学以致用

①E ②C ③B ④A ⑤D ⑥G ⑦F

第四单元

一、热身

1. ①A ②C ③F ④D ⑤E ⑥B
2. ①C1、C2 ②A ③D1、D2 ④B1、B2

三、视听说

1. ①D ②C ③A ④E ⑤B